Population, Law, and the Environment

Robert M. Hardaway

PRAEGER

Westport, Connecticut
London

Library of Congress Cataloging-in-Publication Data

Hardaway, Robert M., 1946–
    Population, law, and the environment / Robert M. Hardaway.
        p.   cm.
    Includes bibliographical references and index.
    ISBN 0-275-94570-7 (alk. paper)
    1. Population—Environmental aspects.   2. Economic development—
Environmental aspects.   3. Environmental law.   4. Population—Law
and legislation.   I. Title.
HB871.H346   1994
304.6—dc20   93-44501

British Library Cataloguing in Publication Data is available.

Library of Congress Catalog Card Number: 93-44501
ISBN: 0-275-94570-7

First published in 1994

Praeger Publishers, 88 Post Road West, Westport, CT 06881
An imprint of Greenwood Publishing Group, Inc.

Printed in the United States of America

The paper used in this book complies with the Permanent
Paper Standard issued by the National Information Standards
Organization (Z39.48-1984).

10 9 8 7 6 5 4 3 2 1

Dedicated
to
Judy Swearingen

Contents

Preface

What do family planning policies, abortion laws, and immigration have to do with the environment?

Governmental environmental policy, as well as private environmental action has traditionally been curative and reactive in nature—that is directed towards cleaning up past environmental disasters, and passing laws to limit the amount and type of pollutants that may be emitted by individuals and enterprises. But what is the cost-effectiveness of such policies at a time when the population of the world continues to expand at an exponential rate? What should be the role of population control in environmental policy?

Up to now both government and private environmental groups have paid little attention to population issues. The meeting of the government representatives and private environmental groups in Rio in 1992 did not invite groups concerned with population issues, and did not even place population issues on the agenda. The recently published book, *Earth in the Balance,* written by high profile politician and Vice-President of the United States, Al Gore, devotes only 27 of its 407 pages to population issues.

But are the Malthusian and Neo-Malthusian doomsayers, such as Paul Ehrlich *(The Population Explosion),* and Donella Meadows *(The Limits of Growth)* to be given credence when so many of their past predictions of disaster have failed to materialize?

This book explores all these questions, as well as attempting synthesis of contemporary population theories in the context of environmental policy.

Although the title of this book is *Population, Law, and the Environment,* it is hoped that the chapters which follow will reveal a relationship not only between population, the law and the environment, but also the relationship to the environment of governmental policies in such areas as abortion, immigration, education, and economic regulation.

Acknowledgements

I wish to thank my dedicated student assistants at the Hastings College of the Law and the University of Denver College of Law without whose background research this book would not have been possible. Mary Stanojevich, Patrick Stewart, Gregory Sheffer, Traci Van Pelt-Johnson, Ansley Westwood and Monica Mejia all worked long hours to accumulate the data, find the sources, and prepared an index used in this book. All of them expressed great interest in the subject matter of the book and this interest and enthusiasm was reflected in their work. However, the opinions and conclusions expressed in the text do not necessarily reflect those of my assistants, and any errors are mine alone.

I also wish to thank my hard working secretary, Frances Nowve, at the Hastings College of the Law, who endured my unreasonable demands and deadlines and went far beyond the duties of a secretary by making many helpful and useful suggestions with regard to syntax and presentation.

I wish to thank Dean Frank T. Read of the Hastings College of the Law for making all the resources of the school available to me during my 1992–1993 visitorship.

I also wish to thank Dean Dennis Lynch of my home institution, the University of Denver College of Law. Dean Lynch approved my research proposal and stipend for this project. Without the generous financial support of the University of Denver College of Law, this book would not have been possible. I thank Elise Oranges and the staff of Publishing Network for their dedicated supervision of the editing and production of the book, and James Dunton of Praeger Press for his support and encouragement throughout this project.

Finally, I wish to thank Judy Swearingen, to whom this book is dedicated. Although it was her interest in the environment, and her tireless and selfless efforts on behalf of preserving the rainforest of Costa Rica which inspired my work, it was her dedication, help, and support which enabled me to complete it.

1 Introduction

The exponential rise in the world's population over the past century has raised great concerns about the effects of this rise on the environment. There is now heated debate between those who warn of impending environmental disaster if population is not brought immediately under control, and those who claim that technology, spurred by population growth, has proved itself capable of both protecting the environment and staying ahead of Malthusian trends in population growth.

Both parties to the debate, convinced of the righteousness of their respective causes, have not been above resorting to some hyperbole. It began in 1798 when Malthus predicted that if the world's population, (then about one billion) were allowed to expand at its natural rate, population growth would soon be checked by starvation and disease, and humankind would be reduced to subsistence. Since that time, mankind—mercifully aided by the opening of the new world, the industrial revolution, and the green revolution—has quintupled in size at the same time that per capita consumption has risen. As for the environment, American forests are thicker than they were 100 years ago,[1] Tokyo's air is cleaner than it was when its population was half its present size,[2] and 23 industrialized countries have cut release of ozone-depleting compounds by 50% since 1987 when the earth contained one billion fewer human beings.[3] Between 1980 and 1989 France and West Germany reduced sulfur dioxide emissions by 50%, and the United States reduced carbon monoxide emissions by 25%, and other forms of air pollution by 33%.[4]

Thus, we can understand the skeptics who say they did not believe Paul Ehrlich when in his 1968 book *The Population Bomb*[5] he warned that failure to stop population growth would cause disaster. Twenty-two years after he published his dire warnings, the population had increased by another two billion people, while at the same time food per capita food production had risen by 10% and the percentage of the population that was starving had declined by 16%. Undaunted, however, Ehrlich wrote a sequel in 1990, entitled *The Population Explosion*,[6] in which he stated that this time he was serious and that any more population growth really would bring catastrophe. Likewise, the skeptics viewed Donella Meadows' 1972 book, *The Limits to Growth*[7] (which used computer models) and her 1992 "I'm really serious now" sequel, *Beyond The Limits*,[8] as just more Malthusian cries of "wolf." (Her computer models had predicted, among other disasters, that gold would run out by 1981, and oil would run out by 1992.)

In *The Population Explosion,* Ehrlich went so far as to suggest that the fall of the Roman Empire had less to do with invading barbarians than with lead poisoning caused by an environmental crisis brought on by water pollution and overpopulation.[9]

The anti-Malthusians and "progrowthers," on the other hand, have suggested that there are virtually no limits to growth, that technological progress is triggered by man's need to overcome shortages caused by population increases, and that people are the ultimate resource because they create other resources of all kinds.[10] They point to zealous environmentalists who are willing to sacrifice thousands of timber industry jobs to save an owl as evidence that the environment movement is anti-growth, antiprogress, and antipeople.

Evidence that over a billion human beings live in squalor, another half billion are starving, that 45,000 children die a day, and that 1.2 billion hectares of land have been eroded and stripped of agricultural productivity since 1945 is dismissed as the product of misallocative economic systems and bad farming methods. Warnings of ozone depletion, and increases in atmospheric greenhouse gases that could lead to global warming, climatic changes, and flooding of coastal areas are simply disbelieved or deemed "unproven"—as if standards of criminal proof must be required before mankind decides to save itself.

If only correct economic theories principles were applied, they argue, pressures of population on the environment could be relieved, and the growth of population could continue unabated. A gathering of bishops assembled to defend the Pope's ban on birth control has asserted that the earth could "theoretically" feed 40 billion people.[11] Such assertions might make the five and a half billion humans now on the planet feel very selfish about not accommodating an additional 35 billion people, until it is revealed that these and other extravagant assertions of the number of people that can be supported on earth are based on assumptions such as that all food is evenly distributed, all available crop land is deforested without soil erosion, heavy use is made of fertilizers containing phosphorus that pours into the oceans, no cash crops are grown (such as cotton or coffee), no livestock is raised, all humans agree to live on a subsistence vegetarian diet, and—in the case of one recent assertion—that all farms are as productive as a specific laboratory farm in Iowa. The latter assumption is particularly unrealistic since productivity of the particular farm referred to in the assumption is unmatched by other Iowa farms, let alone the degraded farms of the third world.

FOOD PRODUCTION

Malthusians note that the world must produce food for an additional 100 million new people each year, and do so with 26 billion less tons topsoil, and ever decreasing supplies of water from rapidly draining aquifers. If, as estimated, food production increases by only 1% per year, there will soon be many more starving people in the world. It remains to be seen how long mankind will be able to pull enough technological rabbits out of the hat to provide enough food to feed an increasing population.

There are some disturbing portents. In 1988, per capita production of cereal declined 6% from its peak in 1985.[12] Developing countries are relying more heavily on imports of food from North America. In 1988, for the first time in recent memory, the United States consumed more grain that it produced.[13] Although that year was one of severe drought, and reserves more than made up for the shortfall, it revealed that, despite new technologies and farming methods, food production is still very dependent on the weather. In 1989, world cereal stocks dropped to the dangerous level of only 17% of annual production.[14]

It can be readily seen that both Malthusian doomsayers and single-minded progrowthers have a wealth of data and statistics to back up their positions. But does either group really believe their own projections? When pressed, even the most zealous progrowther will concede, that at some point, the population cannot continue to double every 25 years. One of Meadows' hypothetical models did not need to rely on controversial assumptions: if one took an ordinary sheet of paper and doubled its thickness by folding it over, and repeated the folding 42 times, the thickness of the paper would reach from the earth to the moon.[15] (This can be verified by using a simple calculator.) It has been shown, for example, that it would not take so many doublings of the human population before the earth would become a ball of flesh expanding outward at the speed of light.

THE EFFECT OF TECHNOLOGY

Likewise, even the most zealous Malthusian must concede that unanticipated advances in technology, food production, and environmental science might delay the dreaded day of reckoning. (Ansley Coale has mused that a Malthusian living in 1890 might have said "there's no way the United States can support two hundred and fifty million people. Where are they going to pasture all their horses?''[16])

It does not appear to be an unfair trivialization of the great debate, therefore, to suggest that it appears to be reducible to simple disagreement about timing. It might be further suggested that continued debate about timing may be counterproductive since it begs the real issue: assuming that the population will indeed stop growing at some point (presumably before the earth becomes a ball of flesh), what forces of law or nature should be relied upon to check the growth of population? Although war, plagues, and famines have operated as temporary checks on growth in the past, is man capable of creating his own checks, hopefully more humane than those checks previously encountered in human history?

There will, of course, be risks in implementing man-created checks at other than an optimum time. Progrowthers will argue that imposing checks prematurely will deprive mankind of advances in technology that might be spurred by the growth of population. Other opponents of birth control will argue that precious new life will be foregone before some divine self-correcting mechanism is allowed to manifest itself. Malthusians will argue that any delay in creating and applying checks will result in imminent encounters with the cruel checks so often encountered in the past—only this time the victims will be not only human beings but the earth itself. But this only brings the debate back to timing.

Resolution of the issue therefore requires two tasks: first, a balancing of the risks posed by both immediate and delayed imposition of checks; and two, an analysis of the kinds of checks that might be created and imposed.

The risks of allowing population to expand without checks are indeed formidable. With each net addition to the human race the amount of land, water, natural resources, and air per human being is proportionately reduced. Thus more intensive use of each resource is required to maintain living standards and prevent or delay Malthusian consequences. Technology can, as it has in the past, enable mankind to make more intensive use of resources. At the margin, technology can even reduce the effect of population on the environment. But the danger signs are becoming increasingly apparent: the holes in the ozone layer, acid rain, the unsustainable depletion of water tables, and the loss of tropical forests.

THE MOMENTUM OF GROWTH

The risk of imposing no checks on population now is that the final limits imposed by earth's resources will be reached while the momentum of population growth continues unabated, thus triggering either the dreaded Malthusian checks, or the equally dreaded inhumane checks imposed by governments. Humane checks on population require planning at least one generation ahead of time. It has been noted, for example, that even in China, where strict family measures are now being applied, the population will continue to grow for at least another generation even if there is no relaxation of current measures.

But what are the risks of imposing population checks at a time when the technological potential exists to maintain an expanding population while at the same time limiting the effects of additional population on the environment? In other words, what if the progrowthers and anti-Malthusians are correct in stating that the limits to growth have not yet been reached? The result would be that certain technological innovations that might have been spurred by the scarcities brought on by population growth will not be developed, and that certain markets will not be stimulated to grow as much as they would have if population growth had increased market demand. In addition, billions of potential human beings will have been denied the right to live on the planet.

THE PHYSICAL LIMITS OF GROWTH

It will be recalled that most anti-Malthusians acknowledge at least some limits to growth (i.e., at some point before the earth becomes a ball of flesh). With this perspective, it is submitted that the risks of not imposing humane population checks now outweigh the risks of imposing them at a time when the potential exists to accommodate additional humans. Since even anti-Malthusians acknowledge the need to impose checks at some time in the future before the earth become a ball of flesh (and thus deny at that time the right of potential humans to live on earth), the question may be raised as to why potential humans numbered 10 to 20 billion should enjoy greater rights to life than potential humans numbered 100 to 200 billion, or 10 to 20 trillion.

The need to take the risks of premature rather than tardy population checks becomes even more apparent when one considers that each new batch of potential humans is purchased only at the cost of billions of living humans who will live lives of desperation and misery. Although it may be countered that the percentage of starving humans has in fact declined since the time of Malthus, the number of suffering people, in absolute terms, has increased geometrically despite general rises in average living standards and dramatic increases in the food supply.

So even if the anti-Malthusians are correct, and technological progress enables mankind to support 20, 30, or even 40 billion people (as asserted by the Catholic Bishops), there is no historical precedent or technological basis for hoping that the number of suffering people in the world will decline as the population increases.

INCOME REDISTRIBUTION

It has been suggested that programs of social justice and fair redistribution can alleviate the suffering of the deprived, particularly in the third world. There is no doubt that such programs could alleviate some of the sufferings of the most deprived at the expense of the privileged few. But even if Americans, who constitute about 5% of the world's population and who hog up to 30% of much of the world's resources could be persuaded to part with their wealth to enrich the world's poor, such a redistribution would not eliminate hunger, increase the per capita amount of land per person, or significantly expand the limits of growth. At most it might permit a few additional billions of humans to inhabit the earth before population checks would inevitably be required.

This is not to suggest that programs of social justice should not be pursued, or that fair distribution of wealth should not be encouraged. Unfortunately, however, long tested economic laws have not resulted in historically significant increases of wealth in many societies professing egalitarian goals (witness the failure of communism and the reluctant resort by such governments to market oriented economies despite the inequalities of capitalism). So while the quest for an egalitarian yet highly productive utopia should certainly continue, the hope that one might someday be achieved should in no way excuse the failure today to address the question of the affect of population on the environment.

In summary, if the controversy between Malthusians and progrowthers can be viewed as a simple dispute as to the timing of the imposition of population checks (that is, a question of when, rather than if), a solution can be reached through an evaluation of the risks of both premature and tardy imposition of checks. Unfortunately, however, no solution is possible without a recognition of the problem. Although such doomsayers as Malthus, Meadows, and Ehrlich have done much to explain the potential effects of population growth on living standards and the environment, their warnings of imminent catastrophe have been proven false time and time again. In this respect, much of their work has been counterproductive inasmuch as it has diminished in the public consciousness the integrity of their basic assumptions. It gives the anti-Malthusians the chance to say again and again "I told you so," and to relegate the Malthusians to the level of the soap box and the religious fanatic carrying the placard "The End is Near."

THE RIO SUMMIT

Indeed, much remains to bring population issues into the mainstream. At the much publicized World Environmental Conference in Rio in 1992, population issues were never even addressed.[17] Although this failure was attributed by some to the influence of the Catholic church, it may more realistically be attributed to both apathy and outright antipathy to population issues by world governments. Thus, the Rio Conference may be viewed as representing a general view held by most countries—that environmental issues can be resolved by laws, clean-up programs, and moratoria.

THE ENVIRONMENTAL PROTECTION AGENCY

In the United States, for example, the government, through the Environmental Protection Agency, spends billions of dollars on the clean-up of toxic waste dumps.[18] Laws require consumers to spend additional billions for a variety of devices such as the catalytic converter in order to reduce certain types of polluting emissions. Despite regulations that give lip service to requiring findings of cost-effectiveness, rarely are all the costs of environmental regulations taken into consideration.

The following hypothetical example illustrates the point: suppose the government mandates that all cars produced must have certain expensive pollution-control devices. Although such devices (like many medications) may have deleterious environmental side effects (such as decreased gas mileage), they nevertheless succeed, at great expense, in reducing certain types of undesirable pollutants by 10%. Assume, however, that at the same time that these improvements in the emissions of pollutants take place, that the number of cars increases by 20%. The result is a net increase in pollution despite the improvement in emissions from each automobile.

This hypothetical example is in no way meant to suggest that environmental laws that reduce individual emissions are bad or undesirable. On the contrary, without them the pollution would be far worse. The point, however, is that the underlying environmental issue is that of population. Like Alice in Wonderland on a treadmill, for each step forward taken through traditional remedial action such as the cleaning up of rivers or toxic dumps, two steps back are taken as population expands exponentially. Unfortunately, however, national public policy in the United States has not recognized the important role that population control should play in solving many environmental problems.

Although the Congressional declaration of national environmental policy set forth in the National Environmental Policy Act of 1969 purported to recognize the "profound influences of population growth," and to set forth the goal of using "all practical means and measures" to "create and maintain conditions under which man and nature can exist in productive harmony," nothing in the substance of that Act sets forth any measures or goals with respect to the growth of population. Neither the Act's index to the Code of Federal Regulations nor the notes of deci-

sions to cases decided under the Act contain so much as one entry referring to population policies of any kind. While the Act created an entirely
new body of administrative law to carry out and implement vast numbers of regulations in such areas as nuclear policy, flood plain control,
land management, air and water pollution, and toxic wastes, there is not
one word implementing federal policies to control population.

POPULATION POLICIES

Indeed, during the 1980s, United States policy on population was perhaps best represented by the Reagan and Bush Administration's policy
of opposing legal abortions and even cutting off aid for family planning
and birth control to countries in which abortion was sanctioned as part
of a family planning program.[19] In short, the policies of the United States
have not only failed to recognize the importance of population in environmental policy, but have actively worked to resist such recognition.
When the issue of population control was taken off the agenda of environmental topics at the Rio Conference, there was no objection or suggestion to the contrary by the United States representatives. In other
words, not only have the nations of the world failed to recognize population control as a major component of a sound environmental policy, they
have chosen to publicly ignore (at least in such public arenas as the
Rio Conference) any suggestion that it plays any role at all. Although
bureaucrats at United Nations Commissions continue to issue vast quantities of periodic reviews and reports on world population, often warning
of environmental consequences, these reports do not purport to reflect
official policy of individual nations.

At its best, traditional approaches to environmental problems have
been curative (cleaning up air, water, and toxic dumps), reactive (requiring installation of catalytic converters in car engines, or scrubbers on
smokestacks), or punitive (punishing polluters, but also innocent victims
of polluters such as landowners).

ENVIRONMENTAL POLICY

At its worst, environmental policy has simply been exclusionary—that
is excluding from a community any newcomers who might make a demand on local resources. In Colorado, for example, representatives of
local communities managed successfully to lobby the federal government to disapprove the Two Forks dam project, which would have provided water for thirsty new Colorado communities.[20] The result of the
disapproval of the Two Forks Dam will almost certainly be the denial of
water taps to many builders and applicants, and increases in the cost of
water. Thus newcomers will be turned away on grounds that there is

insufficient, or too expensive water. Existing residents who already enjoy water taps purchased cheaply years before will enjoy the price rise of their property reflecting the scarcity value of their water taps.

The objections to the Two Forks Dam project were based on some valid environmental objections, and the disapproval of the project no doubt provided some environmental benefit to the residents of Colorado. It was therefore hailed as a great victory for the environmental movement, particularly by politicians seeking the "environmental" vote. Unrecognized, however, was the fact that the environmental benefits for Coloradans had been gained by the simple expedient of excluding (by denying water to new communities) those who would otherwise have come to Colorado to live. The question was never asked as to where those people (who would otherwise have come to Colorado) would go instead. Would they go to Arizona, where their demands for water might contribute to the accelerating and non-self-sustaining depletion of that state's aquifers and underground reservoirs? Would they go to California where water rationing had been introduced and a vicious war for water between farmers and cities was gaining momentum? While those faceless people may have had options, it is certainly not clear that wherever they went, their demand for water and other resources would not have created environmental damage equal or greater to what they would have caused in Colorado.

The environmental "victory" in such cases as Two Forks Dam turns out to be very regional in scope. Implicit in such victories is a population policy, although unrecognized and certainly not advertised as such. That policy is very simple: by keeping people out, pressures on the regional environment can be relieved. Were the people who were excluded simply to disappear from the face of the earth, or take a one-way trip to Mars, the environmental victory would not be limited to one particular region at the expense of another. In fact, however, the people excluded by many self-proclaimed environmentalists do not just disappear, they take their demands for resources somewhere else. In terms of the global environment, therefore, the environmentalists' victory turns out to be a very hollow one indeed. Most of these same "environmentalists" fail to recognize their victory as one based primarily on the distinctly Malthusian premise that there are indeed limits to what the earth can provide for the sustenance of mankind. Why then do they not recognize this and ally themselves with the movement for population control and involve themselves in family planning, birth control, and abortion rights? The answer to this question is addressed in detail in Chapter 4.

Although the examples of regional exclusionary policies masquerading as environmental policies are numerous, and discussed in more detail later in this book, one of the most colorful is that of New York City loading its unwanted sewage on a barge, launching it into the ocean, and trying to sell it to some poor unsuspecting community that values its regional environment less than did New York City.

Other exclusionary policies can be found in local zoning regulations. By limiting the number of lots or water taps per acre, or even attempting to prohibit any building whatsoever, many communities attempt to "protect" their environment by keeping out people who would make demands on their resources, or place any additional environmental burden on the community. The result of such exclusionary policies, put into effect by existing residents who stand to gain from the price rises of their own property reflecting scarcity values, is to exclude undesirable people by raising the cost of property or water taps to such levels that only wealthy and more desirable clientele can afford to join the community. Unfortunately such "yuppie environmentalism" leads to the creation of environmental "ghettoes"—communities in which poor and rejected human beings can afford to live because the environmental regulations are weak or nonexistent. Again, the impact on the global environment is nil, or even adverse, since even one environmental ghetto can create national or global environmental damage out of all proportion to its size.

IMMIGRATION

Some of the worst environmental ghettoes are in third world countries. Toxic dumps, untreated sewage, and eroded land are only some of the environmental conditions that, combined with unfavorable economic and social conditions, make living so intolerable that many inhabitants seek to emigrate. Many of the population pressures that contribute to such conditions are relieved by such emigration, in the same way that similar conditions in Europe were relieved by emigration to the New World. In Mexico, for example, thousands of Mexican nationals pour over the U.S. border each day, seeking better living conditions and making demands on resources in the United States.

Permitting citizens to leave the country turns out to be a far more acceptable internal policy than encouraging family planning, distributing birth control devices to women in rural areas, legalizing abortion, or attempting to overturn cultural traditions of large families. Thus, as long as there are easy policies of emigration, and the United States is willing to turn a blind eye to "illegal" immigration, population and environmental pressures in Mexico will continue to simply be transferred to the United States rather than be dealt with internally by politically unpopular policies.

As of 1993, there appeared to be no political will in the United States to stop the exploitation of Mexican nationals.[21] American corporations have learned that they can achieve higher profits by taking advantage of desperate immigrants willing to work for pittance wages. The technically illegal status of the immigrants makes them subject to blackmail and other forms of exploitation. The Zoe Baird hearings for Attorney General in 1993 revealed that the exploitation of foreign nationals is not limited to large corporations. For the wealthy and privileged in the United States, the advantage of low wages and exploitable labor is too great to permit enforcement of immigration laws. One recent study by the Center for Immigration Studies[22] has revealed another possible reason for the failure to enforce immigration laws. That study has revealed that the failure to enforce immigration laws has provided "an alternative supply of labor so that urban employers have not had to hire available black jobseekers. And the foreign workers have oversupplied labor to low-skilled markets. This has kept the jobs in a seemingly perpetual state of declining real wages which are incapable of lifting black workers out of poverty." The study concluded that the "chief victims [are] black Americans . . . Whether intended or not, the present immigration policy is a revived instrument of institutional racism. It provides a way to by-pass the national imperative to address the employment, job preparation and housing needs of much of the urban black population."[23] When American employers claim that it is not possible to find Americans to fill jobs at the lower end of the pay scale, one wonders if these same employers have taken a look at the unemployment statistics for African Americans, particularly teenagers. Although the study concludes that African Americans are the chief victims of exploitive American immigration policies, it is apparent that other minority groups, including Mexican Americans, also suffer severely.

FREE TRADE

Although immigration laws could be enforced by border fences and a centrally computerized employment documentation system, a far better way would be to help Mexico improve its living conditions and foster employment. The American Free Trade treaty would do precisely that by stimulating employment in Mexican industries producing goods for export, while at the same time stimulating American employment by providing a huge new market for American products. According to the economic laws of comparative advantage, the result would be a significant increase in the wealth of both countries, and a significant reduction in the incentives for immigration. Unfortunately, however, certain interest groups and those whose own particular industries would have to meet competition have lobbied against this treaty. The views of such groups bear a remarkable resemblance to the views of American protectionists who prior to the Great Depression convinced Congress that the way to increase employment was to set up high tariff barriers to "protect'' American businesses. The tragic result, of course, was a reduction in trade and economic activity that led to the Great Depression. Such "protection" is almost always of the type that favors producers (who want to eliminate competition so that they can raise prices and increase profits) over the consumer (who must pay higher prices). Thus, despite a showing that three domestic jobs in export industries will be created for every one job lost in import industries, interest groups representing the industries that lose the one job are often successful in lobbying for protectionist barriers even at the expense of the national interest. For this reason, and the others mentioned above, the influx of illegal workers into the United States will likely continue unabated. As long as it does, there will be no incentive on the part of Mexico to expand its family planning programs or promote wider distribution of birth control devices. Abortion will continue to be prohibited, thus dooming thousands of women to death from unsafe abortions, and others to caring for children who are beyond their ability to support.

Other third world and developing countries do not have a neighboring developed country willing to take all those for whom their own economy cannot provide. Such countries cannot, like Mexico, or Europe in the 1800s, relieve the pressures of population through emigration, and are therefore forced to adopt internal policies of family planning and birth control. China, for example, which for years had no population policy at all (Mao encouraged population growth as a means of increasing political and communist power), finally had to face the fact that its population was approaching one billion people, while its fertile land was rapidly being eroded through overintensive farming. Despite implementation of strict and politically unpopular family planning programs, however, China's population continues to grow and will continue to do so for many years even if its programs continue in full force. China must feed 22% of the world's population by intensive use of 7% of the world's arable soil.

ENVIRONMENTAL PROGRAM

Most environmental programs are one dimensional in that they seek to protect the environment simply by attempting to clean up or repair past damage, or limit the emissions and pollution of individual humans or enterprises. Such one-dimensional policies are ultimately doomed to fail unless they take into account a myriad of other factors, of which population is most significant. Mankind has delayed its Malthusian day of reckoning by emigration to the New World (at the expense of indigenous people in sparsely populated lands), the Industrial Revolution, and the Green Revolution. The effects on human development have been reciprocal. Population growth has created the incentives for innovation, technology, and industrialization, just as those same developments have enabled the earth to support a greater population.

MALTHUSIAN LIMITS

It can be argued that in many parts of the world, Malthusian limits have already been reached—witness the teeming throngs of the starving and dispossessed in many third world countries. But if it is true that there are more people, in absolute terms, who are starving today than there were a hundred years ago, it is also true that the percentage of the total population that is starving is less. While one could argue the philosophical point of which condition is preferable in ethical terms, the fact remains that there are limits to growth. While Meadows, Ehrlich, and other Malthusians may disagree with Simons and the progrowthers as to when those limits will be reached (or whether they have already been reached), no one can deny that it will be reached before the earth becomes a ball of flesh expanding at the speed of light.

If one grants to a potential hundred billionth human no greater right to life than to a potential ten billionth, there appears to be no greater risk to limiting population growth now, than waiting to see if, perhaps, we could not add a few extra billions with no ill effects on the environment. This risk appears particularly well advised to take in light of the fact that at such time as even the Anti-Malthusians perceive the imminent limits to growth, it may take up to a century to stop population growth by humane methods. By that time it could be too late, requiring the use of methods that would be abhorrent to any civilized society. One can imagine, for example, the more humane methods that China might have been able to use had it implemented family planning policies at a far earlier date.

It will be seen that population policies, as an inherent part of any sound environmental program, involve a number of dimensions beyond simple family planning. It will be seen, for example, that abortion is a major part of family planning in many countries (such as Russia), and other countries where religious, legal, cultural, or economic obstacles prevent free dissemination of birth control information and devices. Immigration, emigration, international trade, and education—all play important roles. The chapters that follow attempt to explain the nature of the relationship between these various factors, and answer the question (suggested by the title of this book): what do population policies, family planning, abortion laws, immigration, trade policies, and education have to do with the environment?

PRIVATE ENVIRONMENTAL ACTION

It will be seen that, in many cases, environmental groups have effectively neutralized the influence of each other by their policies of confrontation. Rarely have they taken the opportunity to join forces with population control groups such as Planned Parenthood in order to present a united front on environmental policy. In Rio, for example, the world environmental movement chose not to invite population groups, and population issues were not even on the agenda.[24] High profile environmentalists such as Vice-President Al Gore have chosen to emphasize the curative and reactive aspects of environmental policy. His much proclaimed 1992 book on the environment, *Earth in the Balance,* devotes some 27 of its 407 pages to population issues.[25] When population is addressed toward the end of the book, it comes almost as an afterthought.

This is not to suggest that curative and reactive environmental policies do not have a useful role to play. Cleaning up after past environmental disasters and reducing the number of pollutants per person obviously help the environment. But even the most expensive and zealous curative and reactive policies may not be cost effective if they are nullified by an exponentially expanding population.

Nor are population issues the only ones ignored by most of today's self-proclaimed "environmentalists." Rarely are the more controversial issues of abortion or immigration addressed by environmental groups. It is far more expedient politically to ignore these issues and concentrate on delaying large projects, shutting down industries, or blocking bulldozers. Thus, killing a water project or shipping a barge of sewage to some other community are hailed as environmental victories.

LONG-TERM SOLUTIONS

It will be seen that long-term solutions to population problems are not to be found in policies that merely reduce the standard of living. Democratic governments do not have the power to unilaterally impose such restrictions on the standard of living. In 1988, Rumanian Communist dictator Ceaucescu solved the nation's energy problem by simply issuing a decree that people would get no heat and would have to freeze during the winter. Although democracies can accomplish some analogous results (by, say, denying EPA approval of a water project, thus denying water to new settlers), it has already been noted that such environmental "solutions" are not solutions at all, but accomplish only a shifting of environmental problems from one region to another.

That severe environmental problems exist is not in issue. A wave of new books (including Al Gore's) effectively makes this point. But the indisputable fact of deterioration of the world's environment does not answer the question of what has caused the change, and what is the cure. Nor does it answer the question of what policies will be the most cost-effective.

It will be seen in the chapters that follow that long-term environmental solutions therefore require more than the curative and reactive policies of the kind proposed by contemporary politicians and the majority of "environmental" organizations; they require a recognition of the problems posed by population and solutions that take into account the laws relating to abortion, immigration, education, free trade, and economic activity.

NOTES

1. Charles Mann, How Many Is Too Many?, *The Atlantic,* Feb. 1993, pp. 47, 56.
2. *Id.*
3. *Id.*
4. *Id.*
5. Paul Ehrlich, *The Population Bomb* (1968).
6. Paul Erhlich, *The Population Explosion* (1990).
7. Donella Meadows et al., *The Limits to Growth* (1972); See also Dennis L. Meadows et al., *The Dynamics of Growth in a Finite World* (1974); Dennis L. Meadows and Donella Meadows, *Towards Global Equilibrium* (1973).
8. Donella Meadows and Dennis L. Meadows, *Beyond the Limits* (1992).
9. Ehrlich, *The Population Explosion, supra,* note 6, pp. 53–54.
10. Simon, Why Do We Still Think Babies Create Poverty, *Washington Post,* Oct. 13, 1985.
11. Ehrlich, *supra,* note 6, p. 19.
12. *Id.*
13. *Id.*
14. *Id.*
15. Meadows, *supra,* note 8, p. 15.
16. Mann, *supra,* note 7.
17. See Population Time Bomb Ticks Away at Earth Summit, *Reuters* (June 2, 1992, AM Cycle); Eisner, Earth Summit '92 Population Control Advocates Angered, *Newsday* (June 9, 1992) News, p. 17.
18. See, e.g., *Environmental Protection Agency Manual.*
19. See House Bars Millions for U.N. Fund Bush Says Pays For Abortions, *L.A. Times,* Nov. 15, 1989, p. A13.
20. Robert M. Hardaway, Two Forks Fight Was a Clash with Population, Not the Environment, *Denver Post,* Jan. 19, 1991, p. B7.
21. See, e.g., Evaluating Costs, Benefits of Immigration, *San Francisco Chronicle,* June 23, 1993, p. A5.
22. Vernon Briggs, Jr., Despair Behind the Riots: The Impediment of Mass Immigration to Los Angeles Blacks, 11 *Cent. for Immigr. Stud.* 1 (1992).

23. Id.

24. See, e.g., Earth First Meeting Reflects Gap Between Radicals, Mainstream, *Washington Post,* July 19, 1990, p. A3. Spencer et al., The Not so Peaceful World of Greenpeace, *Forbes,* Nov. 11, 1991; Patt Morrison, 3 Earth First! Defendants Sentenced for Vandalism, *L.A. Times,* Sept. 20, 1991, p. 4A.

25. Albert Gore, *Earth in the Balance* (1993). Population is discussed on pp. 31–33, 74–78, 110, 118, 124, 127, 131, 288, 305–306, 308–309, 311–317.

2   Malthus and the Environment

Every one-third of a second, at about the speed a machine gun fires its bullets, the planet earth makes room to accommodate one additional human being.[1] To provide that one human being with a living that meets minimum standards of human dignity, he must be provided annually with fuel and energy resources which, when consumed, release 3.2 tons of carbon into the atmosphere.[2] To further meet his everyday needs, he will annually require that 2000 m³ of fresh water be drawn from available wells, reservoirs and rivers,[3] and that 207 GJ of energy be produced from nonrenewable resources.[4] For shelter he will demand his per capita share of wood resources, including (if he is born in a developing country) nonrenewable tropical rain forests now being destroyed at an estimated rate of 100 acres per minute.[5] His and his fellow humans' demand for land will require intensive use of available arable soil, resulting in a 2% annual decline in the land available per person,[6] and the creation of deserts and nonproductive land at the rate of 1.25 million acres per year.[7] His waste products will include his share of 355,000 metric tons of phosphorus dumped annually into the world's oceans,[8] and 270,000 metric tons of methane,[9] 30,000 of sulfur,[10] and 80,000 of carbon monoxide released into the atmosphere.[11] To provide living space and resources for this new human and his fellows, one entire living species must be sacrificed every day, including the extinction of one vertebrate species every 9 months.[12] When he dies, his epitaph is written on a monument of waste and garbage 4000 times his body weight.

Every 18 days, the earth's population is increased by a number equal to the entire human population of the world in 5000 B.C.[13] Every 5 months the population increases by a number equal to the population of the world in the year 1575;[14] every decade the population increases by a number equal to the population of the world in 1776; and every two and a half decades, the population increases by a number equal to the entire population of the world in 1950.[15] On July 11, 1987, the earth welcomed its five billionth human.[16] By 1993, the population was fast approaching 6 billion, and headed toward 9 billion by early in the next century.[17]

These cold statistics on population growth and the amount of toxic wastes produced by the human population are not in serious dispute. Precise estimates vary, of course, but serious studies are in basic accord as to what is actually happening at the present time.[18] There is considerable disagreement, however, as to what it all means.[19]

For most of human history, it has been taken for granted that an increasing population is a fundamental ingredient of the wealth and power of nations.[20] Kings and philosophers, and economists alike sought to increase the population of the lands in which they lived. As Schumpeter has observed: "With rare exceptions they were enthusiastic about 'populousness' and rapid increases in numbers. In fact, until the middle of the eighteenth century, they were as nearly unanimous in this 'populationist' attitude as they have ever been in anything. A numerous and increasing population was the most important symptom of wealth; it was the chief cause of wealth; it was wealth itself—the greatest asset for a nation to have."[21]

Up until the seventeenth century, there appeared to be a substantial empirical and historical basis for the populationist view, and little cause to dispute it. By 10,000 B.C., the world's human population of about 6 million had already enlarged its food-gathering range to encompass most of the world's suitable land. Having reached those limits, an expanding population, driven by necessity, began the transition to agriculture in order to exploit lands not suitable for food gathering. In other words, without "overpopulation," the incentive to find new sources of food would not have existed, and mankind might find itself today still gathering berries and roots.[22] Continued "overpopulation" created incentives for new and better farming methods and irrigation systems in order to feed the expanding population.

Historians have noted that "development of irrigation systems in Mesopotamia allowed the few hunter–gatherers living in the Zagros Mountains in 8000 B.C. to evolve into a large population of plain-dwellers in the following millenia."[23] Bosrep has observed that "over a period of 8000 years, Mesopotamia became densely populated . . . Gradually the population changed from primitive food gatherers to people who applied the most sophisticated systems of food production existing in the ancient world."[24]

Continued "overpopulation" led to roads, and "creation of cities which allow[ed] for greater specialization and more efficient organization of the economy."[25] The opportunities created by a large population for the division of labor were recognized by all nations seeking to maximize their wealth and well-being. A theory of labor division was postulated by William Perry: "In the making of a watch, if one man shall make the wheels, another the spring, another shall enlarge the dial-plate, and another shall make the cases, then the watch shall be better and cheaper, than if the whole work be put upon any one man."[26] Adam Smith followed up this theory with his example of pin production in which "a single worker might turn out at most 20 pins a day, a factory employing a team of 10 workers manages to produce 12 pounds a day, or 48,000 pins, 4800 per worker."[27]

It was not surprising, therefore, when, as early as 1589, it was first suggested that there were limits to the earth's resources that could support population expansion, that such suggestions were not seriously entertained.[28] By the end of the eighteenth century, however, such suggestions began to be more precisely articulated. Ricardo, in his *Principles of Political Economy and Taxation,* observed that, even if the technological progress triggered by population growth is taken into account, the finite nature of certain fixed resources (such as land, water, and certain essential minerals) meant that a law of diminishing returns would ultimately check the growth of population: "Although, then it is probable that, under the most favorable of circumstances, the power of production is still greater than that of population, it will not long continue so; for the land being limited in quantity, and differing in quantity, with every increased portion of capital employed on it there will be a decreased rate of production, while the power of poulation continues always the same."[29]

Livi-Bacci has illustrated this concept with the example of a population isolated in a deep valley:

Initially, the more fertile, easily irrigated, and accesible lands are cultivated—those in the plain along the river. As population grows, and so the need for food, all the best land will be used, until it becomes necessary to cultivate more and distant plots on the slopes of the valley, difficult to irrigate and less fertile than the others. Continued growth will require the planting of still less productive lands, higher up the sides of the valley and more exposed to erosion. When all the land has been used up, further increase of population can still be obtained by more intensive cultivation, but these gains are too limited, as the point will eventually be reached when additional inputs of labor will no longer effectively increase production. In this way [population growth] leads to the cultivation of progressively less fertile lands with ever greater inputs of labor, while returns per unit of land or labor eventually diminish.[30]

Although Giovanni Botero first observed the effects of population growth on the availability of resources,[31] these observations were later expanded upon and popularized by the Reverend Thomas Malthus, whom Karl Marx derided as a "plagiarist" and "sycophant of the ruling classes."[32] Less widely known for the distinction of being the world's first professional economist,[33] Malthus' 1798 essay on population declared that "the power of population is indefinitely greater than the power in the earth to produce subsistence for man."[34] In support of this thesis, Malthus relied upon Ricardo's law of diminishing returns: "When acre has been added to acre till all the fertile land is occupied, the yearly increase of food must depend upon the melioration of the land already in possession. This is a fund which, from the nature of all soils, instead of increasing, must be gradually diminshing."[35]

The essay set forth what was essentially an economic hypothesis of the relationship between population and the earth's capacity to provide for it. Its logical conclusion—that mankind was doomed to expand until the limits of food production checked its expansion through starvation—was so pessimistic that its many critics simply refused to accept its premise, condemning it as "libel against the almighty himself,"[36] since it refuted the Christian doctrine that God would always provide. Others could not deny its compelling logic, dubbing Malthus' new economics the "dismal science."[37] According to some reluctant disciples, the most that could be hoped for was to delay the day of reckoning for as long as possible by using new methods and technologies to increase food production and produce greater quantities of goods. Thus even if Malthus was correct in observing that population increased geometrically, his corollary observation that food production increased only arithmetically might be refuted, at least for the foreseeable future.

Had Malthus confined his essay to his central premise concerning the relationship between population and the earth's capacity to sustain it, the compelling logic of his thesis would have been far more impervious to the counterattacks of his enraged critics. If his tone had been less pessimistic, emphasizing the role that new methods and technologies might play in increasing food production geometrically to keep up, at least for a time, with the geometric increase in population, he might not have stirred the resentment that drove his critics to such frenzy. Further, he could have done so without compromising his central hypothesis.

Instead, however, Malthus gilded the lily of his thesis with dogmatic claims that his "laws" were as immutable as those of Newton, and that the inevitable result of their application in nature was starvation, misery, war, and disease. According to Malthus, welfare and poor laws were counterproductive since, far from delaying the day of reckoning, they hastened it by fomenting the expansion of the poor population.

Malthus' failure to spike the bitter pill of his "laws" with any alternatives or hope not only compromised the perception of the integrity of his thesis, but also diminished his reputation. Thus his failure may have been more one of public relations rather than of logic. Even today, critics of family planning and population control programs hold up Malthus as the prime example of the fanatic doomsayer whose predictions never came true. They point out that the population of the earth has more than quintupled since the time of Malthus, but that the percentage of the population that is starving has gone down not up. The "Green Revolution" in agriculture has resulted in an increase in food production that surpasses even the rate of increase in the population.[38] In the United States, for example, food output per acre quadrupled during the period 1903–1976.[39]

ECONOMIC GROWTH

A latter day coalition of anti-Malthusians has many constituent interest groups. Proponents of economic growth insist that far from inhibiting economic growth, population increases are necessary for economic growth to occur. They argue that without such growth in the population, markets for goods will shrink, along with the incentives for technological innovation. According to such theories,[40] population growth creates a larger market and thus a greater market demand for goods. Schumpeter, for example, sees population as playing only a secondary role to technological innovation. "The fundamental impulse that sets and keeps the capitalist engine in motion comes from the new consumers' goods, the new methods of production or transportation, the new markets, the new forms of industrial organization that capitalist enterprise creates."[41]

It is still argued, as it was by Adam Smith, that increased demand permits producers to take advantage of the "economies of scale" of mass production.[42] An example of this theory is car production. If a population is small, say only a few thousand people, there will not be enough demand for cars to justify the creation of a big factory or assembly line. Thus all cars will be built by hand on an individual basis, and production per capita will be very low, resulting in a relatively low standard of living. If the population increases, however, producers will have the economic incentive to build a large factory capable of taking advantage of economies of scale by utilizing an assembly line to mass-produce cars. In addition, because of the greater profit potential of selling in such a large market, the rewards and incentives for technological innovation also increase. The result is higher per capita production of cars with a corresponding rise in the general standard of living for the entire population.

Kuznets, for example, while acknowledging the law of diminishing returns, nevertheless insists that diminishing returns are more than compensated for by the returns of human ingenuity triggered by population growth:

Why, if it is man who was the arthitect of economic and social growth in the past and responsible for the vast contributions to knowledge and technological and social power, a larger number of human beings need result in a lower rate of increase in per capita product? More population means more creators and producers, both of goods along established production patterns and of new knowledge and inventions. Why shouldn't the larger numbers achieve what the smaller numbers accomplished in the modern past—raise total output to provide not only for the current population increase but also for a rapidly rising supply per capita?

In other words, diminishing returns from fixed resources are more than compensated for by the increasing returns of human ingenuity and by the ever more favorable conditions created by demographic growth.[43]

Simon argues that Malthusian theory is based almost solely on the law of diminishing returns—that is, as increased population demands additional resources, each marginal increase in resource production requires ever greater input of labor and capital. To provide the first million people with coal, for example, cheap strip mining can produce what is required. As population increases, however, resort must be made to ever more expensive methods of extraction including digging deeper and deeper into the ground for each additional unit of coal. Simon points out that the law of diminishing returns assumes a fixed resource base. People, he argues, are an expanding resource that can in turn provide other resources of all kinds. He cites the example of the shortage of ivory tusks for billiard balls that occurred when the source of supply from elephants approached exhaustion late in the last century. As a result a prize was offered for an ivory substitute, which resulted in the invention of celluloid.[44] This invention in turn resulted in greatly increased production of billiard balls. Thus shortages of the type that Malthus feared would result in degradation of living standards as population increased, actually result in technological advances that increase the standard of living. Indeed, without increases in population, living standards would be doomed to stagnate or even decline.

Simon cites several examples of his thesis. He notes that Thailand doubled its population between 1950 and 1977, while at the same time enjoying an enviable economic growth rate of 3%. Per capita income increased at the even higher rate of 4% during this period.[45]

It should be noted that Ehrlich refers to this latter illustration as an example of the "Netherlands Fallacy: The Netherlands can support 1,031 people per square mile only because the rest of the world does not. In 1984–1986, the Netherlands imported almost 4 million tons of cereals, 130,000 tons of oils, and 480,000 tons of pulses (peas, beans, lentils). It took some of these relatively inexpensive imports and used them to boost their production of expensive exports—330,000 tons of milk and 1.2 million tons of meat. The Netherlands also extracted about a half-million tons of fishes from the sea during this period and imported more in the form of fish meal.[46]"

ORGANIZED RELIGION

A second group of anti-Malthusians can be found within certain organized religions. Although most such religions originated prior to the time of Malthus and the population explosion of the industrial age, latter day leaders of such religions profess to have found a moral and religious aspect to the question of population and family planning. Since their rejection of Malthusian premises and objections to family planning (in particular "artificial" contraceptives and abortion) are based on perceived moral principles steeped in religious faith, they are, by definition, not subject to economic or scientific refutation. In many cases, however, the revelations to church leaders of the immorality of birth control and abortion have come relatively recently in the development of religious doctrine. As early as 1588, Pope Gregory XIV, the head of the Catholic Church, condoned abortion,[47] and it was not until 1869 that God revealed to Pope Pius IX that Pope Gregory was wrong and that abortion (along with such other horribles as public education) should be condemned.[48] Still later, in 1968, Pope Paul VI issued the encyclical *Humanae Vitae,* which went on to condemn the use of all contraceptives except the one that had been proven to be ineffective—the infamous rhythm method.[49] Although Pope Paul's successor was rumored to be in favor of overturning the contraceptive ban, he died just days after investiture before taking any action, and the present Pope has been steadfast in his condemnation of any kind of artificial birth control. Other religions also condemn abortion (see Chapter 6).

ABORTION AND CONTRACEPTION

A third anti-Malthusian constituency has been, at various times in human history, the legal community. One hundred years ago, birth control was illegal in most countries. Abortion, on the other hand, does not appear historically to have been specifically prohibited by many of the world's legal systems. Neither the ancient Greek nor Roman legal systems prohibited abortion, and the English common law at the time of Malthus permitted abortion up until the time of "quickening." In the United States, the common law permitting abortions until quickening was followed by all the states until 1828, when New York became the first state to make abortion before quickening a crime. Abortion after quickening was declared to be a form of manslaughter. The trend toward illegalization of abortion continued, and legal prohibitions even extended to the distribution of birth control information and devices. In 1873, the U.S. Comstock Law prohibited advertisements of prescriptions for contraceptives. Many states enacted similar laws. As late as the 1960s public restroom vending machines disbursing condoms were required to advise purchasers that condoms were for the prevention of disease only. In many large countries with high fertility rates, such as Mexico, birth control was not even legalized until 1973.

A trend toward liberalization of birth control and abortion laws began in the early 1960s. In 1962, the trials of Sherri Finkbine caught the public's imagination and sympathy. Ms. Finkbine had taken the drug thalidomide, which was subsequently discovered to cause hideous birth defects in children. When she was refused the right to abortion in the United States, she was forced to go to Sweden to get her abortion.[50] Soon thereafter, several states began to liberalize their abortion laws. California, North Carolina and Colorado led the way with liberalizing legislation in 1967, and in 1970 Hawaii, New York, and Alaska abolished all criminal laws against abortions performed in the early months of pregnancy. Finally, in 1973, the United States Supreme Court in Roe v. Wade[51] declared that a constitutional right to privacy ensured a woman's right to abortion in the first trimester of pregnancy. Subsequent decisions of the court addressed state attempts to limit abortion rights. While state laws giving husbands the right to veto a woman's abortion decision were struck down,[52] a variety of other restrictions, such as provisions requiring parental or court consent for abortions of an unmarried minor, have been upheld.[53] In 1992, the basic right to an abortion as set forth in Roe was upheld by a narrow majority of the Supreme Court, although tighter restrictions were also upheld.[54]

By 1993, the trend of the world's legal community was clearly toward greater liberalization of both abortion and contraception laws.[55] Of countries with populations of 1 million or more, 25 now permit abortion on demand, 42 permit abortion on general medical grounds, incest, or rape, and 13 permit it for certain medical or social reasons; 52 countries permit abortion only when the life of the mother is in danger.[56] In Ireland, abortion is prohibited with virtually no exceptions.[57] Despite the Islamic Hadith, which permits early abortions, many Islamic nations in Asia prohibit abortion.[58]

An inventory of laws on the books of the world's nations is somewhat misleading, however. Many governments, such as Mexico, do not vigorously enforce abortion laws.[59] Thus, while legal, religious, and cultural obstacles prevent legal abortions, illegal abortions are commonly performed. Like most countries in which abortion is prohibited, an abortion underground thrives. It is estimated that over one million illegal abortions are performed in Mexico every year.[60] About 50,000 women die each year from septicemia and other complications.[61] One of the reasons for this exceptionally high death rate is that the common method of abortion practiced in the abortion underground is that of inserting a plastic tube into the cervix in order to induce an infection that causes an abortion. Although such a procedure is cheap (usually less than $30), and capable of performance without sophisticated medical equipment, it is the most risky method and often leads to the death of the mother. Other methods used are the insertion of potassium-soaked cotton, the medicinal herb zoapatle, or other concoctions. Dr. Alfredo Rustrian, a surgical gynecologist in Mexico, has observed that the use by women of such unsafe methods reveals "how desperate women get looking for a way out of the problem. They prefer risking their lives with these cures to having the child. This type of patient doesn't go to the hospital for a week, when the infection is over all her body. They often die."[61A]

In countries where abortion is legal and available, the preferred method is suction curettage. In the United States this method has largely replaced the method of scraping the uterus with an implement. The difference in death rates resulting from safe legal procedures, and unsafe illegal ones is significant. In the United States, for example, where abortion is legal, no deaths of women resulting directly from abortions have been reported in recent years,[62] and abortion is "11 times safer than a tonsillectomy or childbirth."[63] Considering that over a million abortions are performed each year in the United States, this appears to be a remarkable medical achievement.

Worldwide, however, it is estimated that over a fifth of a million women die each year from unsafe illegal abortions in countries where it is banned.[64] Many of these deaths are slow and agonizing. A hospital in Nairobi, where abortions are illegal, reports that it admits 40 to 60 women each day suffering from the effects of unsafe abortions.[65]

In countries where the abortion rate is rigorously enforced, there is a secondary cause for increased deaths among mothers—namely, deaths from forced maternity. For example, when Communist Romania in 1966 issued a restrictive abortion decree in an attempt to increase the birth rate, the maternal death rate per million women aged 15 to 44 skyrocketed from 14.3 in 1965 to 97.5 in 1978.[66] Romania's abortion law was so strict that, according to Western diplomats, women were required to undergo gynecological checkups in the presence of police, and pregnant women were put under police surveillance until they gave birth.[67]

Some of the highest abortion rates are to be found in countries in which abortion is illegal.[68] Greece, for example, has one of Europe's highest abortion rates, as does Belgium, where abortion is also illegal.[69] Yet even where abortion is legal, legality is not tantamount to availability of safe abortions. When Spain legalized abortion in 1985, the Catholic Church threatened to excommunicate any woman who had an abortion. As a result, doctors in state-run hospitals refused to perform abortions on moral grounds. When a woman who contracted german measles was forced to travel to a Southern province to get an abortion, the doctors who performed the abortion, and the woman, were excommunicated. Doctors in Badajoz in western Spain refused to perform an abortion on a 14-year-old girl who had been raped.[70]

In West Germany, abortion was, until 1992, illegal except for certain social or "psychological" reasons. Because the law was subject to wide varying interpretations, actual determinations of legality were made on a regional basis. Thus there was considerable internal migration from regions with strict interpretations to those with more flexible ones. As a result over 75,000 legal abortions were performed in West Germany in 1989, more than in the East where abortions were legal on demand. Nevertheless, West Germany's abortion laws became the subject of contention when Germany was reunited. Despite the opposition of the Kohl government, the German Bundestag voted in June 1992 to permit abortion on demand during the first 12 weeks of pregnancy if the mother first submitted to counselling 3 days before the abortion.[71] (In June 1993, however, Germany's highest court ruled that the Constitution made abortion illegal, but that doctors and mothers could not be prosecuted.)

Many countries with the highest abortion rates are those in which birth control information or devices are not for legal, economic, or cultural reasons readily available. Since abortion is widely viewed as a poor substitute for contraception, one might expect to find great support for contraception among those opposed to abortion, particularly among those opposed to abortion on religious or moral grounds. In fact, that does not appear to be the case. It has already been noted that some of the strongest opponents of abortion (such as the Catholic Church) are also strongly opposed to contraception.

A joint committee of the National Research Council and the Institute of Medicine estimates that half of the 1.5 million abortions in the United States are the direct result of contraceptive failures.[72] Thus, there appears to be a significant connection between the availability of contraception and abortion. Why, then, are not the strongest opponents of abortion not also the strongest advocates of contraception? There appear to be two explanations for this.

First, the line between contraception and abortion is often blurred. Many abortion opponents are convinced that many birth control devices are in fact abortificants. In the case of one of the most common birth control devices, the intrauterine device (IUD), they appear to have some medical support for their position. Second, many abortion opponents are convinced that the very availability of birth control information and devices will encourage sexual promiscuity. Third, of course, many are convinced that contraception is inherently immoral (thus the *Humanae Vitae* encyclical of the Catholic Church), and that God intended mankind to propagate the earth without artificial limits.

Although the abortion opponents' position with regard to whether birth control devices are abortificants is often a matter of opinion or philosophy, there is little empirical evidence to support their position that the availability of contraceptive information and devices encourages promiscuity or abortion. Indeed, Holland, which has some of the most liberal laws relating to sex and the availability of contraception, also enjoys one of the lowest abortion rates. In Russia, by contrast, where contraception is legal but contraceptive devices are not widely available (due to economic reasons), the abortion rate is one of the world's highest. Indeed, in Russia abortion is now the primary means of birth control. This unfortunate fact appears to be the direct result of the lack of availability of contraceptive devices. Thus, ironically for those opposing both contraception and abortion, their opposition to contraception appears to result in significantly higher abortion rates.

Although contraception is now legal in the United States and most other countries, actual availability is an entirely different matter. Cultural, economic, and religious barriers still prevent widespread use of contraceptives even in countries where it is legal. In Mexico, for example, where population growth is very high,[73] the use of birth control is not considered to be widespread.[74] Contraceptives can be obtained from the government only by married women, and rural women often have no practical access at all.[75] Women who do have access, but are Catholic, risk violating the Pope's *Humanae Vitae* if they use birth control. Particularly for rural women, cultural attitudes and taboos inhibit the use of contraceptives even where it can be obtained. One observer of family planning in Mexico has observed that "many men still view offspring as a sign of their masculinity, or prohibit their wives from using birth control for fear the women will 'put the horns to them' with other men."[76] In many of the poorer and less developed countries, a large number of children are desired in order that they may be sent to the factories to supplement the income of the family, or to provide for their parents in old age.

Even in the United States, where such cultural attitudes do not pose a major obstacle to family planning, the availability of safe and reliable contraceptives is a problem, and in more recent years has become more rather than less so. The litigiousness of American society, combined with products liability laws that greatly favor plaintiffs has resulted in the disappearance of a large number of contraceptives. For example, five types of IUD, most of which were never proven to be unsafe when properly used, simply vanished from the American market in the 1980s.[77] Even the birth control pill, once hailed as the ultimate contraceptive, has been downgraded, leading many doctors to recommend against its use.

The loss of older methods of birth control would not be so severe, and the resulting number of abortions would be far fewer, were newly developed methods of birth control allowed in the United States. Unfortunately, the groups opposed to birth control have succeeded in blocking the introduction of new types of contraceptives, even where their use has been found to be safe and reliable. Indeed nine new birth control methods have been introduced during the past 10 years in a large number of countries worldwide. Such methods include a monthly nasal spray, and various types of implants. The range of options allowed in the United States have been more limited, although more recently a special kind of IUD known as copper-T380A, a low-dose oral contraceptive, and a contraceptive sponge have managed to reach American consumers.[78] Norplant was made available 8 years after its use and approval in other Western Countries such as Finland, and only after its maker compiled 19,000 pages on 55,000 users in 46 countries and thousands more in clinical trials in the United States.[79] Ever since the FDA's disapproval of thalidomide (which caused birth defects in children) in the face of its approval by European countries, the FDA has used this one example to justify its refusal to approve, even on an experimental basis, drugs and methods, even where such drugs promise to save many lives. In fact, the FDA's policies may be more representative of a bureaucracy's tendency to decline risks in a litigious society. The FDA realizes that it is far less likely to receive blame for keeping out a drug that saves lives than to approve even one that causes harm.

The abortion pill RU-486, developed by a French company and now available in France, has been banned from the United States. Even if the Clinton administration manages to get this ban reversed, there is a serious question as to whether the French company that developed it will allow its import in the United States, as antifamily planning and antiabortion groups have threatened a boycott of the company's products if RU-486 is introduced. Carl Djerassi, who helped develop the birth control pill in 1951, recently observed that the "United States is the only country other than Iran in which the birth-control clock has been set back during the past 10 years."[80]

Many of the most reliable types of birth control require continuous and diligent performance on the part of the woman. Most birth control pills, for example, must be taken daily, and the failure to observe the regimen can result in an unwanted pregnancy. For this reason, many family planners favor more passive methods of birth control that do not depend upon daily diligence for their effectiveness. Although suitable only for those who wish to have no children in the future, voluntary sterilization provides such a passive means. For this reason it has gained considerable popularity over the past two decades. In the United States, for example, the lack of other acceptable methods has made voluntary sterilization the leading method of contraception (33%).[81] In many other countries, however, laws and cultural taboos have inhibited the use of sterilization. It is therefore unavailable in many countries that have the most severe problems of overpopulation. In most of Latin America, for example, sterilization is available only for medical reasons.[82] The procedure is almost unheard of in Africa, and most doctors there refuse to even discuss it as a contraceptive option.[83] Although most countries in Western Europe have recently legalized the procedure, the state of the law in France is at present unsettled. It seems ironic that many countries that permit abortion on demand are still uncomfortable with permitting sterilization, which might reduce the demand for many abortions. Fortunately the procedure is permitted in many countries with severe problems of poverty and overpopulation (such as Bangladesh).[84]

The failure of the United States to permit many of the most effective and reliable birth control methods within its own borders might be more palatable if its policies did not extend to inhibiting the use of birth control in other countries that desperately need them. In 1989 the Bush administration resisted funding the United Nations Funds for Population Activities on grounds that the groups foster abortion.[85] In addition, the U.S. Agency for the UN Population for International Development withheld its 25 million contribution to the UN Population fund for similar reasons.[86] This ban on family planning assistance applied even to organizations operating in countries where abortion was legal. The tragic result of this policy was that abortions overseas increased dramatically due to the cut-off of funds available for birth control.[87] Many of these additional abortions, even in countries where abortion was legal, were of the primitive type, thus causing large increases in the deaths of pregnant women. Although the Clinton administration in 1993 was dedicated to reversing many of these shortsighted policies, the work of private domestic groups continues to inhibit family planning overseas. Antiabortion groups, for example, have succeeded in pressuring the Hoechst Corporation of Germany from licensing and marketing RU-486.

The fourth constituency of anti-Malthusianism may be generally described simply as "political." The term is here used more broadly to include not only statements and positions taken by those seeking votes and pursuing political office, but also statements and positions taken of nonpoliticians seeking to espouse a particular ideology. Although such statements often espouse the passage of certain laws and policies, they are not limited to such statements, and therefore are addressed here separately from the constituency of the law. The term "political" as used here therefore includes the activism of groups working outside the law, such as antiabortion groups blocking access to abortion clinics, as well as positions taken by leaders who have an interest other than the achievement of political office.

An example would be the position taken by Mao Tse Tung prior to the cultural revolution in Communist China. Mao proclaimed that it was in the interest of China for the population to increase as much as possible so that its armies might be supplied with soldiers to assert its political will. (That position was dramatically reversed by Mao's successors.) In Nazi Germany, Hitler proclaimed a policy of encouraging German women to have as many children as possible, both to man Germany's armies and to spread the ''Aryan'' race across the globe. Stalin too made such proclamations, handing out special medals such as ''hero of the Soviet Union'' to women who had eight babies.

Political leaders of some developing nations have not disguised their suspicion that the Western nations' ''family planning'' policies for the third world are a plot to reduce the population, and therefore also the worldwide political clout of the third world. Leaders of minority groups have charged that family planning programs hide a hidden racist agenda to reduce their numbers, and therefore the political power of their race.[88] Medical ethicists have expressed concern that such birth control measures as Norplant might enable political or legal authorities to impose involuntary birth control on those considered undesirable by society. They point to a 1990 Florida case in which a judge, as punishment, imposed 10 years of mandatory birth control on a criminal defendant.[89]

It should be noted that the four anti-Malthusian constituent groups discussed above do not represent monolithic forces. Not all religions oppose abortion, for example, just as not all countries' laws forbid abortion or birth control, and not all economists agree with Simon (most do not). It has also not been suggested that the reasons behind laws, policies, or religious dogma are the same. (Stalin's and Mao's reasons for encouraging population growth and rejecting birth control were obviously different from that of the Catholic Church.) Nor would all the groups described necessarily identify themselves as ''anti-Malthusians.'' They do, however, share one common denominator, and that is the implied belief that increases in population, even geometric ones, do not necessarily lead to Malthus' four horsemen of starvation, disease, war, and poverty.

To a large degree this belief is supported by historical evidence. No one would deny, for example, that the average human's general standard of living is higher today in a world of five and a half billion people than it was 5000 or 10,000 years ago, when the population did not exceed a few million people. The difference in the average life span of a human living today compared with 10,000 years ago (when a human was lucky to reach the ripe old age of 25) would refute any contention that population increases inevitably lead to lower living standards.

But it should be recalled that Malthus' central thesis was that ''the power of population is indefinitely greater than the power in the earth to provide subsistence for man.''[90] Although Malthus did not set forth a precise prediction of the time period over which this law would manifest itself, it is clear that he had a far shorter time period in mind than has been proven to be the case. It should further be recalled that an essential assumption of Malthus' thesis was that food production increased only arithmetically, while population increased geometrically. Even the most fervent adherents of Malthusian economics now concede that these two assumptions, particularly the latter one, have not been shown to be valid over the short term (say several hundred years or so). Several historic developments, presumably not envisioned by Malthus at the time he wrote his famous essay, have caused these assumptions to be invalid over the short term.

With regard to the first assumption regarding population, Malthus clearly did not foresee the enormous relief that immigration to the new world would provide for expanding populations of the old world. For every new immigrant to the new world, the population of the old world was similarly reduced by one. If space travel were advanced enough to allow travel to other worlds in space, a similar effect could be achieved today if all people representing increases in total population emigrated to other planets. (There are some who argue that such effects can take place today without space travel by encouraging emigration of people to underpopulated areas of the world such as the desert or Antarctica. Such arguments will be addressed later in this chapter).

With regard to Malthus' second assumption, that of arithmetical increases in the supply of food and goods, two historical developments have served to invalidate its application over the short term. First, the industrial revolution served to increase the output of goods and services to a degree that can only be described as "geometric." Indeed, to the extent that the industrial revolution increased the average per capita income of the world's humans, it can be stated that the production of goods and services exceeded the increase in population.

THE GREEN REVOLUTION

The second development unanticipated by Malthus was the "Green Revolution." The first year of this revolution is generally acknowledged to be 1944, the year in which the Rockefeller Foundation in cooperation with the Mexican government built a "plant-breeding" station in Mexico.[91] One of the first products of the Green Revolution initiated at this station was the development of a high-yield wheat plant, which almost singlehandedly transformed Mexico from a country that imported half of its wheat, to one that was almost entirely self-sufficient in wheat. This success led to the development of similar high-yielding rice strains in India and the Philippines. As a result, these countries doubled their rice and wheat production within 10 years. This doubling of food production within the span of but 10 years was, understandably, not the kind of development envisioned by Malthus in 1798.

Anti-Malthusians point to the failure of Malthusians to envision such developments as support for their theory of virtually infinite population limits. Pre-Columbian Europeans no more dreamed of a New World in the Western Hemisphere than short-sighted provincialists today dream it is possible to colonize the solar system or even the planets of other stars. A disinterested observer in the England of 1066 distressed about the denuding of that country's forests could never have conceived of the possibility that one thousand years hence there were be both many more trees and many more people. The steam engine, electricity, nuclear power and fusion, and genetic engineering were beyond the power of human thought and experience at that time in history to conceive of them.

But the anti-Malthusians may be as guilty as the Malthusians of fighting the last war. If Malthusian doomsays are appropriately chastised for crying "wolf" once too often, it should be recalled that there were two morals to be learned from the ancient fable. The first is that one who cries "wolf" will not be believed; but the second is that those who, having been tricked again and again, assume that the wolf will never come may lose all their sheep. That the one who cried "wolf" is in part to blame for the loss of the sheep can be of little consolation to all the others.

ECONOMIES OF SCALE

There is, of course, some substance to the anti-Malthusian argument that a certain threshold level of population is necessary to justify production at a level that takes advantage of economies of scale. Certainly it is also true that advances and developments not yet within the capability of human imagination may permit still greater increases in the growth of population while at the same time improving the standard of living of the average citizen of the world. It may even be possible to accomplish this expansion, for a time, without further deterioration of the environment of the planet. Indeed, the past 20 years have shown that this is possible.

SYMPTOMS AND CURES

But all these suppositions avoid the central thesis of Malthusianism that there are limits to growth, and that the expenditures of vast quantities of intellectual energy on the question of when those limits will be reached diverts energies better spent on planning and preparation. Worse of all, however, avoidance of the population issue in the area of environmental policies and laws has resulted in severe misallocations of both public and private treasure spent on environmental causes. Perhaps most harmful is that many governments of the world have not seen fit to advise their citizens of the cost effectiveness of the "environmental" programs they are asked to support, nor of the deleterious side effects of many of those policies. The reasons for such failures range from political expediency (the fear of a backlash to lost jobs or short-term economic harm), the avoidance of controversy (abortion, family planning, and sex education), to outright demagoguery (the "environmental president" or the "environmental candidate"). Very often exclusionary policies are advertised as environmental crusades, the environmental costs of policies exceed the environmental benefits, and the cost of environmental programs results in the diversion of funds that could make substantial contributions in addressing the root causes, rather than the symptoms of the twentieth century's environmental crisis. Thus while population lies as a root cause, the bulk of the earth's treasure devoted to the cause of environmentalism is used to treat the symptoms: water and air pollution, nuclear contamination, and toxic wastes.

Even the symptomatic solutions are often misdirected. Although the chapters that follow will document many examples of this misdirection, a few are noted here to close this preliminary analysis.

ENVIRONMENTAL COSTS

One persistent criticism of environmental policy has been the failure of economic and political systems to reflect the actual costs of environmental damage. For example, an industrial polluter might find it inexpensive to dump toxic wastes on the nearest available land. While this expedient might save the company a few dollars in disposal costs, the environmental costs to society might be severe, ultimately requiring a toxic cleanup costing a thousands time more than was saved by the company in conveniently dumping the waste. The economic principle involved is that if goods, rights, or privileges are not properly priced (i.e., they are priced either above or below their marginal cost), they are not properly valued and valuable resources are ultimately misallocated. Thus, if dumping privileges are sold too cheaply (less than the marginal cost of treating or disposing of the waste), inefficiencies result, and—in the case of environmental policy—programs are initiated that are not cost effective. Proposed solutions include determining the actual cost of environmental damage to society and then imposing those costs on those who seek to purchase the right or privilege to pollute.

Although the real problem with such solutions is the translation of theory into practice, the theory itself has not gone unchallenged by some environmental groups. Why, they ask, should anyone be allowed to pollute, even if they pay their fair cost of the privilege? The answer, of course, is that every human being, whether or not engaged in corporate or productive endeavor, pollutes and makes demands on the earth's non-renewable resources. Humans have to breath, consuming oxygen produced by rapidly declining inventories of forests, and spewing out carbon dioxide, which contributes to global warming and the greenhouse effect. Humans also have to drink, move, and be sheltered, and, in the case of humans living in developed nations, do it in style.

Current environmental laws include requirements that human waste be cleaned up. But between 1986 and 1991, four dump sites were closed for every one that was opened. One that has remained open is a New Jersey site within sight of the Statue of Liberty, which is fast reaching the size and height of the Great Pyramid of Giza. Unfortunately, environmental policy and expenditures are often directed not at resolving the overall problem of waste disposal, but in making sure that any dump is located somewhere else. In the United States, a large percentage of funds spent on "the environment" is in fact spent on such costs as financing a political campaign to persuade a local community to open a dump, and on the costs of applying for a permit (the cost of which now averages about half a million dollars). Under the EPA's Superfund Program, which costs taxpayers over a billion dollars a year, 88% of the sums spent by polluters and their insurers to settle pollution claims went toward legal fees and paperwork costs. In 1989 almost half a billion dollars was spent on such expenses—money that might otherwise be spent on actually cleaning up the environment. But when American representatives at Rio proudly proclaimed to the world that America was the leader in environmental expenditures and protection, little was said about how much of these expenditures were lawyer's fees, political campaigning, lobbying, and application fees spent with the purpose of simply making sure that the inevitable emissions of an industrial society went into someone else's backyard.

Although many self-proclaimed environmentalists claim that existing political and economic systems fail to impose on polluters the actual costs of pollution, the regulations many of them espouse in fact result in distortions of the costs of environmental protection. Some environmentalists freely concede that they prefer government environmental regulation to market-based incentives, on grounds that only through regulation can the actual cost of environmental protection be concealed. (Such views are presumably based on the assumption that if voters were aware of the true costs of environmental protection they would not vote for it.) For example, an NBC poll revealed that only 27% of Americans would support a gas tax to deter use of polluting gasoline or pay for the environmental consequences of motor vehicle operation.[92]

The Economist has reported that "America's 1989 Clean Air Act tightened the rules on air emission to the point where typically half the capital cost of a new (incineration) plant goes on air-pollution control equipment. As landfill prices rise, they influence waste-to-energy prices, since disposing of the ash generated can be as much as one third of the operating costs of the plant."[93] When federal legislation in 1988 banned New York City from dumping its sewage at sea, the City proceeded to spend $2 billion on a sludge conversion plant.[94] This great expenditure of taxpayer funds was hailed as a great environmental victory, and the salvation of New York's beaches, until it was later revealed that most of New York's beaches were polluted from overloaded storm drains. Needless to say, there were no proposals to ban all the cars from New York City, the leaking oils from which went straight into the storm drains.

WASTE AND RECYCLING

Despite some environmentalists' predictions that the world is running out of municipal waste sites, a recent study concluded that, "If America continues to produce municipal solid waste at present rates for the next 1000 years, the whole lot will still be containable in a space 100 yards deep and 30 miles square."[95] For much of the environmental movement, the question is not so much the problem of waste itself, but which region can be identified as politically weak enough to accept a waste site in its vicinity. Environmentalists in New York State have found that with dumping fees of $150 a ton at New York's Fresh Kills dump, it pays to send New York's refuse to Ohio and Indiana where local authorities charge only $21 a ton and are glad to have the business. A study by Resources of the Future found that New York and New Jersey alone accounted for over half of interstate dumping.[96]

Despite the economic advantages of being a dumping ground for waste of East Coast environmentalists, many of the mid-Western states have adopted their own brand of environmentalism by demanding that waste imports be certified medically as free of toxic wastes. France recently enacted similar environmental legislation in response to German waste exports.[97]

The distortion in perceived costs and benefits of governmental environmental regulation has led some environmentalists to favor market-based incentives to achieve environmental benefits. Again, the theories are seductive, as they purport to provide economic incentives to individuals and enterprises to adopt environmentally sound policies. Although such programs are anathema to many of the more radical environmental groups the members of which see no reason why anyone should be al-

lowed to destroy the environment for a price, such programs do have
the advantage of creating less distortions in the cost and benefits of environmental programs. The basic premises of such programs are simple.
They involve a political determination of just how much pollution a community can tolerate. Once this determination is made, the "pollution
rights" are rationed (sometimes with appropriate grandfathering provisions), and then sold or distributed to the highest bidder. The price ultimately paid may or may not be rationally related to the costs to society
of the pollution thus produced.

Other varieties of market-based incentive programs include recycling
credits, landfill taxes, refundable deposits, and, in at least one American
city, a "pay to throw" scheme. The latter program, versions of which
have been adopted in over 200 cities, involves the imposition of a sur-
charge on any extra bags of trash produced by municipal residents. Unfortunately, all of these programs have revealed serious drawbacks. In
Seattle, for example, which had adopted "pay to throw," municipal
dwellers soon learned the "Seattle stomp,"[98] squeezing ever greater
quantities of trash into a single bin. Landfill taxes, designed to encourage alternative methods of waste disposal (such as recycling), have instead encouraged incineration with resulting increases in air pollution.
Recycling credits have caused costs to rise, thereby siphoning funds that
might have had a greater and more direct beneficial environmental impact. As one Waste Management officer observed: "We lose money on
recycling . . . It costs $150–200 a ton to collect from the curbside and
sort household refuse. We might make $40 a ton from selling waste ma-
terials, and we might avoid a $30 a ton of landfill charges. But the bot-
tom line is that it's not profitable."[99]

If companies are forced to absorb such costs by law, as some state
laws have mandated, the costs of recycling become absorbed in the price
of the product produced by the company. Although such a tax may be
justified as reflecting an environmental cost, the fact remains that, by
being hidden, it is virtually impossible to make the kind of cost-effectiveness analysis necessary to maximize the environmental benefits of each
dollar expended, or to compare those costs with other environmental
programs.

On the private, or public relations side, environmental propaganda
and misleading claims continue to distort the environmental agenda.
Commercial products tout their "biodegradable" characteristics, with
little or no uniform standards for making such claims. A Professor of
Archaeology at the University of Arizona recently dug up a typical municipal trash dump to examine its contents, and found the single greatest
part of the landfill's bulk to be in the form of newspapers, many of which
were over 25 years old.[100] Other types of paper products took up much
of the remaining bulk, while plastics came in a distant third.

ALTERNATIVE ENERGY SOURCES

Environmentalists are constantly looking for new cleaner sources of energy, alternatives to the internal combustion engine that spews so many contaminants into the world's atmosphere, and to the use of such polluting fuels as coal, oil, and wood. Thus the quest for an electric, nonpolluting automobile. Unfortunately, even if an electric car with sufficient power and range could be developed, the results would likely be as disappointing as the gasoline automobile engine that was hailed as the environmental solution to sewage and manure that fouled the streets of major cities that relied on animal transport. For the fact remains that any electric car will have to obtain its energy from some source that pollutes the environment. Will the electricity come from generating plants that use coal, spewing acid rain into the environment? Will it come from nonrenewable sources of natural gas; from nuclear energy with its deadly waste that threatens deadly contamination for thousands of years; or from dams, which threaten the delicate and fragile ecosystems of so many living creatures? One environmentalist has suggested that it might come from the ultimate clean source: wind power. Although such power, along with solar power, can hope, in the foreseeable future to provide only a tiny percentage of mankind's energy demands, it seems that even such utopian energy sources may be grist for an environmentalist's crusade. A 1993 article in *USA Today* carried a long story on the environmentalists battling California's windmills.[101] In 1983, 17,000 100-foot-high wind turbines were built across the state, producing the impressive amount of 1% of its energy needs. Ten years later, environmentalists were decrying the windmill fields as something worse than ravages of surface mining, a landscape worse than "Salvador Dali's worst nightmare."[102] But worst of all, proclaimed environmentalist lobbyist Paul Thayer, "these huge wind turbines are virtual Cusinarts for birds." Another concerned spokesman said, "Wind energy is great, but we can't go around killing the environment."[103] In England, environmentalists have launched a campaign against windmills. So far environmentalists have not yet begun throwing themselves in front of windmills to protest "clean" windpower, but the fact that even this source of power has stirred up environmental resistance reveals the illusion of finding any energy source that will enable mankind to continue its exponential expansion without ultimately adversely affecting the environment.

There are, of course, some possible energy sources that might at some time in the future prove to be far less polluting than present sources— solar and fusion power coming to mind. But the notion that any source of energy is going to permit the pollution-free, but exponential, expansion of the human race is clearly an illusion.

SUMMARY

It is not for a moment to be suggested that mankind has no interest in implementing environmental strategies, policies, and programs. The $2 billion dollars spent by New York to build a sludge plant certainly did some good for the environment. (In Europe, of course, most of the largest cities still dump their sewage into the ocean, and keep their $2 billion dollars while New Yorkers share the same big ocean.) New Yorkers probably benefitted even more when their excess sewage was sent on barges to be dumped somewhere else in the world. Residents in Colorado will not have to put up with all those people who might have come into the state if the Two Forks dam project had not been killed by the EPA. Power plants can stop burning coal (which causes acid rain) by converting to nuclear power, and nuclear power plants producing their deadly radioactive wastes can convert back to coal—all depending on which environmentalist's toes one happens to step on. But if traditional environmental policies are ultimately self-defeating, or self-neutralizing, is there really any solution? One typical proposed solution is that governments, rather than trying to clean up after the world's consumers, should instead try to persuade them to "buy less and consume less." The Romanian dictator Ceaucescu certainly had no trouble following this advice. He simply turned off the lights and cut off the heat.

It is suggested in the chapters that follow, however, that there is a third alternative involving policies of population control, family planning, abortion, immigration, and free trade. It is the understanding of the relationship between all these elements of human endeavor and activity that will provide a basis for an enduring and constructive environmental policy.

NOTES

1. Sadik, The State of World Population: *Choices For the New Century* (UNFPA, 1990), p. 7; see also Sadik, Three People Born Every Second—250,000 Daily, *L.A. Times,* Feb. 22, 1990, p. 10.

2. *Id.,* p. 11.

3. World Resources Institute, *World Resources* (1992), p. 316, Table 22.1.

4. *Id.,* p. 316, Table 21.2.

5. Hurst, *Rainforest Politics: Ecological Destruction in South-East Asia* (1990), p. viii.

6. Based on 1980–1990 data; Sadik, *supra,* note 1, p. 8.

7. *World Resources, supra,* note 3, p. 348, Table 24.2.

8. *Id.*

9. *Id.,* p. 351, Table 24.5.

10. *Id.,* p. 351, Table 24.6.

11. *Id.,* p. 338, Table 23.2.

12. Chiras, *Environmental Science: Action for a Sustainable Future* (1991), p. 5.

13. Hamil, The Arrival of the 5-Billionth Human *The Futurist,* July/Aug. 1987, p. 36.

14. *Id.*

15. *Id.*

16. *Id.*

17. Bureau of the Census, U.S. Department of Commerce, Economics and Statistics Administration (1991).

18. See, e.g., Charles Mann, How Many Is Too Many, *The Atlantic,* Feb. 1993, pp. 47–67; Emily Smith, Growth v. Environment, *Business Week,* May 11, 1992, p. 66.

19. See, e.g., Eugene Linden, Too Many People: Beyond 2000, *Time,* Fall, 1992 special issue, p. 64; Gregg Easterbrook, Green Cassandras, *The New Republic,* July 6, 1992, p. 23; Linda Kamamine, U.N. Report Warns of Population "Catastrophe," *USA Today,* April 30, 1992; D'vora Ben Shaul, World Population Growth Must Stop, *The Jerusalem Post,* June 1, 1992; Stenley Meiser, World Population to Soar to 10 Billion, Agency Says, *L.A. Times,* May 14, 1991, p. 4; Orville Freemen, Meeting the Food Needs of the Coming Decade, *The Futurist,* Nov.–Dec. 1990, p. 15; William Stevens, Humanity Confronts Its Handiwork: An Altered Planet, *N.Y. Times,* May 5, 1992, p. C-1.

20. See generally Schumpeter, *History of Economic Analysis* (1954).

21. *Id.,* p. 251; cited in Massimo Livi-Bacci, *A Concise History of World Population* (1989), p. 86.

22. See, e.g., Cohen, *The Food Crisis in Prehistory. Overpopulation and the Origin of Agriculture* (1977); cited in Livi-Bacci, *supra,* at p. 90; see also Childe, *Man Makes Himself* (1951).

23. Livi-Bacci, *supra,* p. 96.

24. Boserup, *Population and Technological Change* (1981), p. 65.

25. Livi-Bacci, *supra,* p. 97.

26. Petty, *The Economic Writings* (C. H. Hull, ed., 1963), p. 437; cited in Simon, *Theory of Population and Economic Growth* (1986).

27. Livi-Bacci, *supra,* p. 95, citing Adam Smith, *The Wealth of Nations* 5 (1964).

28. Mann, *supra,* note 18, p. 50.

29. Ricardo, *The Principles of Political Economy and Taxation* (1964), p. 56; cited in Livi-Bacci, *supra,* p. 75.

30. Livi-Bacci, *supra,* p. 75.

31. Mann, *supra,* note 18, p. 49.

32. *Id.*

33. *Id.* Malthus held the first University Chair in Economics.

34. Thomas Malthus, *Essay on Population* (1798).

35. Malthus, *Essay on the Principle of Population* 8 (7th ed., 1967).

36. Mann, *supra,* note 18, p. 50.

37. *Id.*

38. Chiras, *supra,* note 12, p. 152.

39. *Id.*

40. Professor of Business Administration, University of Maryland. His works

include *The Economics of Population Growth, The Ultimate Resource,* and *The Economic Consequences of Immigration.*

41. Schumpeter, *Capitalism, Socialism, and Democracy* (2nd ed. 1947), p. 83.

42. Simon, Why Do We Still Think Babies Create Poverty, *Washington Post,* Oct. 13, 1985, p. B1.

43. Kuznets, *Population, Capital and Growth* (1973), p. 3.

44. Simon, *supra* at B1.

45. *Id.*

46. Ehrlich, *The Population Explosion,* p. 39.

47. Ancient Practice, *Star Tribune,* July 4, 1989, p. 11A.

48. *Id.*

49. *Id.*

50. *Id.*

51. Roe v. Wade, 410 U.S. 113 (1973).

52. Planned Parenthood v. Danforth, 428 U.S. 52 (1976).

53. *Id.*; Colautti v. Franklin, 439 U.S. 379 (1979); Hartigan v. Zbaraz, 484 U.S. 171, 108 S.Ct. 479, 98 L.Ed.2d 478 (1987).

54. Planned Parenthood v. Casey——U.S.——, 112 S.Ct. 2791, 120 L.Ed.2d 674 (1992).

55. See, e.g., Anti-Abortion Movement Steps Up Campaigns in Western Europe, *Star Tribune,* June 28, 1989; U.S., World Abortion Practices Studied, *L.A. Times,* Nov. 16, 1986, p. 9; The Court's Decision on Abortion Out of the Mainstream: More Is at Stake Than the Rights of the Woman v. the Rights of the Fetus, *Philadelphia Examiner,* July 19, 1992, p. C5; see generally Mary Glendon, *Abortion and Divorce in Western Law* (1987).

56. Where Other Nations Stand, *Star Tribune,* June 30, 1992, p. 8A.

57. *Id.*

58. Faith and Abortion; Where the World's Major Religions Disagree, *Washington Post,* Jan. 23, 1990, p. 212.

59. Machismo, Church Complicate Issue: Tradition Poverty Shape Mexico Abortion Debate, *L.A. Times,* April 9, 1989.

60. *Id.* Estimate by Dr. Alfredo Rustinian.

61. *Id.*

61A. *Id.*

62. *Id.* Barth, U.S. Abortion Policy Abroad Is Disastrous, *Star Tribune,* June 7, 1989, p. 15A.

63. Jodi Jacobson, Abortion in a New Light, in *The World Watch Reader on Global Environmental Issues,* p. 287.

64. *Id.* Barth, U.S. Abortion Policy Abroad Is Disastrous, *Star Tribune,* June 7, 1989.

65. *Id.*

66. European Countries Beg to Differ on Abortion Laws, Ethical Issues, *Miami Herald,* Oct. 21, 1985, p. 3B.

67. *Id.;* see also Overplanned Parenthood: Ceaucescu's Cruel Law, *Newsweek,* Jan. 22, 1990, p. 35.

68. American Teenagers Have Highest Rate of Abortion, *San Francisco Chronicle,* Dec. 16, 1988, p. B6.

69. European Countries, *supra,* note 58, p. 3B.

70. *Id.*

71. In Defeat for Kohl, Germany Adopts Liberal Abortion Law, *Christian Science Monitor,* June 29, 1992, p. 3; see also Reunited Germany Is Divided on Abortion, *Chicago Tribune,* Feb. 16, 1992; Germany Approves Liberal Abortion Law, *San Francisco Chronicle,* June 26, 1992, p. A10.

72. UN Surveys Global Sex, Fertility Trends, *Boston Globe,* June 25, 1992, p. 85. See also Abortion Rate in U.S. High: Report Examines Fertility Issues, *Miami Herald,* June 3, 1988; Abortion Around the World, *Time,* May 4, 1992, p. 32; About Women: U.S., World Abortion Practices Studied, *L.A. Times,* Nov. 16, 1986, p. 9; Antiabortion Movement Steps Up Campaign in Western Europe, *Star Tribune,* June 28, 1989, p. 4A; Exporting Misery: A U.S. Abortion Ruling Affects Women's Health Worldwide, *Scientific American,* Aug. 1991, p. 16.

73. Machismo, Church Complicate Issue: Tradition, Poverty Shape Mexico Abortion Debate, *L.A. Times,* April 9, 1989, p. 1.

74. *Id.*

75. *Id.*

76. *Id.*

77. Leslie Roberts, U.S. Lags on Birth Control Development, *Science,* Feb. 23, 1990, p. 909. See also Dourten-Rollier, Family Planning and the Law, *World Health,* April, 1989, p. 7.

78. Doug Podolsky, Sorry, Not Sold in the U.S. (Birth Control Options), *U.S. News and World Report,* Dec. 24, 1990, p. 65; see also Your Health Focus on Birth Control, *Newsday,* Feb. 28, 1989, p. 7.

79. *Id.*

80. Sorry, Not Sold, *supra,* p. 65.

81. See notes 69–70, *supra.*

82. Machismo, *supra,* note 65, p. 1.

83. Family Planning, *supra,* p. 2.

84. *Id.*

85. Ann Devroy, Bush Hints at Veto of Foreign Aid Bill; President Renounces Provision to Fund Population-Control Agency, *Star Tribune,* Oct. 10, 1989, p. A28.

86. Randolph Schmid, U.S. to Withhold Funds for U.N. Family Plan, *Philadelphia Inquirer,* Aug. 28, 1986, p. D8.

87. *Id.*

88. Sorry, Not Sold, *supra* note 70, p. 65.

89. *Id.*

90. *Supra,* note 23.

91. Chiras, *Environmental Science* (1991), p. 152.

92. Gutfeld, Shades of Green, *Wall Street Journal,* May 14, 1991, p. A1.

93. A Survey of Waste and the Environment, *The Economist,* May 29–June 4, 1993 Supp., pp. 1–18.

94. *Id.*

95. *Id.*

96. *Id.*

97. *Id.*

98. *Id.*

99. *Id.*

100. *Id.*

101. Maria Goodavage, Battling Safe Windmills: Bird Deaths in Turbines Spur Outcry, *USA Today,* May 27, 1993, p. 3A.

102. *Id.*

103. *Id.*

3 Environmental Laws and Policies

This circle game (of transferring pollution from one medium to another) has got to stop. At best it is misleading—we think we are solving a problem and we aren't. At worst it is perverse—it increase(s) . . . pollution.

Former EPA Administrator Lee Thomas

Prior to 1970, responsibility for administering governmental laws and regulations relating to the environment were scattered among a number of different federal and state agencies. In January 1969, however, a local environmental disaster prompted demands for more comprehensive environmental laws. An oil spill off the coast of Santa Barbara, California resulted in miles of beach being contaminated with oil, and the death of thousands of birds and fish.[1]

In response to the disaster, President Nixon in June 1969, established an Environmental Quality Council. This did not satisfy Congressional demands for more dramatic action, however, and on January 1, 1970, Congress passed the National Environmental Policy Act of 1969.[2] Additional executive action on the environmental front followed with the President's Reorganization Plan No. 3, which created the Environmental Protection Agency (EPA).[3] Under this plan, responsibility for coordinating federal environmental laws was consolidated under the EPA, and William Ruckelshaus was appointed as the first EPA Administrator.

As the responsibility for more and more new environmental laws came to be assigned by law to the EPA, questions arose as to the ability of any one agency to assume such broad responsibilities. One former EPA Administrator has commented that "many of EPA's difficulties over the years can be traced to the fact Congress loaded the agency with far more statutory responsibilities within a brief period of time than perhaps any [one] agency could effectively perform."[4]

Within 2 years of the passage of the Environmental Policy Act, while President Nixon was preoccupied with Watergate, Congress passed a rash of environmental laws, including the Federal Environmental Pesticide Control Act,[5] the Water Pollution Control Act Amendments,[6] the Noise Control Act,[7] the Water Quality Improvement Act,[8] and the Clean Air Act Amendments.[9] Although this frenzy of environmental activity was slowed somewhat by the 1973 Arab Oil Embargo (which revealed to some legislators the need for greater consideration of the economic impact of environmental laws), a number of important environmental laws were passed in the following 3 years: the Safe Drinking Water Act of 1974,[10] the Toxic Substances Control Act of 1976,[11] the Resource Conservation and Recovery Act of 1976,[12] and the 1977 Amendments to the Water Quality Improvement Act.[13]

The most controversial environmental legislation during this period was the Comprehensive Environmental Response, Compensation and Liability Act of 1980,[14] which set up a Hazardous Response Trust Fund (popularly known as "superfund") to be used for the clean up of toxic contaminants. It was the intent of the Act to avoid a substantial federal financial commitment by extracting 86% of the funds from business and industry.[15]

The early 1980s were a time of controversy and administrative turmoil within the EPA. President Reagan's appointee as EPA Administrator, Anne Buford, soon alienated many members of Congress who were already skeptical of the administration's commitment to environmental protection. Dissatisfied with EPA's cost cutting programs and what it regarded as lax enforcement of environmental laws, a House Committee subpoenaed documents relating to the EPA's management of the Superfund. When Buford refused to produce the documents, the House of Representatives cited her for contempt on December 16, 1982. Although a compromise eventually resulted in the dropping of the contempt citation, Buford resigned on March 9, 1983, and the head of the Superfund program, Rita Lavelle, was convicted later that year of perjury and obstruction charges relating to the Congressional investigation of the EPA. In a move obviously intended to restore confidence in the EPA, William Ruckelshaus was reappointed as EPA Administrator, and unanimously confirmed by the Senate on May 17, 1983.[16]

The new administrator pushed through a number of strong environmental measures, including a 91% reduction in the lead content of gasoline, and the banning of the pesticide ethylene dibromide.[17] Because some alternative pesticides were available, this action did not meet fierce resistance. Attempts to control power plant emissions that allegedly contributed to acid rain, however, were a different story.

A number of studies had linked coal-burning power plants with acid rain, which damaged forests and lakes, particularly in Southern Canada and in the Northeast United States. Although amendments to the Clean Air Act were proposed that would reduce emissions causing acid rain, environmental commitment was severely tested when a Report by the Energy Information Administration concluded that the costs imposed by the proposed amendments would raise utility bills by over 6%.[18] The Director of Office of Management and Budget calculated the cost per fish of the proposed legislation, but was faced with zealous environmentalists who demanded maximum emission reductions. Ruckelshaus backed down and agreed to support only "additional research" on acid rain.

In 1984, Ruckelshaus resigned, stating that "This ship called EPA is righted and is now steering a steady course again."[19] He was succeeded by Lee Thomas, one of whose first major accomplishments was the extraction of one-tenth of a billion dollars from the Westinghouse Corporation for alleged toxic dumping.[20] His agency soon issued new regulations forcing utilities to cut sulfur oxide emissions by 1.7 million tons a year at a projected cost to the industry and its consumers of three quarters of a billion dollars.[21]

THE CIRCLE GAME

Criticism of the EPA continued, however. In 1985 a Congressional Report revealed that while over "200 hazardous chemicals were being routinely leaked into the air in the United States, [o]nly five of the compounds were regulated by the EPA."[22] In 1993, studies reviewed by the EPA and the Harvard School of Public Health revealed that the worst air pollutant is soot, breathable particulates that cause 50,000–60,000 deaths a year. But the EPA, which has almost no budget for epidemiology, had not even identified soot as a major pollutant, with the result that it is "found in most urban areas, without violating legal standards."[23]

But perhaps one of the most revealing criticisms of the EPA was made by the Director himself when he alleged that most "pollution cleanup" did not result in a net benefit to the environment, because all such controls did was transfer pollution "in one medium, such as the air . . . to another, such as soil or water."[24] He went on to state that "This circle game has got to stop . . . At best it is misleading—we think we are solving a problem and we aren't. At worst, it is perverse—it [increases] rather than reduce[s] pollution."[25]

Thus, Thomas had revealed that despite enormous costs, much of what passed as environmental protection was an illusion—giving the impression to voters concerned about the environment that the environment was being protected by laws, when in fact those laws did nothing more than transfer pollution from one medium and dump it into another. While a reduction in a particular contaminant in the air might be hailed as an environmental victory, the simultaneous appearance of that same contaminant in another medium (such as the soil) is rarely greeted as a defeat, or even acknowledged by the environmental community.

Other illusions about environmental policy have also become manifest. For example, studies have revealed that attempts to impose on industry and business steep costs for toxic dumping have resulted in dramatic increases in illegal and "midnight" dumping in areas that before had been free from contamination.[26] It is by means of such illusory legislation and environmental policy that questions about the ultimate source of all pollution are deflected and not addressed.

The fact is that the greatest source of all pollution is people—most of all people with high rates of consumption. It is people who demand power for heat, and light, and movement. Viable energy resources (those needed for a civilization with high rates of consumption) result in the emission of contaminants into the atmosphere—only a small number of which are controlled or within the power of the EPA to control. Although a small percentage of these contaminants can be transferred from one medium to another, and their visibility thereby reduced, any such small gains, reaped at high cost, are more than outweighed by the increases in demand for energy and resources of an exponentially rising population. But as long as the appearance of legitimate environmental action is maintained, controversial issues relating to population—abortion, birth control, sex education—can be addressed outside the context of environmental policy.

For those who oppose population control policies, it is important that population issues never be linked to environmental issues. The reason for this is apparent: a clean environment is like mom and apple pie—everyone is in favor of it. As long as voters can be persuaded that the environment is being taken care of by transferring pollution from one medium to another—or by imposing huge fines on legitimate businesses (who pass their costs on to consumers in the form of a hidden, and thus politically acceptable tax) while less financially viable firms, unable to pay the costs and stay in business, resort to "midnight" dumping in previously pristine areas—population issues can be isolated. Advocates of birth control, family planning, abortion, and population control then become vulnerable to emotional arguments unrelated to the environment. If the link between population and the environment was revealed and acknowledged, however, true concern for the environment might threaten to undermine resistance to population control policies.

It was not surprising, therefore, that antiabortion and antifamily planning advocates worked so urgently in 1992 to ensure that population issues were not on the agenda at the Earth Summit in Rio.

The fact that much of environmental policy is ineffective and illusory, however, does not mean that all current environmental efforts should be discarded. For the time being, it may be better for humans that some contaminants in the air are neatly tucked into the ground, and that at least a few cities of the world are required to treat their sewage before dumping it into the ocean. It cannot be denied that some environmental benefits are achieved even by current policies, and the argument can certainly be made that honest efforts, even ineffective ones, give hope and sustenance to all members of the human race. Doctors know that even placebos help many patients.

That some benefits may be derived from current policy, however, in no way excuses the failure to come to grips with the ultimate sources of pollution: that is, the world population itself. It remains, therefore, to examine the extent to which current laws and policies consider population factors as part of solutions to environmental problems.

ENVIRONMENTAL LAW

The National Environmental Policy Act of 1969 sets forth the following Congressional declaration of purpose: "The purposes of this act are: To declare a national policy which will encourage productive and enjoyable harmony between man and his environment; to promote efforts which will prevent or eliminate damage to the environment and biosphere and stimulate the health and welfare of man; [and] to enrich the understanding of the ecological systems and natural resources important to the nation.[27]"

Although this statement of Congressional purpose makes no reference to population or its consideration as a factor in protecting the environment, the Act's separate declaration of national environmental policy does make such a reference: "The Congress, recognizing the profound impact of man's activity on the interrelations of all components of the natural environment, particularly the profound *influences of population growth*, high-density urbanization, industrial expansion, resource exploitation, and new and expanding technological advances . . . declares that it is the continuing policy of the Federal Government . . . to use all practicable means and measures . . . to create conditions under which man and nature can exist in productive harmony"[28] (emphasis added).

Having made this one reference to population, no further reference to population is made in the remaining 245 pages of the Act.[29] Indeed, there is not even an index entry under the Act's notes of decisions on any matter or case relating to population. Although other federal legislation does address population issues, it does so not in the context of the environment, but in the context of promoting public health.

For example, the Family Planning Services and Population Research Act of 1970[30] states that grants may be awarded for the purpose of assisting in the establishment of "voluntary family planning methods and services (including natural family planning methods, infertility services,

and services for adolescents)."[31] Unlike environmental laws, for which
compliance is mandatory and noncompliance punished, the Population
Research Act specifically provides that acceptance by any individual of
family planning services "shall be voluntary and shall not be a pre-requi-
site to eligibility for . . . any other assistance in any other program."[32]
Lest the obvious omission of any reference to abortion not be fully understood, a specific provision of the Act states that "none of the funds
appropriated under this title shall be used in programs where abortion is
a method of family planning."[33] A 1991 Supreme Court decision has
upheld this provision insofar as it denies funds to recipients who engage
in abortion-related activities.[34] At least one Federal Circuit Court, however, has struck down the provision, along with 1988 regulations prohibiting abortion counselling (the "gag" rule), insofar as it purports to prohibit recipients from advising women of abortion as a medical option if
birth control devices should fail, or if the woman is already pregnant.
The Court cited both the First and Fifth Amendments of the U.S. Constitution in support of its decision.[35]

Likewise, the National Urban Policy and New Community Development Act of 1970[36] originally stated findings that "the rapid growth of
urban population . . . seriously threatens our physical environment."[37]
Although perhaps not intended as such, this language stated that federal
policy recognized a link between population growth and the environment. It was not long, however, before it was realized by some conservative politicians that such language might be used as the basis for linking such population issues as family planning and abortion with
environmental policy. Before the Act's policy statement could be used
as the basis for further legislation linking population issues with the environment, however, an Amendment changed the "growth of population"
language to read instead "rapid changes in patterns of urban settle-
ment."[38] Though the change in language appears to be subtle, the intent
is clear. According to the amendments, it is not the growth in population
itself that raises environmental problems, but only "patterns of development" (which presumably can be remedied by such measures as zoning
and exclusion). Just as efforts by a conservative worldwide political and
religious community were successful in keeping population issues off the
environmental agenda at the 1992 Earth Summit, so internal domestic
policies have been successful in keeping population issues off the environmental agenda in the United States.

Other references in this Act to population issues have also been deleted by subsequent amendments. For example, §710 of the Act originally stated Congressional findings that "this Nation is likely to experience during the remaining years of this century a population increase
of about seventy-five million persons . . . . [This] anticipated increase in
population will result in 1) inefficient and wasteful use of land resources

. . . 2) destruction of irreplaceable natural and recreational resources and increasing pollution of air and water . . . 5) unduly limited options for many of our people as to where they may live, and 6) . . . decreasing employment and business opportunities."[39] Obviously such language required more than subtle word changes in order to retract the direct assertion by Congress of a link between population and the environment. Under the Reagan administration, this section was simply repealed in its entirety.[40]

THE ENVIRONMENTAL PROTECTION AGENCY

As an independent agency of the executive branch of government, the Environmental Protection Agency is responsible for administering environmental laws and coordinating governmental action affecting the environment. Its duties and obligations include coordinating antipollution research activities, assisting other federal agencies in assessing environmental impacts of their actions, and making independent determinations of environmental impact. Further duties include the development of national programs, and the development and enforcement of national standards (such as emission standards for motor vehicles, air pollutants, lead levels in gasoline, drinking water standards, disposal of waste material, registration of insecticides, disposal of radiation wastes, and the monitoring of radiation in drinking water and the air). In addition, the EPA administers grant programs to assist states and subsidizes the cost of such projects as sewage treatment plants.[41]

Section 102 of the National Environmental Policy act requires that government agencies proposing a "major federal action" prepare an environmental impact statement including the following:

(i)   the environmental impact of the proposed action
(ii) any adverse environmental effects which cannot be avoided should the proposal be implemented
(iii) alternatives to the proposed action
(iv) the relationship between local short-term uses of man's environment and the maintenance and enhancement of long-term productivity, and,
(v)   any irreversible and irretrievable commitments of resources which would be involved in the proposed action should it be implemented.[42]

"Major federal actions" are to be identified after considering the "overall, cumulative impact of the action proposed."[43] Such an action requires "substantial planning, time, resources, and expenditure."[44] However, even "minor" federal actions can be considered "cumulatively considerable when one or more agencies over a period of years puts into a project individually minor but collectively major resources."[45] Actual determinations of what constitutes a major federal action appear to be somewhat arbitrary, subjective, and unpredictable. Thus a proposal for a 272-unit low- and moderate-income housing project,[46] and the continuing operation of a dam,[47] have been held not to constitute a major federal action, while the use of an airport runway for a new flight path has been held to constitute a major federal action.[48]

With regard to the required factors to be set forth in an environmental impact statement, one factor is significant by its omission in the Act, namely a cost–benefit analysis. This omission appears to have been a deliberate attempt by its advocates to avoid a specific requirement that the interests of the environment be balanced against the economic costs of protection. As one Court interpreting the Act has observed, "We find no requirement in the [Act] for the placement of dollar values on environmental impacts."[49] The D.C. Court of Appeals has held that the Act "does not require that a cost benefit ratio be included in [an environmental impact statement]; the [Act] only requires consideration of the ecological costs in deciding whether depletion of irreplaceable natural resources should proceed in the manner suggested or not at all."[50]

At least one Court, however, while conceding that the Act does not require any "formal and mathematically expressed cost–benefit analysis"[51] has nevertheless suggested that cost may be considered as a factor pursuant to §102 (B), which states that agencies must "identify and develop methods and procedures" that will "insure that . . . environmental values may be given appropriate consideration in decision-making along with economic and technical considerations."[52] Although the Court did not explain how such "appropriate consideration" could be given to economic values if such values were not even included as factors to be set forth in an environmental impact statement, Judge Skelly Wright has opined that "environmental amenities will often be in conflict with economic and technical considerations. To consider the former along with the latter must involve a balancing process. In some instances environmental costs may outweigh economic and technical benefits and in other instances they may not. But the [Act] manages a rather finely tuned and 'systematic' balancing analysis in each instance."[53]

Although the Act implicitly suggests the need for consideration of economic impact, the failure to require a cost–benefit analysis in the environmental impact statement has led to the filing of statements of conclusions without corroborative data. One critic has observed: "The Environmental Impact Statements usually contain the results of economic conclusions concerning a proposed action, but not the data or assumptions used to arrive at those conclusions. This omission is one of the more serious problems in the implementation of the [Act]."[54] In fact, as previously noted, the omission is even more serious since the lack of a specific requirement for a cost–benefit analysis in the impact statement has led some courts to conclude that no such analysis at all is required.[55]

In any case, it is clear the economic cost of a particular environmental law or regulation is not given high priority under current law. In none of the cases cited under the Act, for example, has any consideration been given to the costs of family planning or population control as an "alternative means" of protecting the environment.

Most federal projects, whether they are dams, water projects, airports, or highways, are undertaken in response to population pressures. More cars require more and expanded highways, greater numbers of air travellers require greater numbers of airports, and expanding communities need additional sources of water, power, and electricity. Under current law, there exists no provision for considering family planning, or other measures of population control as an alternative means of protecting the environment.

SPECIAL ENVIRONMENTAL LAWS

"When I use a word" Humpty Dumpty said, in rather a scornful tone, "it means just what I choose it to mean—neither more nor less."
  Chief Justice Warren Burger, citing Lewis Carroll's *Through the Looking Glass*, in *TVA v. Hill*[56]

The National Environmental Policy Act has been described as an Act that imposes primarily "procedural requirements; once an adequate Environmental Impact Statement is prepared, the [Act] grants no authority to enjoin an action adversely affecting the environment."[57] Injunctions have been granted under the Act, however, where the procedures have not been followed. In such cases as the *Environmental Defense Fund v. TVA*, for example, Federal Courts have enjoined the completion of a federal project on grounds that an environmental impact statement had not been filed.[58]

A number of other specific pieces of federal legislation have provided for more substantive remedies. Examples of such other legislation include the Toxic Substances Control Act,[59] the Federal Water Pollution Control Act,[60] the Clean Air Act,[61] the Noise Control Act,[62] the Atomic Energy Act,[63] the Marine Protection, Research and Sanctuaries Act,[64] the Scenic Rivers Act,[65] the Fish and Wildlife Coordination Act,[66] the Resource Conservation and Recovery Act,[67] the Federal Land Policy and Management Act,[68] the Federal Insecticide, Fungicide and Rodenticide Act,[69] the Safe Drinking Water Act,[70] and the Coastal Barriers Resource Act—to name but a few. It is beyond the scope of this chapter to cover all the substantive law in the environmental area, but there are a number of excellent works that provide such coverage.[71]

An analysis of one typical environmental act suffices to reveal the consequences of the failure of environmental laws to consider the cost effectiveness of their policies. The point to be made is not that environmental laws do not create some beneficial results; rather the point is that existing laws do not maximize environmental benefits with the resources that are allocated by society for that purpose. The reason for this failure can in large measure be attributed to the failure to consider alternatives in the area of family planning and population control.

Consider, for example, the cost and effectiveness of one particular environmental law: the Endangered Species Act of 1973.[72] The stated Congressional purpose of this Act was to "provide a program for the conservation of . . . endangered species, and threatened species, and to take such steps as may be appropriate to achieve the purposes of [international treaties relating to endangered species]."[73] The Act further declared that "All federal agencies shall seek to conserve endangered species and threatened species and shall utilize their authorities in furtherance of the purposes of this chapter."[74] The Act authorized the Secretary of the Interior to declare a species to be "endangered" due to such causes as destruction of habitat, predation, disease, or other natural or manmade factors. Although population is not specifically addressed, there is an oblique reference to the additional factor of "overutilization for commercial [and] recreational" purposes.[75] Unlike the National Environmental Policy Act, however, the Endangered Species Act charged all federal agencies to take "such action necessary to insure that actions funded by them do not jeopardize the continued existence of endangered species."[76] The Act, in somewhat "humanly" chauvinistic fashion, exempts only those species that most humans dislike (i.e., the "Class Insecta determined by the Secretary to be a pest"). This latter provision was mercifully inserted to ensure that taxpayer money would not be used, say, to protect an endangered subspecies of cockroach.

One commentator has compared the two acts by observing that unlike the National Environmental Policy Act, which "allowed a balancing of factors and values," the Endangered Species Act "mandates a non-balancing approach . . . The values have been pre-balanced."[77]

The first test of whether the Act could be used to stop major projects in the interests of protecting a species came in 1975. In that year, a conservation group, a regional association of scientists, and a group of citizens living near the Tennessee Valley area petitioned the Secretary of Interior to list a species of snail darter as an endangered species. Although the precise motives of all the petitioners will never be known, they all had one common goal, namely to permanently block the opening of a dam that had already been built at a taxpayer cost of $100 million.

In any case, it is doubtful if any of the petitioners had nursed any lifelong attachment to the snail darter, since this particular species of darter had been discovered only a few months before the petition. The year before, an injunction blocking the dam project on grounds that an environmental impact statement had not been properly filed[78] had been dissolved after a statement was duly filed by the Tennessee Valley Authority (TVA).[79] The belated discovery of a tannish, three-inch long fish (a species of snail darter)[80] seven miles from the mouth of the Little Tennessee river gave new life to the petitioners' crusade to block the opening of the dam. Although over 130 known species of darter were already known to exist,[81] trained ichthyologists had difficulty in differentiating one species from another. New species of snail darter were being discovered at the rate of one a year.[82] This particular species, however, was destined to go into snail darter history.

The object of the petitioner's ire was the Tellico Dam and Reservoir Project, the construction of which had begun in 1967 after Congress appropriated funds.[83] The purposes of the dam included providing a clean energy alternative to coal-burning power plants by providing sufficient hydroelectric current to heat 20,000 homes, and improving economic conditions, particularly for many of the poor and impoverished residents of the area.[84] Although the dam was "virtually completed and essentially ready for operation," the tangle of lawsuits and administrative hearings woven by the petitioners had, prior to the discovery of the snail darter, prevented the opening of the project. With the final dissolution of the injunction against the dam's opening in 1974, the snail darter's status as an endangered species was the only tool left in the petitioner's arsenal of obstruction.[85]

In October 1975, in response to the petitioner's request, the Secretary of Interior listed the snail darter as an endangered species, finding that "the snail darter is a living entity which is genetically distinct," the habitat of which would be destroyed by the dam project.[86] Suggestions that the snail darter be transplanted to the Hiwassee River were dismissed by statements from Dr. Etnier (the darter's discoverer) and the Fish and Wildlife Service that "it may take from 5 to 15 years for scientists to determine whether [the transplant would be successful]."[87]

Armed with the snail darter's entry on the Secretary's list of endangered species, the petitioners filed an action under the Endangered Species Act on grounds that the opening of the dam would cause the extinction of a species of snail darter.[88] Although the District Court agreed that the snail darter's habitat would be destroyed, it denied the request to block the dam on grounds that "at some point in time a federal project becomes so near completion . . . that a court should not apply a statute enacted long after its inception of the project to reach an unreasonable result."[89] To grant the permanent injunction, said the Court, would require "impoundment of water behind a fully completed dam if an endangered species were accidentally discovered in the river on the day before such impoundment was scheduled to take place."[90]

The petitioners appealed to the Court of Appeals, which reversed the District Court and issued the injunction, holding that nothing in the Act suggested it was not meant to "encompass the terminal phases of ongoing projects,"[91] and that it was not to be unexpected that new species might be discovered well after a project was underway and millions of dollars already expended. "Courts are ill-equipped," added the Court, "to calculate how many dollars must be invested before the value of a dam exceeds that of endangered species."[92]

In 1978, the case found itself before the United States Supreme Court in *TVA v. Hill*.[93] The Court began its opinion by stating "It may seem curious to some that the survival of a relatively small number of three-inch fish among all the countless millions of species extant would require the permanent halting of a virtually completed dam for which Congress has already expended more than $100 million."[94] It concluded, however, by stating that "the explicit provisions of the Endangered Species Act require precisely that result."[95]

The Court conceded that the result of its decision would be the "sacrifice of the intended benefits of the project and of many millions of dollars in public funds." Nevertheless, the Court insisted, the Endangered Species Act commanded all federal agencies to "insure that actions . . . funded by them do not jeopardize the continued existence" of an endangered species, and that this language must be read literally to apply to any of the 1.4 million species of animals and 600,000 species of plants in the world. Further, the fact that $100 million was already spent to provide clean energy and help the poor, and would now be wasted, was totally irrelevant. To rebut the dissent's view that the language of the Act could not reasonably be interpreted as applying to a project well under way long before the Endangered Species Act was even passed, Chief Justice Burger professed a lack of understanding as to how the words of the Act could possibly be so interpreted. He was reminded, said the Chief Justice, of the lines from Lewis Carroll's *Through the Looking Glass:* " 'When I use a word,' Humpty Dumpty said, in rather a scornful tone, 'it means just what I choose it to mean—neither more nor less.' "[96]

The dissent, led by Justices Blackmun and Powell, quoted the statement of the Attorney General in support of its argument that the Act was not meant to apply to projects that had already been built: "the dam is completed; all that remains is to close the gate . . . the dam is finished. All the landscaping has been done."[97] The dissenting Justices submitted that the result that would follow the majority's decision makes it "unreasonable to believe that Congress intended that reading." Moreover, they suggested, the Act could be construed in a way that would avoid "an absurd result" without doing violence to the language of the statute. The word "actions" in the statute referred to actions that an agency *might* take in deciding whether to fund a project—that is actions not yet carried out. Such an interpretation is further reinforced by the legal presumption against giving statutes retroactive effect. According to the majority, the dissent observed, "the only precondition to destroying even the most important federal project would be a finding by the Secretary that the continuation of the project would threaten the survival of a newly discovered species of amoeba."[98]

The dissent's views went unheeded. The Court shut down the Tellico Dam and Reservoir Project.

LESSONS LEARNED

The case of *TVA v. Hill* serves as an excellent case study, and is representative of all that is wrong with existing environmental laws and policies. It is true of course that after the expenditure of millions of dollars, and after years of delays, Congress, in the aftermath of the *Hill* case, passed Amendments to the Endangered Species Act that permitted the application of an exemption for such projects as the Tellico Dam. Notably, among the factors to be considered for any such application, were the "irretrievable and irreversible commitment of resources" to a project, and an inquiry was required as to "reasonable and prudent alternatives."[99] And perhaps Congress, more than the Supreme Court (which was only doing its best to carry out its perceived will of Congress) is to answer for the result in *Hill*.

The point, of course, is not that measures should not be taken to prevent the extinction of species. It has already been noted that the spread of human population over the globe is crowding out habitats of other species and causing the extinction of one living species per day, including the extinction of one vertebrate species every 9 months.[100] But is the cause of the extinction of any particular species to be attributed to any one man-made project built to provide energy to a rapidly expanding human population and to alleviate poverty and human suffering? Environmentalists have chosen such battlegrounds as the Tellico dam project to press their agenda. Environmental groups' supporters of the lawsuit no doubt sent newsletters to their contributors that their money had been well spent on a grand environmental cause. The wastage of $100 million expended for the purpose of providing clean energy and alleviating poverty was hailed as one of the greatest environmental victories of all time, and a proud feather in the cap of the entire environmental movement.

But important issues concerning the Tellico project were never addressed by either the government or the environmentalists. For example, who were the 20,000 people who lived in the and around the dam area? Where did they come from, and how did they come to require energy, heat, electricity, and shelter? That their needs might have been met in other ways (burning wood, coal, gasoline) is beside the point. Doubtless the extinction of many living species can be directly attributed to the loss of forest habitat caused by burning wood for fuel, or burning coal that causes acid rain. For every snail darter discovered by a crusading ichthyologist, there may be thousands of other species who are quietly being crowded out of their living space by a human population expanding at the rate of one new human every one-third of a second.

If environmentalists are brought to account for their willingness to waste $100 million already expended on a project for clean energy, so should the government be brought to account for failing to explore alternatives. In 1972, at a time when Congress was in the process of funding the Tellico dam, it was also appropriating $60 million (a little more than half what was finally appropriated for Tellico) for voluntary family planning.[101] This meager funding, combined with cut-offs of funds to all family planning groups counselling abortions, meant that many women were denied the means to plan their families. The result was hundreds of thousands of unwanted pregnancies, the offspring of which will no doubt demand power from future Tellico dams.

Cutting off sources of clean energy and the means for economic survival of thousands of human beings in the name of saving one species of snail darter at a cost of $100 million is certainly one alternative. Another, not considered by present laws or policies, would be to provide humans with the incentives and means of planning their families, thereby reducing unwanted pregnancies and moderating the exponential expansion of population and the demand for ever increasing quantities of water, energy, and resources. How many unwanted pregnancies would be prevented by the expenditure of $100 million on contraceptives and family planning information? What effect would this have on the total population? Likewise, what would $100 million spent on enforcement of immigration laws (preventing the exploitation of humans for profit and maintaining incentives for other countries to adopt family planning policies) have on population expansion? Would such expenditures have resulted in a population reduction of 20,000 people? (It will be recalled that 20,000 human beings were denied the electrical power that the Tellico dam would have provided.) Such questions have not been answered, because environmental policy makers have never asked the questions. The cost effectiveness of family planning measures has never been con-

population and the environment has not yet been acknowledged and accepted in the development of environmental policy.

POPULATION LAWS AND POLICIES

Although existing environmental laws and policies take little or no account of population issues or the cost-effectiveness of family planning programs in exploring alternatives, there are federal laws relating to population. The Family Planning Services and Population Research Act of 1970,[102] and the Family Planning and Population Research Act of 1975,[103] authorized grants to "public or nonprofit entities to assist in the establishment and operation of voluntary family planning projects which shall offer a broad range of acceptable and effective family planning methods and services."[104] Other provisions of these and other related federal acts authorize the conduct of research on "biomedical, contraceptive development, behavioral and program implementation fields related to family planning and population."[105] However, no funds are permitted to be expended on programs where abortion is a method of family planning.[106]

There are several problems with such programs. First, the restriction of funding to programs that use abortion means that many family planning organizations are deprived of funds. Second, the funding is insufficient to enable all women to plan their pregnancies. Finally, and most important, none of the federal population policies and programs is in any way tied to environmental programs. Thus population and environmental issues are dealt with separately and without coordination. The consequences of such lack of coordination will be encountered again in the remaining chapters of this book.

NOTES

1. Russell Train, EPA Administrator 1973–1977, *Environmental Protection Agency Manual,* p. 111 (hereinafter cited as EPA Manual).

2. Pub. L. No. 91-190; 83 Stat. 852; codified at 42 U.S.C.A. §4321.

3. 35 Fed. Reg. 15623, 84 Stat. 2086 (Dec. 2, 1970, amended Aug. 23, 1983); Pub. L. No. 98-80, 2(A)(2)(2),(c)(2), 87 Stat. 485, pursuant to 5 U.S.C.S. §901.

4. EPA Manual, *supra* note 1, p. 111.

5. 7 U.S.C. §135.

6. 33 U.S.C. §1251; 52 ALR Fed. 788.

7. 42 U.S.C. §4901.

8. 42 U.S.C. §1600.

9. 42 U.S.C. §7401.

10. 42 U.S.C. §1600.

11. 15 U.S.C. §2601.

12. 42 U.S.C. §§6901–6992K (1982 and Supp. v. 1987).

13. 33 U.S.C. §1251.

14. 15 U.S.C. §2055.

15. EPA Manual, p. 112.

16. *Id.*, pp. 112–114.

17. *Id.*, p. 115.

18. *Id.*, p. 115.

19. *Id.*

20. *Id.*, p. 116.

21. *Id.*

22. *Id.*

23. Hilts, Soot: The EPA Discovers the Worst Killer in the Air, *N.Y. Times,* July 25, 1993, p. E2.

24. *Id.*

25. *EPA Manual,* p. 117.

26. *Id.*

27. Pub. Law No. 91-190; 83 Stat. 852; 42 U.S.C.A. §4321 (1970).

28. 42 U.S.C.A. §4331(A).

29. 42 U.S.C.A. §4321.

30. Pub. Law No. 91-572; 84 Stat. 1504 (1970); codified 42 U.S.C.A. §§300–300 A-8.

31. 42 U.S.C.A. §300(A).

32. 42 U.S.C.S. §300A-5.

33. 42 U.S.C.S. §300A-6.

34. *Rust v. Sullivan,* 111 S.Ct. 1759; 114 L.Ed. 2d 233 (1991).

35. *Planned Parenthood Federation v. Sullivan,* 913 F.2d 1492 (10th Cir. 1990); see also *New York v. Sullivan,* 889 F.2d 401 (2nd Cir. 1989), cert. granted, 110 S.Ct. 2559 (1990); *Mass. v. Secretary of Health and Human Services,* 899 F.2d 53 (1st Cir. 1990) (en banc).

36. Pub. Law No. 91-609; 84 Stat. 1791; 42 U.S.C.A. §4501. (Dec. 31, 1970).

37. 42 U.S.C.A. §4501.

38. Pub. Law No. 95-128 (1977).

39. Pub. Law No. 91-609 §710; 84 Stat. 1793 42 U.S.C.A. §4511 (1970).

40. Pub. Law No. 98-181, Title VI §474(e), 97 Stat. 1239 (1983).

41. EPA Manual, *supra* note 1, pp. 109–110.

42. Pub. Law No. 91-190 §102; 42 U.S.C.A. §4332.

43. *Sierra Club v. Morton,* 427 U.S. 390, 514 F.2d 856 (1975), rev'd on other grounds.

44. *Natural Resources Defense Council v. Grant,* 341 F.Supp. 356 (E.D. North Carolina 1972); but see *Joseph v. Adams* ELR 20468.

45. *Sierra Club v. Morton,* supra, note 42.

46. *Hiram Clarke Civic Club v. Lynn,* 476 F.2d 421 (5th Cir. 1973); but see *Andrus v. Sierra Club,* 440 U.S. 347; *Sierra Club v. Sigles,* 695 F.2d 957 (5th Cir.)

47. *Grand Canyon Dorries Inc. v. Walker,* 500 F.2d 588 (10th Cir. 1974).

48. *Irving v. FAA,* 539 F. Supp. 17 (N.D. Tex., 1981).

49. *Environmental Defense Fund Inc. v. Costle,* 439 F.Supp. 980 (1977), p. 993.

50. *South Louisiana Environmental Council v. Sand,* 629 F.2d 1005 (5th Cir. 1980), as summarized by Note of Decision to 42 U.S.C.S. §4332 n. 113.

51. *Trout Unlimited v. Morton,* 509 F.2d 1276 (1975), p. 1286.

52. *Calvert Cliff's Coord. Com. v. U.S.A.E. Com'n,* 449 F.2nd 1109 (1971).

53. *Id.,* p. 1113: see also *National Wildlife v. Andrus,* 440 F.Supp. 1245 at 1253 (1977).

54. Paul Roberts, Benefit-Cost Analysis, Its Use (Misuse) in Evaluating Water Resource Projects, 14 *Am. Bus. L. J.* 73, 76 (1976); see also Gen. Acct. Off., *Improvements Needed in Making Benefit-Cost Analysis for Federal Water Resources Projects,* Rep. B-167941 (Sept. 20, 1974).

55. See notes 48–49, *supra;* see also Gillham Dam Cases, 2 ERC 1261 (1971); but see *E.D.F. v. U.S. Corps of Engineers Civ. Act. IVO.* 71-652-Civ. J. (M.D. Fla., Feb. 4, 1974, p. 26) (unpublished), cited in Roberts, *supra,* note 53, p. 77: "Among other things, I am not able to see how such an EIS properly could escape having a current cost/benefit evaluation made of the whole project."

56. *Tennessee Valley Authority v. Hill,* 437 U.S. 153, 98 S.Ct. 2279, 57 L.Ed.2d 117 (1978), p. 173 (n. 18).

57. Roberts, *supra,* note 53, p. 76.

58. 371 F.Supp. 1004 (E.D. Tenn. 1973), aff'd 492 F.2d 466 (6th Cir., 1974)

59. 15 U.S.C. §2601.

60. 33 U.S.C. §1251.

61. 42 U.S.C. §7401.

62. 42 U.S.C. §4901.

63. 42 U.S.C. §2021(h).

64. 33 U.S.C. §§1401–1402, 1411–1421, 1441–1444; 16 U.S.C. §§1431–1434.

65. 16 U.S.C. App. §1271.

66. 16 U.S.C. §661.

67. 42 U.S.C. §§6901–6992K (1982 and Supp. v. 1987).

68. 43 U.S.C.S. §1701.

69. 7 U.S.C.S. §135.

70. 42 U.S.C. §300 n 3.

71. See, e.g.,
Environmental Law: National Environmental Policy Act, 20 *Harv. Int. L. J.* 175, Winter, 1979. Haug, Determining the Significance of Environmental Issues under the National Environmental Policy Act, 18 *J. Environ. Mgmt.* 15, 1984. Bockrath, Environmental Law, 43 *La. L. Rev.* 403, November 1982. Environmental Law: Standing to Challenge Federal Agency Action under National Environmental Protection Act., 57 *Minn. L. Rev.* 404, 1972. Goplerud, NEPA at Nine: Alice and Well, or Wounded in Action?, 55 *N.D. L. Rev.* 497, 1979. Fairfax and Barton, A Decade of NEPA: Milestone or Millstone? *Renewable Resources J.* 22, Summer 1984. Environmental Bill of Rights: The Citizen Suit and the National Environmental Policy Act of 1969, 24 *Rutgers L. Rev.* 230, 1970. The National Environmental Policy Act and the Revised CEQ Regulations: A Fate Worse Than the "Worst Case Analysis?", 60 *St. John's L. Rev.* 500, Spring 1986. Environmental Law: A Symposium, 19 *Santa Clara L. Rev.* 513, Summer 1979. McGarity, The Courts, the Agencies, and NEPA Threshold Issues, 5 *Tex. L. Rev.* 801. Murchison, Does NEPA Matter?—An Analysis of the Historical Development and Contemporary Significance of the National Environmental Policy Act, 18 *U. Rich. L. Rev.* 557, Spring 1984. All cited in 42 U.S.C. §4321, n.2.

72. 84 Stat. 884; 16 U.S.C. §1531.

73. 16 U.S.C. §1531(b). The international treaties referred to were (A) migratory bird treaties with Canada and Mexico; (B) the Migratory and Endangered Bird Treaty with Japan; (C) the Convention on Nature Protection and Wildlife Preservation in the Western Hemisphere; (D) the International Convention for the Northwest Atlantic Fisheries; (E) the International Convention for the High Seas Fisheries of the North Pacific Ocean; (F) the Convention on International Trade in Endangered Species of Wild Fauna and Flora; and (G) other international agreements.

74. 16 U.S.C. §1531(c).

75. 16 U.S.C. §§1533(A)(A)(E).

76. 16 U.S.C. §1536.

77. Zummo, Comment, The Mandate of Section 7 of the Endangered Species Act of 1973: The Darter Meets the Dam, 47 *U. Cin. L. Rev.* 613, 616 (1978).

78. *Environmental Defense Fund v. TVA,* 339 F.Supp. 806 (E.D. Tenn.), aff'd, 468 F.2d 1164 (6th Cir. 1972).

79. *Environmental Defense Fund v. TVA,* 371 F.Supp. 1004 (E.D. Tenn. 1973), aff'd, 492 F.2d 466 (6th Cir. 1974).

80. The snail darter is a species of perch known as *Percina (Imostoma) tanasi;* see 88 *Biol. Soc. Wash.,* 469–488 (Jan. 22, 1976).

81. *TVA v. Hill,* 437 U.S., p. 159.

82. *Id.*

83. Public Works Appropriation Act, 80 Stat. 1002, 1014 (1967).

84. See Hearings on Public Works for Power and Energy Research Appropriation Bill before a Subcommittee of the House Committee on Appropriations, 94th Cong., 2nd Sess., 261 (1976).

85. 437 U.S. at 158.

86. 40 Fed. Reg. 47505-47506 (1975); 50 C.F.R. §17.11(i) (1976).

87. 40 Fed. Reg. 47506 (1975).

88. 419 F. Supp. 753 (E.D. Tenn. 1976).

89. *Id.* at 760.

90. *Id.* at 763.

91. 549 F.2d at 1070.

92. *Id.*

93. 437 U.S. 153.

94. *Id.* at 172.

95. *Id.*

96. *Id.* at 173 (note 18).

97. Tr. of Oral Arg. 18, at 437 U.S. 196 (note 1).

98. 437 U.S. at 203-204.

99. 42 U.S.C. 1536 (h)(A)(i)-(iv)

100. See Chapter Two, note 12, supra.

101. 42 U.S.C. 300A-6, 3505A-3505(c) (1970).

102. 42 U.S. 201 note, 300 A-1 to 300 A-4 (1975)

103. 42 U.S.C. § 300 (A)

104. 42 U.S.C. § 300 A-2

105. 42 U.S.C. § 300 A-6.

106. *Id.*

4 Private Environmental Action

The environmental organizations courted disaster when they "succeeded" American style. When they got too big, too rich and too remote from the environmental effects of their actions. Most of all when we abandoned moral appeal for fund-raising appeals, when we substituted holy war against the infidel for the sweet science of swaying souls. Like our competitors in organized religion, especially in the televangelists, we enviros lost our credibility when we bought into the junk-mail business. When the salvation we offered lost out to our insatiable need for money. Poverty, chastity and obedience wilted before the prospect of empire and power, "careers" in the institutionalized environmental movement.[1]

Tom Wolf

It has been noted that major governmental involvement in protecting the environment began in 1970 with the passage of the Environmental Policy Act. The passage of major legislation did not occur in a vacuum, however; rather it was the culmination of a long political and cultural history.

The relationship between man and his environment was recognized as early as 500 B.C. by Plato, who observed in Attica the erosion of soils caused by deforestation.[2] However, the intellectual roots of the "environmental movement" are traditionally traced back to the transcendentalism of Thoreau and Emerson. A more popular brand of environmentalism in the form of the conservation movement can be traced back to President Theodore Roosevelt. The early conservation movement, founded in an era when property rights reigned supreme, spawned the formation of conservation trusts, founded by private groups with the purpose of purchasing land and open space to preserve the wilderness area from the encroachments of civilization and development. The oldest of such trusts, the Trustees for Reservations in Massachusetts, still owns 71 properties containing 17,500 acres.[3] Over 700 land trusts still exist in the United States today, protecting 8 million acres.[4]

It is perhaps not surprising that a movement with such origins has remained primarily a movement of the upper classes. A Roper poll has revealed that "active support for environmental initiatives is concentrated in the wealthier and most-schooled upper fifth of the population."[5] This appears to be the case despite the fact that, according to studies, "a disproportionate number of toxic waste dumps and waste burning incinerators are in minority and low-income neighborhoods,"[6] and that "three out of five blacks and hispanics live in areas with one or more toxic sites."[7] The *National Law Journal* has reported that "the needs of low-income communities have been largely ignored by enforcement agencies and mainstream environmental lawyers."[8]

Thus, despite the evidence that the poor and disadvantaged suffer the most from environmental deterioration, the environmental movement remains an upper-class enterprise. There are several possible explanations. First, it may be that those who are already adequately fed, clothed, and sheltered have the luxury, not enjoyed by the poor, of contemplating the long-term trends of a global environment. The uneducated and poor may be too involved in immediate economic survival to devote their time and energies to environmental causes, particularly when many of the goals of those causes appear to be in conflict with their own economic well-being.

Second, many environmental groups reject any responsibility for the economic consequences of the actions they seek. A former prominent member of the Sierra Club has observed that the environmental movement now consists of "rich, educated people so high up the needs hierarchy that they actively seek to mock and disdain lower needs, such as food and shelter."[9] According to this view, the environmental movement has deteriorated into a kind of class warfare.[10] After Greenpeace's successful campaign against sealing led to the loss of livelihood of many Newfoundlanders, a Greenpeace activist was asked if his organization intended to take any responsibility for the economic hardships caused by their actions. The response was typical of many such groups: "We blame the federal government for not finding alternatives for these people besides sealing."[11]

When Hispanic shepherds (known as the Gandos De Valle) lost traditional grazing pastures as a result of Nature Conservancy purchases, and Indians in Acoma Pueblo lost tribal lands to a national park lobbied for by the Sierra Club and Wilderness Society, their desperate protests were dismissed as obstructions of the environmental agenda.[12]

In October 1991, Indian, Black, and Hispanic activists convened the first "National People of Colour Environmental Leadership Summit," presenting their case that the mainstream environmental organizations had not made adequate efforts to recruit minority employees or recognized the racial element in environmental issues.[13]

A Labor Institute study has revealed that 30% of the labor force of New Jersey work in the "toxic economy"—namely, industries that produce large quantities of toxic wastes. To those with jobs in this industry, calls for major reductions in toxic waste are tantamount to the elimination of thousands of jobs.[14] Although such workers are often told that there will be better jobs available in a nontoxic economy, their view is that "a job in the hand is worth two in the plan. Workers prefer the jobs they've got now to the ones they might get later on."[15]

One observer has suggested that "the environmental movement has little or no realistic prospect of significantly reducing the use of toxics without offering some believable alternative to the people whose paychecks would be directly affected by their proposals."[16] According to this view, the failure of environmentalists to couple their environmental proposals with realistic economic guarantees for those who will lose their livelihoods is the movement's "achilles heel."[17] At the very least it has cost the support of much of the middle and lower-middle class.

Another explanation for upper-class predominance in the environmental movement is that much of the present environmental agenda is focused on medium transference and the practice of "nimbyism." The words of former EPA Director Thomas may be recalled—that most environmental action takes the form of simply transferring pollution from one medium (such as the air), to another (such as the soil, or water).[18] Nimbyism ("Not In My Backyard") has become the political vehicle for medium transference. The most frequent victims of nimbyism are the economically deprived and the politically unempowered. Much of the funds used to support "environmentalism" are in fact used to transfer pollution from communities with wealth and political power to poor communities with little political power.

Although cases of environmental Nimbyism abound, the case of the State of Arkansas is an illustrative case in point. It is perhaps not coincidental that Arkansas, one of the poorest states, has been identified as the nation's third most polluted state by the Green Index.[19] (A hazardous-waste incineration company in the Arkansas town of El Dorado was known to be importing garbage and waste from 48 states and foreign countries.[20]) A group called the Environmental Congress of Arkansas (representing 16 local environmental groups) sprang into action when an Arkansas community learned that a 300-acre landfill was to be located nearby. The Environmental Congress was "successful" in its efforts to prevent the location of the dump near its community. As a result of its efforts, the landfill was relocated in the Ouachita River Basin where, according to one observer, "one flood will spread garbage and God-knows-what downstream for 60 or 100 miles."[21]

Near Jacksonville, Arkansas, a chemical company sought to dispose of 28,300 barrels of toxic waste that had been piling up for 30 years at the site of an abandoned pesticide factory.[22] Again, the environmental groups leaped into action, forcing the chemical company into filing for bankruptcy (whereupon the company relocated to Memphis, Tennessee). Ten years of lawsuits and political action prevented dioxin burning for 10 years, prompting the United Nations to call their efforts "an environmental success story."[23] Unheralded, however, was the exhibition of community Nimbyism, when, after the expenditure of vast sums by all sides concerned, the EPA in January 1992 granted the Jacksonville site a license to incinerate the toxins. This decision was apparently based on findings that other disposal technologies would be too expensive. According to the Environmental Congress, the burning of the toxins, even after compliance with the Clean Air Act, will result in "releasing the smoke into the atmosphere, where they don't know what it will do."[24] Thus the net result of what was hailed as an "environmental success story" was the transfer of pollution from the soil to the air.[25]

Additional examples illustrate what happens when Nimbyism meets Nimbyism. In the case of the Environmental Congress, it will soon have its work cut out for it. It was recently reported that the hazardous-waste disposal company in El Dorado, which had sought to build a toxic incinerator in a community in Arizona, had been defeated by a Nimby group in Arizona. The company was now seeking to build the plant in El Dorado instead.

It has been suggested that Nimby groups are not true environmentalists, as their interests do not extend beyond the horizons of their own immediate self-interest to the environment at large.[26] Allan Mazur, a sociology professor at Syracuse University, has opined that "as soon as an area is off the list [of candidates for an unwanted facility], it fades out of the picture. Noble Niaby (Not in Anyone's Back Yard) aspirations suddenly disappear. Meanwhile illegal, dangerous 'midnight dumping' by unscrupulous waste haulers run rampant."[27] Be that as it may, the methods of community Nimbyism have been emulated by the national environmental groups. Piller has observed that "the cumulative efforts of Nimbys have produced a new social and political trend, called Nimby gridlock—the consequences of a multitude of communities rejecting any plan regardless of its characteristics. The national environmental organizations have effectively adopted this gridlock approach by opposing almost all available technologies of hazardous waste disposal."[28]

A classic example of the perversity of Nimbyism is that of Peter Calthorpe, a California developer, who says Nimbyism is the greatest obstacle to him building a new kind of residential community built around pedestrian malls and mass transit as an alternative to communities based on the culture of the automobile.[29]

ENVIRONMENTAL BACKLASH

Perhaps the most unfortunate result of the environmental movement's failure to take responsibility for proposing alternatives to the economic hardships caused by the policies they promote is the environmental backlash movement. This backlash movement soaks up funds, which then compete directly with environmental causes. In many cases, the net effect of each movement's tax-deductible funds is simply to cancel out each other's efforts, and neutralize each side's agenda.

The origins of the backlash movement have been traced to the so-called "sagebrush rebellion" of the late 1970s, which represented the political efforts of some interests in Western states to have Western federal land transferred to local control.[30] The modern version of this movement, labeled generically as the "Wise Use" movement, began in 1988 as a coalition of mining, ranching, and energy industries.[31]

In 1988 this movement began with a series of conferences sponsored by the Center for the Defense of Free Enterprise.[32] Groups represented at the first "Multiple Use Strategy Conference" were of the type to make any environmentalist's hair stand on end: the National Rifle Association, the Jackalopes Motorcycle Club, and the Cougar Mountain Snowmobile Association.[33] The "Wise Use" agenda produced by that conference included such goals as clear-cutting old growth forests, opening all public lands to mineral exploitation, development of national parks by enterprises such as Walt Disney, and the imposition of civil penalties against anyone challenging development of federal lands.[34]

In the early 1990s, Alan Gottlieb organized the "Alliance for America," coordinating over 125 groups. Gottlieb describes his coalition as fighting "an evil empire. For us, the environmental movement has become the perfect bogeyman."[35]

Former Secretary of the Interior Stewart Udall has suggested that the First Use movement should be called the "Me-First" movement, arguing that their very use of the term "Wise-Use" is a perversion of history. He notes that Theodore Roosevelt's chief forester, Gifford Pinchot, first coined the term to describe the alternative to the private exploitation of public lands. In contrast, he quotes a leader of the Wise-Use movement as having the goal "to destroy, to eradicate the environmental movement in a decade,"[36] and expresses concern over an estimate by Canada's Library of the Parliament that there are over 250 "Me-First" organizations in the United States.[37] The Library's Report quotes as typical of the "Wise-Use" movement the attitude of the Wilderness Impact Research Foundation, which "sees environmentalists as anti-Christian; a writer in *Land Rights Letter* who identifies the supreme appreciator of nature, Ralph Waldo Emerson as 'a fallen away Unitarian minister'; a Mormon rancher who can't understand why 'environmental-ists want to go against the Bible, which says (in Genesis) that Man shall have dominion over the Earth.' ''[38]

In 1990, Mike Nichols launched the "Grassroots for Multiple Use." Since then, dozens of similar groups have been formed with much the same agenda. As promoters of "wise use," these organizations repre-sent what has been described as a "movement with more than 50 million potential members, bound by a fervent belief that designating public land as wilderness is elitist, unnecessary, un-democratic, even vaguely un-Christian."[39]

Other groups have professed to be more confrontational, such as the "Sahara Club" purporting to represent a coalition of bikers, ranchers, and miners who actively oppose environmentalists. One member has been quoted as boasting of a special division of "Sahara Clubbers; I'm the smallest, at 220 pounds. Our biggest are ugly, 300 pound desert rid-ers. If we find Earth Firsters setting traps, we're going to take care of them with baseball bats."[40] According to one journalist, the Club's third newsletter issue "offers a $100 'bounty' for the arrest of any Earth First! member breaking the law."[41]

Although the Wise-Users are sometimes dismissed as having insuffi-cient financial and political clout to affect policy, several bills have been introduced in Congress reflecting the Wise-Use agenda, including such bills as the Recreational Trails Fund Act, which would use gas taxes to build motorized vehicle trails in National parks.[42] In September 1989, a number of advertisers, including Ford Motor Company, were pressured into withdrawing their ads for the Turner Broadcasting presentation of "Rage Over Trees," an Audubon documentary about logging operations in the Northwest.[43]

Joining forces with the Wise-Use movement have been a number of conservative groups such as the American Freedom Coalition, which among other goals opposes abortion and unregulated art work.[44] This group planned numerous conferences around the country, and during the Bush administration petitioned the President to open the National Wild-life Refuge to oil and gas development.[45]

U.S. News and World Report recently noted that "wise-use members have increasingly outnumbered environmentalists at key public hearings, scuttling both a new protection plan for the Greater Yellowstone region and a unique timber-cutting pact between conservationists and loggers in Montana."[46] The political success of wise-use groups prompted Susan Tixier of the Southern Utah Wilderness Alliance to express concern that "these folks are very clever, they know Washington and they know lo-cal politicians. I give them credit for doing what we should be doing. I just wish we had their big money."[47]

It does not yet appear that the antienvironmental movement has the same amount of direct funding as environmental groups, although industries locked in battles with particular environmental groups can often outspend their opponents. While it is true that conferences of the movement have been given support by major corporations,[48] it is equally true that major corporations have supported the environmental movement as well.[49] Of course considerable money is raised and expended by both sides anytime a major confrontation or legal action develops over a particular proposed project or piece of major legislation.

It is an unfortunate result of the confrontation between the two movements that millions of tax-deductible dollars are spent on the confrontations themselves, both legal and political, rather than on actual programs that protect the environment. One cannot help but wonder whether the contributions of environmentally minded citizens have not in fact encouraged such confrontations by subsidizing them. Without such funding, the confrontations would have to give way to cooperation and compromise. Indeed, if the money spent on confrontations had instead been used to fund economic alternatives for those dislocated by the environmental agenda, much of the resistance to the environmental movement might not have arisen in the first place.

PRIVATE ORGANIZATIONS

In the United States alone, the environmental movement has been described as splintered into over "10,000 hopelessly decentralized groups competing for funds."[50] The 1991 Resource Guide to Environmental Organizations lists 150 *major* environmental organizations covering every conceivable aspect of a very diverse environmental agenda. These organizations range from the Xerces Society,[51] which promotes the preservation of insects, snails, and slugs, to the National Campaign to Stop Radiation Exposed Food.[52] The "Environmental Movement's Mainstream" has been identified as a group composed of 10 large organizations known as "The Group of 10."[53]

The Group of 10 includes the Natural Resources Defense (annual budget of $16 million; membership of 130,000; the primary legal advocate of the environmental movement), the Sierra Club ($32 million; 553,000; founded by naturalist John Muir, it addresses a broad range of environmental issues), the Sierra Club Legal Defense Fund (independent of the Sierra Club; $8.3 million; 120,000; it often represents other environmental groups), the National Wildlife Federation ($85.6 million; 3 million members; seeks to protect wildlife preserves, but also interested in such other issues as global warming), the Wilderness Society ($20 million; 360,000; seeks to protect public lands), National Parks and Conservation Association ($3.28 million; 125,000; seeks to preserve the national parks), National Audubon Society ($35 million; 580,000; promotes hunt-

ing and fishing), Izak Walton League ($1.64 million; 50,000; promotes
hunting and fishing), Environmental Defense Fund ($15 million; 150,000;
promotes novel solutions, such as market-based principles), and Friends
of the Earth ($2.5 million; 50,000; merged with Environmental Policy
Institute and the Oceanic Institute, advocates grass-roots environmental
interests in Washington).[54]

Other important environmental groups include the controversial
Greenpeace (1990 budget: $157 million), and private foundations such as
the MacArthur Foundation and Pew Charitable Trust, which contribute
to environmental causes. In 1991 the Mellon Foundation made a $21
million land gift to the United States. Other foundations, such as the
Nathan Cummings Foundation (assets: $200 million) and the Sundra
Foundation (assets: $300 million), have announced new environmental
programs.[55]

The goals and tactics of each of these environmental groups vary significantly. The Nature Conservancy, for example, does not use lawsuits,
picketing, or confrontation to achieve its goals of wilderness preservation. Instead it simply buys the land it seeks to save from development,
and dedicates it as a preserve. Although criticized by other environmental groups for cooperating with business and for not being confrontational, the Nature Conservancy has achieved success where more confrontational methods have failed. In 1988, for example, when members
of Earth First! were chaining themselves to bulldozers in a vain effort to
stop development of a wilderness area near Austin, Texas, the Nature
Conservancy presented a compromise plan that set aside 29,000 acres as
a preserve funded by fees on developers. In support of the plan, several
large companies donated funds, including the 3M Company, which contributed $1 million. An officer of the U.S. Fish and Wildlife Service later
observed that "The Conservancy was absolutely critical to the plan's
success. Average people can relate to an environmental group that is
also entrepreneurial."[56]

When more extreme environmental groups threatened to block a $17
billion development project near Palm Springs, California, the Conservancy presented a plan under which developers agreed to pay $600 for
each acre developed. This money was then used to finance a preserve
for the habitat of an endangered lizard, which is now known as the
Coachella Valley Preserve, and in which the lizard now thrives. An attorney for the developers acknowledged that "We couldn't have accomplished any of this without the Nature Conservancy. The business community responded to its approach because it works."[57]

The Conservancy's approach has attracted a number of very helpful
contributors, such as the Reynolds Metal Company, which contributed
97 acres for a rare-plant habitat in Kentucky, and the National Gypsum
Co., which gave 150 acres in Vermont for a cave habitat for brown

bats.[58] Allied Energy Services financed the acquisition of 140,000 acres of tropical rainforest in South America.[59] In the past 2 years, the Conservancy has acquired over a million acres, mostly from private individuals.[60]

The Director of Communications for the Conservancy has explained the group's philosophy of cooperation as follows: "In evaluating potential for corporate associations, the Conservancy sticks to what it knows. And what it knows nothing about is sportswear, cars, and breakfast cereal. As a result, we eschew corporate relationships based on product endorsement or an implied 'green seal' of approval. . . . Most recently, we've begun building a partnership with Honda of America that is not only making cash donations to our exosystem preservation model on the Big Darby Creek in Ohio, but is also independently mobilizing its workers to participate in tree planting along the Darby."[61]

If all of the environmental groups used the methods employed by the Nature Conservancy, it is doubtful if the environmental backlash movement would have attracted many adherents. However, many environmental groups, including Nimbys, prefer lawsuits and aggressive legal advocacy to advance their goals. The motto of the Environmental Defense Fund has been "Sue the Bastards"[62] (although more recently it has adopted a less confrontational approach, as when it worked with McDonald's to persuade it to use biodegradable containers).[63] In 1991 four environmental groups, including the Conservation Law Foundation, sued to block a $5 billion highway project to rebuild an underground freeway and construct an underground tunnel under Boston Harbor, claiming that the project would violate the Clean Air Act.[64] The result of another such lawsuit (TVA v. Hill) was described in Chapter 3. It has already been noted that many of the "environmental victories" of such courtroom battles are phyrric, often only delaying the inevitable and almost always waking a sleeping tiger and mobilizing powerful antienvironmental forces.

Some groups, such as Greenpeace, have chosen an even more confrontational approach when the results of democratic decision-making have not coincided with their own preconceived environmental agenda. Greenpeace's tactics have included the delivery of dead stinking fish to annual board meetings of companies accused of polluting rivers, climbing smokestacks, plugging industrial sewage pipes, blockading a chemical plant, and sailing small boats into nuclear test sites.[65] Even such actions as these did not satisfy some members. In 1977, one of the original Greenpeace members charged that Greenpeace had become more interested in raising funds than triggering confrontations. He left to form the Sea Shepherd Society.[66]

Although the 1990 revenues of Greenpeace exceeded $156 million, there is some debate over whether the confrontations funded by it have been successful. Reductions in nuclear testing had to await the fall of communism in Russia, and it is doubtful if receiving stinking fish made corporate board members more sympathetic to Greenpeace's causes. However, the destruction of the seal hunting business has been attributed, at least in part, to the disruptive tactics of Greenpeace. In any case, however, such tactics have given ammunition to the antienvironmental movement, and become the focus of a backlash. The Chairman of Noranda Forest Inc. has charged that members are "zealots. Society is being forced to defend practices which shouldn't require defense and to spend time fixing non-problems."[67] Powerful business interests, led by *Forbes Magazine,* have recently traded charges and countercharges with Greenpeace in the national media.[68] A former Greenpeace member told Reuters that Greenpeace "has betrayed its original objectives. It is a drag on the environmental movement, sucking up funds that could better be used by smaller groups."[69]

Nevertheless, Greenpeace has its supporters. The *Toronto Star* recently ran a published story in which it gave Greenpeace credit for its role in pushing for a recent international treaty, signed by 23 nations, banning mining in Antarctica, and observing that Greenpeace "now offers solutions. Recently in Toronto, Greenpeace delivered a four-ton roll of glossy, magazine-grade paper, made without chlorine bleach, to the head of Canada's largest publisher, to embarrass the company into using a less-polluting product. But the stunt was possible only because Greenpeace had worked with a German paper mill to develop a new process for making the paper."[70]

Greenpeace is by no means the end of the spectrum. Some fringe groups have found inspiration in a 1975 novel, *The Monkey Wrench Gang,* in which four "ecoteurs" blow up dams, bridges, and other structures they believed detracted from the scenic beauty of the Colorado River. The founder of one such group has been reported as having written "two editions of 'Ecodefense: A Field Guide to Monkeywrenching' which offers detailed advice on how to drive spikes into trees to shatter chain saws and sawmill blades; scatter caltrops on roads to flatten tires; disable construction equipment; pull up mining markers and survey stakes . . . which are 'highly vulnerable to monkey-wrenching.' "[71] The common rationalization of such groups appears to be based on a philosophy of "deep ecology" in which the interests of nature are placed above those of mankind. One member of such a group has described this as a philosophy that the "wilderness has a right to exist for its own sake," and that monkey-wrenching is "a form of worship toward the earth. It's really a very spiritual thing to go out and do."[72]

Doug Bandow, a Cato Institute fellow has warned that "With groups apparently prepared to bomb sawmills, down electrical towers, and decapitate cyclists—and ads placed for terminally ill volunteers to launch kami kaze attacks on dams—ecoterrorism can no longer be dismissed as minor. We risk the development of an ecological guerilla movement."[73] While such warnings may be an overreaction, there have been numerous reports of tree-spiking in the Northwest, and vandalization of ski lifts.[74] At a Court hearing in 1991, a defendant convicted of vandalizing ski-lift supports sang, "We must fight them with our spirit, with our life, and with our guile. We must show them that the answer is to stay forever wild."[75] After the defendant was sentenced to a 3-year term, the U.S. attorney working on the case said that the sentence would help crush "this radical deviant pseudo-environmental movement that has besmirched legitimate environmental movements."[76]

Although several groups have been accused of using such tactics, Mike Rosell, a founder of Earth First! says "We believe in confrontation, yes, but violence, no,"[77] and claims that Earth First! people are targets, and not the instigators of violence.

FINANCING ENVIRONMENTALISM

The need for financing has created a dilemma for many environmental groups. Their environmental agenda requires funding, but the greatest source of funds is controlled by many of their opponents—in particular, business and industry.

During the years of the Reagan administration many environmental groups were able to exploit the "Watt Factor."[78] James Watt, Reagan's controversial Secretary of the Interior, became the Darth Vader of the antienvironmental movement. Environmentalists responded by sending millions of dollars in contributions to environmental groups.

After Watt's departure, however, contributions first began to fall off; but each new environmental disaster triggered new waves of contributions. Two months after the Exxon Valdez spilled 11 million gallons of oil on pristine Alaska beaches in March 1989, the National Wildlife Federation received 21,000 new applications in the space of 19 days,[79] and a "Fund for Alaska" campaign (to "monitor the oil spill") raised $633,000. The Wilderness Society received $50,000 in unsolicited donations after sending out letters urging people to write the President about the oil spill.[80]

But the 1990–1991 War in the Gulf, and an economic recession, caused a flattening out of contributions and memberships. In 1991 the Wilderness Society reported that the average donation was down 12%, and the National Wildlife Federation projected a $4 million shortfall for their 1991 budget. The unexpected layoff of 56 National Wildlife employees shocked not only that organization, but other environmental groups as well.[81]

Nevertheless, many environmental groups have continued to grow, requiring ever greater sums of money to support an ever expanding internal bureaucracy. The need of many groups to devote a large percentage of their activities to fund-raising has caused some disillusionment among members. Tom Wolf, an environmentalist who writes about the West, has written that

the environmental organizations courted disaster when they 'succeeded' American style. When they got too big, too rich and too remote from the environmental effects of their actions. Most of all, when we abandoned moral appeal for fund-raising appeals. Like our competitors in organized religion, especially the televangelists, we enviros lost our credibility when we bought into the junk-mail business. When the salvation we offered lost out to our insatiable need for money. When the enticement of tax deductibility led to abuses of our nonprofit status.[82]

Wolf's disillusionment went to the very heart of what environmentalism was supposed to be about: "Our culture of narcissism spread its sickly, sweet smell through environmental board rooms in the '80's, as former radicals changed overnight into yuppies, as small organizations became huge and unwieldy. Poverty, chastity and obedience wilted before the prospect of empire and power, 'careers' in the institutionalized environmental movement."[83]

Brad Knickerbocker has observed that

Mainstream environmental organizations have begun to narrow their focus, excluding or deprioritizing any target, issue, objective, or analysis that does not raise money or build membership. Worse still, these organizations are extremely reluctant to alienate existing members, directors, funders, cabinet secretaries, congressional leaders, or corporate executives with whom they might one day have to negotiate an accord.[84]

Most of the largest environmental organizations have become political action groups, requiring the support of large staffs and lobbyists. With some groups having budgets approaching one-tenth of a billion dollars, some have turned to money from the very corporations considered to be their adversaries. It has already been noted that some corporations have made donations in kind as part of a compromise plan. In other cases, however, corporations have become voluntary financial backers of a particular environmental group.

For example, contributors to the World Wildlife Fund/Conservation Foundation include Philip Morris, Mobil, Chevron, Exxon, and Morgan Guarantee Trust.[85] Among those who have paid $10,000 each to join the National Wildlife Association's Corporate Council are the likes of Dupont and Arco.[86] The Wilderness Society has received $100,000 in a licensing agreement with the Timberland Company, and $50,000 from an

Ohio brewer in return for the use of the Society's emblem on beer six-packs.[87] Waste Management Inc. has contributed over $900,000 to environmental organizations, and has been admitted to the Environmental Grantmakers Association (which supports environmental groups).[88] One critic of this arrangement has asserted that Waste Management "is now in the position that the fox might envy; guarding, and even financing, the henhouse . . . Grass-roots groups, such as the Citizen's Clearinghouse for Hazardous Wastes, Inc., are already suspicious of the three way revolving door connection of many large environmental organizations, government regulatory agencies, and big business."[89] A member of Greenpeace (which does not accept corporate money) claims that "these corporations claim to be environmentalists, but they are buying off the groups who are opposing them."[90]

In 1988 a federation of 40 environmental groups (including Friends of the Earth and the Sierra Club) was formed under the name "Earth Share." Conducting corporate workplace drives using methods similar to United Way, it raised $8 million in 1991.[91]

While the corporate sponsors claim they are just being good citizens showing interest in the environment, and the environmental groups assert that their independence is not compromised by corporate contributions, the reliance on corporate funding has at times proved awkward, as when General Electric, citing recession woes, declined in 1991 to renew a $3 million contract to underwrite National Audubon Society televised specials.[92] The *New York Times* cited this as an example of the "vulnerability to sudden cuts in financing from a source that is becoming increasingly important. More than that, it demonstrated the importance of the closer ties between environmental groups and the businesses that are often thought of as their adversaries."[93]

Not all corporate contributions are accepted, however. The Sierra Club has adopted guidelines prohibiting the acceptance of contributions from "major polluters," and in 1991 the Environmental Defense Council refused a $5000 check from Procter and Gamble Co., which manufactures disposable diapers, explaining that "We aren't ruling out . . . corporate contributions . . . [b]ut we don't want to take contributions from people who are directly involved in manufacturing—particularly products that may have environmental consequences."[94]

THE GREEN MARKETING INDUSTRY

Environmental groups can take credit for increased awareness among Americans of environmental issues. Some environmental groups around the world franchise or authorize the use of a green type "stamp" on products considered environmentally sound. A recent *Wall Street Journal*/NBC poll reported that 8 of every 10 Americans consider themselves to be "environmentalists."[95] Corporate marketing strategists have been quick to pick up on this wave of environmental consciousness, and now tout the environmental attributes of a myriad of their products. Marketing Intelligence Service reports that over a quarter of all manufactured household products in the United States now boast on their labels that they are "ozone-friendly, recyclable, biodegradable, compostable, or some other shade of green."[96]

"Recycling" is one of the most commonly touted attributes of a product. Unfortunately, the fact that a product is theoretically recyclable has no relation to whether actual recycling facilities exist. California has recently considered a bill that would prohibit recycling claims unless there is a showing that recycling facilities exist within easy access of the consumer.[97] Since many products are marketed nationally, however, such attempts at regulating enviromarketing reveal the need for national, rather than local laws.

The attempt by state attorneys-general to issue guidelines for making environmental claims in compliance with state laws does not appear to be an adequate substitute for such national law. The "Green Report II," issued in May 1991 by 11 state attorneys-general, states that "There is no more pressing issue facing our society than the need to change the way we live, work, and do business to protect our natural environment."[98] The Report asserts that since "no reliable and meaningful methodology exists for conducting complex product life assessments,"[99] product life claims should be restricted. The Report also states that "environmental claims should be as specific as possible, and not general, vague, incomplete or overly broad."[100]

The kind of detail sought by the Report is indicated by the information that must accompany a claim of product recyclability: "(The claim) must indicate the maturity of the recycling infrastructure for that material, the number of locations where the product is being recycled, the nature of the collection sites utilized if there is no curbside pick-up available, and the states where collection and recycling facilities are located."[101] It remains to be seen whether the inclusion of such detailed information is practical on one small label, particularly when it is considered that much other information is already required on many products (such as nutrition information on food products).

Although the Report asserts that there is no meaningful method for conducting product life assessments, there are in fact many studies that have attempted to do precisely that. Thus a strict interpretation of the Report would appear to restrict findings such as those made by Franklin Associates to the effect that "the manufacture and disposal of 128-ounce paperboard milk containers generate twice as much air pollution, nearly five times more water pollution, 48 times more industrial waste and almost twice as much solid waste as the manufacture and disposal of 128-

ounce high-density polyethylene (plastic) milk containers."[102] Certainly, manufacturers of plastic containers would be well advised to seek legal counsel before making such claims if their products are marketed in one of the 11 states represented by the attorney-generals who wrote the Report.

Another study, conducted by Professor Rathje of the University of Arizona, has concluded that in the food products industry, consumer packaging reduces waste by 33% since it enables consumers to consume a higher percentage of their food.[103] Likewise, a manufacturer of foam cups (condemned by environmental groups) claims that their foam cups "contain no CFC's, are better for incineration, preserve our trees and forests, use fewer resources, are better for landfill, are recyclable."[104] Again, it is doubtful if such claims would pass muster with the drafters of the Report.

Nevertheless, such reports do call into question the value of the consciousness-raising attributed to environmental groups. For example, the perception exists, whether or not due to campaigns of environmental groups, that paper packaging is good, and plastic is bad. In fact, the reverse may be true. It has already been noted that an archeological dig of a 25-year-old landfill revealed that unbiodegraded newspapers and paper containers compiled the bulk of the landfill, with plastic containers a distant third as a percentage of bulk.[105]

Although many environmentalists have condemned the use of disposable diapers as not environmentally correct, a recent study has concluded that it is the reusable diapers that cause the most environmental damage since they require "9,620 gallons of water per child per year. If you employ a diaper service, the delivery trucks add to the town's air pollution."[106]

If nothing else, however, the publicity campaigns of environmental groups have caused a wave of collective guilt among housewives. When a reporter doing a story on environmental products interviewed a housewife in a supermarket, "she look[ed] startled and trie[d] to cover the offending items (disposable diapers and juice boxes) with her hands. 'Normally you would never see these things in my basket—never!' she exclaim[ed]. 'The only reason is that we're going on a six-hour trip. I don't know what to expect on the road, or what to expect when I get there.' "[107] A 42-year-old school teacher says her 9-year-old would not let her walk out of a fast food restaurant with a foam container.[108]

Consumers often get caught in the middle of conflicting information, and use environmentally touted products selectively. William Booth has described the activities of a typical family that "recycles their cans and bans six-pack plastic rings in their house, but drives itself to a shopping mall two blocks away, and drenches their lawn with chemical fertilizers leaching into the same waterways as the six-pack rings."[109]

Despite environmental campaigns, not all Americans are willing to pay for environmental benefits. According to an NBC Poll, only 27% of Americans are willing to support a gas tax to discourage driving, and 51% (to 34%) think jobs in the Northwest are more important than the spotted owl; however, by a 51–42% margin they say they are willing to drive less safe cars if it would help the environment.[110]

Environmental groups, employing advertising and publishing a multitude of glossy environmental magazines,[111] spend considerable time and energy on campaigns against products they consider to be environmentally unsound. The Environmental Defense Fund, for example, recently called for a boycott of Hefty trash bags produced by Mobil because Mobil had dared to claim that the bags were biodegradable.[112] Although this claim was in fact true (if the bags received air and sun) it was also true that 90% of the bags ended up underground in landfills where they did not biodegrade any more than the 25-year-old newspapers found by the University of Arizona archaeologist in old landfills. Under additional pressure from the Minnesota Attorney General, Mobil deleted the claims on its trash bags.[113]

Some manufacturers have expressed frustration over their attempts to be environmentally correct. The head of a packaging company has complained that "As soon as you go out on a limb and say you're doing something, a consumer group attacks the validity of your claim."[114]

A REEXAMINATION

Although the environmental movement is currently undergoing a reexamination, the debates are centered more on the question of methods and tactics than controversial funding methods or the cost-effectiveness of their proposed policies. They have, however, asked whether they should be more confrontational, or actively seek compromises and whether money should be spent more on legal action or publicity campaigns. For example, the Natural Resources Defense Council recently discovered the advantages of a slick publicity campaign over expensive litigation and lobbying. After the latter efforts had proved unsuccessful in banning the pesticide Alar from the food supply, the Council paid $40,000 to a public relations firm for a television commercial featuring Meryl Streep in a kitchen explaining to a child why it was necessary to wash vegetables. Within days, schools across the country banned apples from lunch programs, and supermarkets pulled juices from their shelves until the manufacturer of Alar agreed to pull its stocks.[115]

Other environmental initiatives have proved counterproductive and at cross-purposes with each other. In 1992, for example, the Sierra Club gave its support to some wilderness bills that would have buried bills supported by other environmental groups. As part of a "compromise," the bill would have restricted the right of private citizens to appeal the decisions of federal agencies. The Club's position was justified, according to its director of field services, because "we are of the incremental school. You can not get all the wilderness and all the biological diversity protected at once. That doesn't work in Congress. . . . Its worth putting a lot of resources in to frame the debate."[116] Such policies have spawned a dissident organization calling itself the Association of Sierra Club Members for Environmental Ethics,[117] and has triggered an angry response from a Club Chapter: "Frame the debate? What does that mean? The framing begins when environmentalists come to the table with a compromise, and the timber industry asks for everything it wants."[118] A similar debate in tactics occurred when the National Wildlife Association announced it had no opinion on a controversial bill making 1 million acres of wilderness eligible for cutting. This prompted the Executive Director of the Native Forest Council to respond that "They talk like Rambo in their fund-raising letters but the big national groups are wimps when it comes to dealing with the bad guys."[119]

The large size of many mainstream organizations leaves many of them open to charges of nonresponsiveness and unaccountability. Marshall Ingwerson has opined that "the tension between compromise and confrontation over environmental issues emanates from a variety of environmental and neighborhood groups uncomfortable with the deal-making of a few of the largest, most established groups."[120]

One recent type of expenditure by environmental groups appears to be more cost-effective than some of the others. In 1992 the World Wildlife Federation negotiated a deal with the DKB Bank of Japan under which DKB donates to the Federation the right to claim $1 million of debt with Ecuador. The money will then be used by the Federation to protect wildlife on the Galapagos Islands owned by Ecuador.[121] Similar "debt-for-nature" agreements have been worked out between J. P. Morgan Bank and the Nature Conservancy involving the debt of Bolivia, and proceeds have been used to fund environmental projects.[122]

Despite such success stories, other environmentalists are less optimistic. George Reiger has bemoaned that "a lot of what is ballyhooed as education or problem-solving amounts to little more than environmental basket-weaving."[123] He cites the all too typical example of small school children who are shown how to make bird baths from containers thrown away in the garbage: "The children help their teachers create the clever designs, which are then taken home, and for the most part thrown away, since few parents want 'trash' in their backyards, when more elaborate, more durable, and—best of all—newer products can be purchased from catalogs."[124] He cites the fruitless efforts of an army of environmental volunteers mindlessly recruited to "monitor" water quality in the Chesapeake tributaries, only to find that the problem is not finding an environmental disaster, but getting someone to do something about it.[125]

NEW PRIORITIES

It is suggested that the debate currently going on in the environmental movement is fundamentally misdirected. The American people contribute millions of dollars to support a large number of private environmental organizations. By necessity, much of these funds must be plowed back into fund-raising activities and, particularly in the case of the larger organizations, into supporting large and unwieldy bureaucracies. The focus of these organizations is often very narrow—witness the Xerces Society, discussed above, which is dedicated to preserving the slug. Often such organizations are unable to look beyond the horizons of their own particular agenda, or to attempt to understand how their agenda might affect human beings. The result has been polarization and mobilization of antienvironmental forces, and a backlash movement that threatens to neutralize many environmental efforts.

Rarely do such groups involve themselves in the fundamental question of the ultimate source of environmental damage and deterioration. It is not just slugs, whales, porpoises, snail darters, or spotted owls that are threatened by the encroachments of man. As the population expands, diminishing returns require humans to expand their range of habitat and intensify their use of existing resources. As humans continue to expand their habitat on the planet, environmental activity can have only limited long-term effect on the condition of the environment. Litigation, costing environmental contributors and taxpayers alike billions of dollars, can result in a road project being deferred, or a toxic dump transferred from point A to point B. But ultimately, to the extent that economic activity makes it affordable, all human passengers on the earthship will demand a standard of living commensurate with traditional notions of human dignity.

It has been suggested that the key element of environmentalism is consumption. Al Gore addressed this point in his acclaimed book *Earth in the Balance,* stating that our addictive need to consume is the mark of a "dysfunctional civilization," and that the environmental crisis is "an outer manifestation of an inner crisis that is, for lack of a better word, spiritual crisis."[126] The biggest polluters are the wealthy who spew 11 tons of carbon into the air every year, followed by middle-class Americans who spew out 3.5 tons, followed by the teeming masses of the world's third world poor who produce only one-tenth of a ton of carbon per person per year.[127] According to Gore, if the wealthy could only be induced to consume substantially less, and the poor induced to give up their dreams of wealth, many of the world's environmental problems would be solved.

The first problem with this analysis is that, historically, it has been man's quest for wealth that has driven the engine of innovation and technological progress that up until now has provided the only hope of delaying the onset of the more extreme effects of diminishing returns and the day of environmental reckoning. Kuznets and Simon are correct on one point—that technological innovation, including both the Industrial and Green Revolutions, has delayed the onset of some of the predicted Malthusian consequences. (Where Simon and Ehrlich part company is on the more fundamental question of whether it can continue to do so indefinitely, or whether there are limits.) Thus it is not simply a question of "educating" or persuading the masses of the great benefits of lower consumption. To take away the carrot of wealth is to deprive mankind of the incentive for the very kind of technological change that is needed to defer environmental catastrophe.

The second problem with Gore's consumption thesis is that, at least in democratic societies, declines in consumption cannot be mandated. A Romanian dictator can simply turn off the lights and turn off the heat. Congress cannot. Nor can those in the first world expect much sympathy for the environmental need for poverty among the wretched poor living in the third world countries.

Rather than trying to find ways to reduce the consumption of people already on earth, it would be far better to find humane ways of limiting the number of people who arrive. Although the cliche of "rearranging the deck chairs on the Titanic" is much overused, it is particularly descriptive of present environmental policy. Environmentalists are busy transferring a deck chair of toxic wastes from the promenade deck to the engine room, or shuffling garbage from the first class to the third class living areas. Each environmental group is interested in a particular deck chair, and the groups fight among themselves, or with the captain, about which chair will be moved, who will get to use the chairs, or whether it would be better if people used fewer chairs per person. Others see salvation in producing more deck chairs. The passengers spend billions of dollars supporting one group or another in their bid to move the chairs or determine who may use them. Meanwhile the entire ship is sinking under the weight of humanity because the ship acknowledges no limits to the number of passengers it can accommodate.

In the context of a sinking ship the debate between Ehrlich and Simon fades into irrelevance. They are really only arguing about timing—what will be the exact moment that the ship will sink. The debate as to the effects of population on the environment is also rendered moot. Everyone knows that *at some point,* regardless of deck chair production or rearrangement, the ship will ultimately sink if people board her at an exponentially increasing rate.

None of the foregoing is meant to imply that deck chair re-arrangements may not be desirable. Toxic wastes are probably better off in the engine room, and the efforts of first class passengers to get their garbage dumped in third class is understandable if not admirable. As the ship sinks, efforts to save as many chairs (endangered species) as possible are also to be commended. But it is suggested that the main effort should be directed toward preventing the ship from sinking. And only programs directed toward population control can have that long-term effect.

To their credit, some environmental groups have at least put population control on their agenda. The Environmental Defense Fund has pledged to boost "public awareness" of population issues.[128] Population groups, such as Zero Population Growth, the Population Crisis Committee, and the Population Institute, all support the cause of population control. But their organizations are underfunded, their efforts dispersed, and, most significantly, they lack cooperative and conceptual links with the environmental movement. The need for such links, as well as links with family planning and abortion groups, is documented in the chapters that follow.

NOTES

1. Tom Wolf, The Rise and Fall of the Environmental Movement, *L.A. Times,* Mar. 24, 1991, p. M6 (ellipses indicating deletions are omitted).

2. "[Attica] was covered in rich soil, and there was abundant timber on the mountains, of which traces may still be seen. Some of our mountains at present will only support bees. But not so very long ago trees fit for the roofs of vast buildings were felled there, and the rafters are still in existence. There were also many other lofty cultivated trees which provided unlimited fodder for beasts.

The soil got the benefit of the yearly 'water of Zeus.' This was not lost, as it is today, by running off a barren ground to the sea. A plentiful supply was received into the soil and stored up in the layers of clay.

By comparison with the original territory, what is left now is like the skeleton of a body wasted by disease. The rich, soft soil has been carried off. Only the bare framework of the district is left."

Plato, *Critias,* 111b-d (A. E. Taylor trans.), in *Plato, Collected Dialogues* (1963); cited in Harrison, *The Third Revolution* (1992), p. 115.

3. Knickerbocker, Land Stewardship, *Christ. Sci. Mon.,* Nov. 6, 1990, p. 15.

4. *Id.*

5. Merrill, When the Pill Is Worse Than the Poison, *L.A. Times,* Dec. 4, 1990, p. 6.

6. Hayes, New Specialty Helps Poor, *Wall Street J.,* Oct. 9, 1991, p. B5.

7. Black Marks for Greens, *The Economist,* Oct. 19, 1991, p. 29.

8. Hayes, *supra,* note 4, p. 135.

9. Ron Arnold, as quoted by Margaret Knox, *The Progressive,* and cited in The New Face of Environmentalism, *UTNE Reader,* July/Aug. 1992, pp. 105, 109.

10. *Id.*

11. Frontline Fighters: A Bigger, More Influential Greenpeace Begins Its Third Decade, 46 *MacLeans,* Dec. 16, 1991, p. 47.

12. Black Marks for Greens, *supra,* note 7.

13. *Id.*

14. Merrill, When the Pill Is Worse Than the Poison, *supra,* note 5.

15. *Id.*

16. *Id.*

17. *Id.*

18. See Chapter 3, note 1.

19. Webster, Sweet Home Arkansas, *UTNE Reader,* July/Aug. 1992, p. 112.

20. *Id.,* p. 116.

21. *Id.*

22. *Id.,* p. 112.

23. *Id.,* p. 116.

24. *Id.,* p. 113.

25. Under EPA standards, some waste is permitted to be returned to the atmosphere. The effects of the discharge of small or even infinitesimal amounts of deadly toxins are a matter of some debate.

26. Piller, Nimbymania: Are Not In My Backyard Groups Really Environmentalists?, adopted from *The Fail-Safe Society: Community Defiance and the ENP of American Technological Optimism* (1991), in Webster, *supra,* note 17, p. 114.

27. *Id.*

28. *Id.*

29. *Id.*

30. Any Color But Green: A New Political Alliance Is Battling the Environmental Movement, *U.S. News & World Report,* Oct. 21, 1991, pp. 74, 75.

31. *Id.,* p. 74.

32. Baum, Wise Guise, *Sierra,* May/June 1991, pp. 71, 72.

33. *Id.,* p. 72.

34. *Id.*

35. Egan, Fund Raisers Tap Anti-Environmentalism, *N.Y. Times,* Dec. 19, 1991, p. A18.

36. Udall and Olson, Me First, God and Nature Second, *L.A. Times,* July 2, 1992, p. B5.

37. *Id.*

38. *Id.*

39. *Id.*

40. *Id.*

41. *Id.,* p. 73.

42. *Id.*

43. *Id.*

44. *Id.*, p. 92.

45. *Id.*

46. Any Color But Green, *supra*, p. 75.

47. *Id.*

48. *Id.*

49. See, e.g., Schneider, Natural Foes Bankroll Environmental Groups, *N.Y. Times*, Dec. 23, 1991, p. A12.

50. Milbank, Despite Appeal, Saving the Earth Lacks Donors, *Wall Street J.*, July 11, 1990, p. B1.

51. Seredich, *Your Resource Guide to Environmental Organizations* (1991), p. 439.

52. *Id.*, p. 171.

53. Weiskopf, From Fringe to Political Mainstream: Environmentalists Set Policy Agenda, *Washington Post* April 19, 1990, p. A1.

54. *Id.*

55. Milbank, Despite Appeal, Saving the Earth Lacks Donors, *Wall Street J.*, July 11, 1990, p. B1.

56. Fitzgerald, Quiet Savers of the Land: With Little Fanfare, They Preserve Millions of Acres—Without Blocking Development or Destroying Jobs, *Readers Dig.*, June, 1992, pp. 129, 132.

57. *Id.*, p. 133.

58. *Id.*, p. 131.

59. Hall, Building Green Corporate Partnerships, *JABC Comm. World,* April, 1992, p. 25.

60. Quiet Savers of the Land, *supra*, p. 131.

61. Building Green Corporate Partnerships, *supra*, p. 26.

62. Gutfeld, Environmental Group Doesn't Always Lick 'Em; It Can Join 'Em and Succeed, *Wall Street J.*, Aug. 20, 1992, p. B1.

63. *Id.*

64. Environmental Groups Sue to Block Highway Project, *Wall Street J.*, Aug. 22, 1991, p. A14.

65. DeMont, Lowther, Frontline Fighters: A Bigger and More Influential Greenpeace Begins Its Third Decade, *Macleans,* Dec. 16, 1991, pp. 46–47.

66. *Id.*

67. *Id.*

68. Spencer et al., The Not So Peaceful World of Greenpeace, *Forbes,* Nov. 11, 1991, p. 174; but see O'Sullivan, Against The Gain: Capitalist Tool, *The Humanist,* May/June 1992, p. 47.

69. Quoting Paul Wilson's statement to Reuters, and cited in the *Toronto Star,* and republished in *World Press Review,* Dec. 1991, p. 50.

70. *Id.*

71. Bandow, Ecoteur's Credo: To Save the Trees, Cut Down People, *Wall Street J.*, June 20, 1990, p. A14.

72. Wells, Earth First! Group Manages to Offend Nearly Everybody, *Wall Street J.*, June 19, 1990, pp. A1, A8.

73. Ecoteur's Credo, *supra*, note 71.

74. *Id.;* see also Goltz, Earth First Meeting Reflects Gap Between Radicals, Mainstream, *Washington Post,* July 19, 1990, p. A3.

75. Moorison, Laughlin, 3 Earth First! Defendants Sentenced for Vandalism, *L.A. Times,* Sept. 20, 1991, p. A4.

76. *Id.*

77. Earth First!, *supra,* note 72.

78. President Reagan's controversial Secretary of the Interior.

79. Mohr, Environmental Groups Gain in the Wake of Spill, *N.Y. Times,* June 11, 1989, p. L31.

80. *Id.*

81. Lancaster, War and Recession Taking Toll on National Environmental Organizations, *Washington Post,* Feb. 15, 1991, p. A3.

82. *Id.*

83. Wolf, The Rise and Fall of the Environmental Movement, American-Style, *L.A. Times,* Mar. 24, 1991, p. M6 (ellipses indicating deletions are omitted).

84. Knickerbocker, 'Green' Groups Need Deeper Grass Roots, *Christ. Sci. Mon.,* May 28, 1992, p. 11.

85. Pell, Buying In: How Corporations Keep an Eye on Environmental Groups That Oppose Them—By Giving Big Wads of Money, *Mother Jones,* April/May 1990, pp. 23.

86. *Id.*

87. Schneider, National Foes Bankroll Environmental Groups, *N.Y. Times,* Dec. 23, 1991, p. A8.

88. *Id.,* p. 23, quoting David Rapaport.

89. Buying In, *supra,* note 85.

90. *Buying In, supra,* note 85.

91. Schneider, Natural Foes Bankroll Environmental Groups, *N.Y. Times,* Dec. 23, 1991, p. A8.

92. Environmental Groups Find New Sources of Funds, *Christ. Sci. Mon.,* Oct. 5, 1992, p. 7.

93. *Id.*

94. Bennett, The 'Green' Bandwagon Brings Ethical Choices, *Wall Street J.,* May 21, 1990, p. B1.

95. Gutfeld, Eight of 10 Americans Are environmentalists, At Least So They Say, *Wall Street J.,* July 10, 1991, p. 2A.

96. Fierman, The Big Muddle in Green Marketing: From Ketchup Bottles to Garbage Bags, Companies Are Making Products They Claim Will Spare the Environment, *Fortune Magazine,* June 3, 1991, p. 91.

97. *Id.,* p. 92.

98. Cited in Taylor, Bossy States Censor Green Ads, *Wall Street J.,* Aug. 8, 1991, p. A12.

99. *Id.*

100. *Id.*

101. *Id.*

102. *Id.,* finding summarized by Taylor.

103. See Chapter 2, note 93.

104. *Id.*

105. *Supra,* note 103.

106. Findings as summarized by Fierman, in The Big Muddle, *supra,* note 96.

107. See Chapter 2, note 92.

108. *Id.*

109. Booth and Cohn, Sharing the Environmental Burden, *Washington Post,* April 18, 1990, p. 1.

110. *Supra,* note 107.

111. Ho, Environmental Magazines Defy Slump, *Wall Street J.,* Sept. 10, 1991, p. A1.

112. The Big Muddle, *supra,* note 96, pp. 91–92.

113. *Id.*

114. Statement of John Lister, quoted by Jaclyn Fierman, in The Big Muddle, *supra,* note 96, p. 92.

115. Weiskopf, From Fringe to Political Mainstream: Environmentalists Set Policy Agenda, *Washington Post,* April 19, 1990, p. A1.

116. Trouble At the Sierra Club, *The Progressive,* July 1992, p. 13.

117. *Id.*

118. *Id.*

119. Schneider, Selling Out? Pushed and Pulled, Environment Inc. Is On the Defensive, *N.Y. Times,* Mar. 29, 1992, p. G1.

120. Ingwerson, Environmentalists Debate Tactics: Hardline Activists Reject the Compromises Negotiated by Traditional Organizations, *Christ. Sci. Mon.,* April 12, 1989, p. 1.

121. Japan's Biggest Bank Sets a 'Debt for Nature' Swap, *Wall Street J.,* Mar. 27, 1992, p. 9A.

122. Bank to Swap Bolivian Debt For Environmental Funds, *Wall Street J.,* Feb. 8, 1992, p. 5A.

123. Reiger, The Basket Weavers: One Way to Maintain the Status Quo Is to Keep Reformers Busy with a Project That Will Never Be Put to Any Meaningful Use, *Field and Stream,* July, 1992, p. 19.

124. *Id.*

125. *Id.*

126. See Chapter 1, note 27, *supra;* cited and discussed in Green Ticket or Thicket, *Commonweal,* Aug. 14, 1992, p. 4.

127. *Id.*

128. Edward, Environment, *Wall Street J.,* Sept. 13, 1991, p. B1.

5　Family Planning

"They're all mine" Mohammed said, with a large smile.
"How many?" I asked.
"Fifteen!" Mohammed said. I swore I could see his chest swell with sexual pride.
"Fifteen! Why do you need so many children?"
"It is God's command. Besides, I need all the help I can get for my farm. And my children will provide for me in my old age . . . ."
"How many children have you fathered in all?"
"Twenty-one! But six have died. There is much illness around Kaduna. Not enough clinics. Few doctors."
"Are you planning to have more children?"
"Of course . . . "
"Have you considered family planning?"
"What for? Who am I to refuse Allah's gifts?"
"But what about the children? Are they getting the proper care?"
Mohammed shrugged . . .
"Why do you keep producing so many children?"
Mohammed grinned and whispered hoarsely to Jennifer, my translator.
She giggled.
"It is a matter of my manhood" was what Mohammed had said.

Interview with Mohammed Abusaza of Kaduna,
Nigeria by Pranay Gupte[1]

When I first informed my colleagues and associates that I was planning to write a book having to do with population, several of them discouraged the idea. First, one cautioned me, you will never resolve the debate over optimum population; and second, if you are going to talk about family planning, you will be preaching to the converted because everyone is already in favor of it.

On the first point, the advice was well taken. There are too many complex variables to make a determination of an "optimum population" as it relates to economic growth and protection of the environment. For this reason, I have chosen to document only the debate. I have not attempted to resolve the apparently insoluble problem of determining an optimum population, but have instead suggested that it can be reduced to a debate about timing. I have left the problem of optimum population to the Ehrlichs, the Meadows, and the Simons, who disagree strongly on this question. I have, however, attempted to compare the risks of controlling population too soon (in which case the consequences predicted by the populationists may or may not occur) with the risks of controlling population too late or not at all (with the possible consequences being those predicted by the neo-Malthusians.) Having determined that the risks of acting too late or not at all outweigh the risks of acting too soon, I have been free to pursue my objective of finding a common policy denominator in government and private programs relating to both the environment and population, while at the same time identifying areas in which policies and programs have been inefficient and counterproductive.

On the second point, however—that everyone is already in favor of family planning and that I would be beating a dead horse—I was at first inclined to agree, and thought that the subject might require only a passing reference. During the course of my research, however, I was genuinely surprised by the volume and depth of literature I encountered, much of it "scholarly," vigorously opposing the whole idea of family planning as a vast conspiracy to depopulate the earth for racist or other evil ends. In fact I found that even mainstream society has come to accept family planning and birth control only very recently.

For many years family planning was identified with anarchism and radical revolution. As late as 1993, when a modest bill was introduced in Congress (The International Population Stabilization and Reproductive Health Act), which would have spent no more money on voluntary international family planning programs than is spent on a single B-1 bomber,[2] opponents vigorously opposed it on grounds that "Nobody has the right to tell people how many children they should have."[3]

Some of the literature opposing birth control is directed toward the more extreme and arbitrary forms of family planning that have been implemented at various times in such countries as India, or policies implemented today in countries such as China.[4] But much of the remaining literature is directed against the whole concept and philosophy of family planning. The interest groups for opposing birth control vary— from the religious, to the philosophical, to the political. United, however, the coalition against birth control, though weaker than 100 years ago, is still formidable.

On the forefront of the campaign against the use of any kind of "artificial" birth control are certain religious groups, particularly the Catholic

Church. In 1930, Pius XI, in *Casti Connubii,* declared intercourse to be for the sole purpose of "generation of children."[5] Archbishop Roberts has explained that it is the Catholic Church's position that "intercourse is unlawful and wicked where the conception of the offspring is prevented."[6]

A number of medical doctors also oppose the use of contraceptives. Dr. John Cavanaugh, for example, wrote in his "medically oriented" book *The Popes, the Pill and the People,* that "the most convincing proof of the natural law arguments against contraception are to be found in the teaching of the Popes . . . They would appear to be . . . clear and authoritative teachings."[7] Typical of those opposing family planning is Dr. John J. Billings, an Australian neurologist who argues vigorously for the outlawing of all "artificial" birth control, and opposes all international birth control programs on grounds that, among other evils, they discriminate against poor people. Overpopulation is not an immediate concern, he asserts, and the earth could easily support 10 times as many people.[8]

Dr. Billings has in recent years spearheaded an anti-birth control campaign that has caused considerable consternation among many family planning groups worldwide who are struggling not only for funds but against local superstitions and cultural traditions. Pranay Gupte has warned that "Billings' worldwide anti-birth control campaign could well play a key role in eventually dismantling global population projects."[9]

Dr. Billings has claimed to have refined the Vatican-approved rhythm method of birth control with his own method, which relies on a woman's examination of her own mucus to predict periods of fertility (the "Billings method"). Although many physicians who have heard of the method say that "the scientific basis for [it] is quite shaky,"[10] the main criticism of it is the same as that of the rhythm method, namely that it requires an unrealistic amount of diligence and recordkeeping, as well as discipline, particularly from husbands who may come home drunk or surly demanding sex from their wives during fertile periods of required abstinence. Lest his method be dismissed as being on the fringe, however, it should be noted that many regional governments in India have gone on record as recommending his method as the sole means of birth control, and the method has even drawn some support from the health and natural food movement in the United States.[11]

Dr. Billings is also spokesman for those who see family planning as a conspiracy by drug companies to obtain profit even at the cost of depriving the world of its population. Pranay Gupte reports a conversation with him in which Billings alleged that "Propagandists for the pharmaceutical industries have cleverly persuaded many people that opposition to their programs represents an attempt by a minority to impose their morality upon the world. Of course it is the exact opposite. The persons who stand to receive financial gain from the birth control programs are seeking to impose their perverted morality upon the rest of the world."[12]

In fact, those representing the anti-family planning coalition, whom Ehrlich dismisses as those who "whisper in the ears of politicians all kind of nonsense,"[13] remain a powerful political force. Although it is spearheaded by such self-proclaimed crusaders as Dr. Billings, it is represented in the political arena by such advocates as James Miller, Director of research of the Population Research Institute in Gaithersburg, Maryland.[14] Miller has stated that "the current population of the world and any foreseeable population that we might have over the next century can easily be accommodated."[15] Such views inhibit international aid to help other countries provide family planning services. For example, Miller attributes the political problems of the United States with Iran in the 1970s not to such factors as the Shah's policies, but to U.S. birth control policies: "One of the reasons the U.S. faced such furor in Iran (in the 1970's) was outrage that the U.S. was promulgating birth control among Iranian women."[16] International birth control programs, he asserts, undermine the cultural traditions of other nations, and create hostility toward the United States.[17]

Others, even respected academics, have attempted to taint family planning programs by association with Nazi-type "eugenics." Jacqueline Kasun, a Professor of Economics, in her chapter on the history of the population movement in her book *The War Against Population*,[18] recounts the work of Karl Pearson who believes that "the sterilization of sections of the community is of small civic worth,"[19] and characterizes Margaret Sanger not as the founder of the family planning movement, but as the most "enthusiastic eugenicis[t]" of her time.[20] She refers to the "confession" of Edward Pohlman that "some Indians regard this foreign control of their population as a form of 'genocide.' "[21] (Interestingly, she does not also note that Nazi Germany had the strictest anti-abortion laws in history, and gave awards for womanly feats of reproduction.)

If such references are not frightening enough to potential recipients of family planning programs, Kasun warns that sex education, particularly

the assault of sex teachings, and life-limiting services on our own people and those abroad—are, according to influential and highly placed American officials, only a prelude. Even more coercive measures are likely to be necessary . . . As frightening as it is to watch the government assiduously at work reducing the number of people, the deeper danger lies in the frank, explicit aspiration to improve the quality of the biological product. Genetic screening and genetic counseling accompanied by selective abortion and sterilization, are gaining ground, a haunting historical reminder.[22]

Kasun acknowledges that environmental pollution in the United States increased 267% while population increased only 40% during the period 1947–1970, but attributes the increase in pollution not to population itself but to the "shift away from older, less-polluting technologies."[23] Thus increases in population are not to blame for increases in pollution, and the environment can instead be saved by a "direct attack on the polluting engines . . . and other activities responsible for environmental degradation."[24] This latter view expresses quite succinctly the rationale and philosophy of most existing environmental laws, despite the fact that most such laws do little more than play the "circle game" (see Chapter 3). Indeed, it is not very different from the views of some of today's most prominent environmentalists including Vice-President Al Gore, who despite his reference to population as one ingredient in environmental policy,[25] nevertheless places high reliance on similar direct attacks, as well as changes in consumptive patterns (see Chapter 4).

Kasun decries modest government expenditures on family planning, such as the 1986 $238 million funding for the U.S. Agency for International Development, and the $2 billion in other "population assistance" appropriations.[26] Especially galling to Kasun was President Carter's acknowledgment of the problem of "overpopulation" in his January 14, 1981 farewell address.[27] Equally disturbing to Kasun was the statement of Peter McPherson, administrator of the Development Agency, in which he requested $235 million, stating that, "Rapid population growth in the developing countries is one of the primary obstacles to the expansion of food production, reduction and malnutrition and chronic disease, and conservation of dwindling non-renewable resources."[28] It seems clear, however, that it is not the amount of money involved in such appropriations that offends Kasun and Miller (the amount of funding for population programs would barely suffice to purchase a few high-tech bombers), but rather the uses to which the money is put.

Kasun concludes that the "vitalizing inspiration for government birth control is, and always has been, eugenic. The slick, professional booklets of the likes of Planned Parenthood and the Gutmacher Institute are profusely illustrated with pictures of pot-bellied, dusky women surrounded by hordes of children living in slums here and abroad. To explore the rationale of the eugenics movement—scientific racism—would fill another volume."[29] She continues with an alarming plan for action: "Only a radical operation on our fundamental policy would reverse this accelerating trend . . . in which the prevailing philosophy of social planning is thoroughly repudiated. And the disavowal must be total—encompassing the religious, social, and economic thinking that has ravaged our traditions and values."[30]

Kasun joins Simon, Miller, Billings, and others in claiming that "[e]ight times, and perhaps as much as 22 times, the world's present population could support itself at the present standard of living,"[31] and notes that "there would be standing room for the entire population of the world within one quarter of the area of Jacksonville, Florida."[32] However, she does not answer (nor does she ask) the question of what policies she would advocate once *those* limits were reached. When the world reached a population of 132 billion (22 × the earth's present 6), would she then wholeheartedly join the neo-Malthusians in advocating family planning and birth-control? (Or would she wait until there was standing room only?) And if she did then finally concede the need for family planning, what would she say to diehard anti-family planning opponents who told her that such policies were repugnant to "traditions and values?" Would not the potential 133 billionth person not have a "right to life"?

One would certainly expect that followers of Julian Simon would approve of Kasun's work, and in fact Simon has done so, calling it "an eye-opener. The material Kasun presents is invaluable,"[33] and acknowledging that "I had thought the sex education movement was more benign and less insidious."[34] Perhaps more disconcerting, however (especially to those who, like my colleague, are under the impression that "nobody today could be against family planning"), is the response to Kasun's work by the Hoover Institution, Stanford University, which praised her work as a "shocking account of the multi-billion movement of the population controllers and their efforts to enforce global population control;"[35] or a Professor of Law who saw revealed in her work that "one of the best kept secrets in the world is the evil nature of the population control movement."[36] The Editor of *Human Life Review* said her book was "about much more than the 'over-population myth—for instance the bare facts about 'sex-ed,' "[37] and the author of *Conflict of Visions* said her work "carefully exposes two of the leading frauds of our time—the 'overpopulation' hysteria and the false pretense of 'sex education.' "[38]

I have chosen to discuss Kasun's 1988 work, the *War Against Population,* as but one example of many works and opinions opposing policies of population control.[39] I have done this both to show the depth of resistance to population control policies, as well as to begin to suggest an explanation as why there has been as yet so little linkage and cooperation between the environmental and population movements. To those aged over 40 who are reading this book, however, and who kept abreast of the news even as a child, Kasun's and Miller's views might appear as a logical progression in a long, but more recently familiar history of societal and cultural opposition to family planning.

HISTORY OF THE FAMILY PLANNING MOVEMENT

Over 1700 years has passed since the legendary Galen first wrote about contraception in one of history's first medical treatises.[40] The earliest contraceptive techniques ranged from withdrawal (sometimes associated with the "onanism" of the Bible), and the practice of sodomy, to the ingestion of magical potions. Most of the earliest devices were what would today be classified as of the "barrier" type, and included primitive condoms made of crude, and oftentimes unspeakable kinds of material, some of it animal by-product. By and large, however, it has historically been the lot of women who engaged in intercourse to undergo the physical pains of childbirth, whether or not the child was wanted or could be adequately cared for. The "irrepressible urge" to perpetuate the species, observed by Malthus, is found in the intercourse phase of the reproductive process, and not in the childbirth phase, and if the evolutionary process of human physiological development had mistakenly reversed the pain and pleasure aspects of each, it is doubtful if mankind would have survived, let alone grown to six billion.

In one of those ironic twists so frequently encountered in history, the first important advocacy of family planning in modern times took place not as a preconceived idea, but in the course of a heated exchange of ideas in which a defender overreached his defense by contradicting the one defended. After Malthus wrote his Essay on Population,[41] William Godwin in 1820 wrote a rebuttal in which he argued that mankind could provide for itself even as it multiplied in numbers.[42] Francis Place then took it upon himself to defend Malthus in *Illustrations and Proofs of the Principle of Population* in 1822, but in doing so went far beyond Malthus's urging of deferred marriage, and advocated birth control as a means of avoiding Malthusian consequences: "If, above all, it were once clearly understood, that it was not disreputable for married persons to avail themselves of such precautions as would . . . prevent conception, a sufficient check might once be given to the increase of population beyond the means of subsistence."[43] Kurt Back has credited this work with "transforming an academic discussion into a social movement."[44]

Francis Place soon began distributing what were later known as the "diabolical handbills" that set forth three types of contraception (withdrawal, condoms made from animal guts, and sponges).[45] Place soon converted a young John Stuart Mill to his cause. Shortly before meeting Place, Mill had been traumatized by the sight first of a strangled, newborn baby he had found wrapped in old rags, and then by the sight of the remains of hanged prisoners outside the Old Bailey Prison. He readily adopted Place's view of how to prevent unwanted children and their "train of misery and vice."[46]

After a collaboration between Sanger and Richard Carlile produced a more specific manual advocating contraception (*Every Woman's Book,* 1926),[47] there followed a number of works on contraception by other authors, including *Moral Philosophy* (1830), *The Fruits of Philosophy: An Essay on the Population Question* (1832), and *The Elements of Social Science* (1859).[48]

Fruits of Philosophy was written by Charles Knowlton of Massachusetts. In discussing contraception the book dealt with matters of sexual behavior. As a result, Knowlton was charged and convicted with obscenity, fined heavily, and sentenced to hard labor.[49] Nevertheless, his book was later published in England, selling out nine editions. When Henry Cook published an illustrated version in England, however, Cook too was sentenced to 2 years of hard labor.[50] After Cook's conviction, two family planning advocates, Annie Besant and Charles Bradlaugh, defiantly reissued the book. A trial followed that rivaled in notoriety the famous Monkey trial that took place later in the United States. The event was widely publicized, and, according to contemporary accounts, attracted over 20,000 people.[51] Although Besant and Bradlaugh were both convicted of the crime of obscenity, the conviction was reversed on appeal on a technical point (the prosecutor had not identified the specific passages in the book that were alleged to be obscene).[52]

Such events outraged much of decent society, which still equated contraception with obscenity. In response, Anthony Comstock in 1872 introduced a bill in the U.S. Congress to outlaw as unmailable "every obscene, lewd, lascivious, indecent, filthy or vile article . . . and every written . . . notice of any kind giving information . . . by what means conception may be prevented or abortion produced."[53] The Act also made it a crime to "sell, lend or give away any article whatever for the prevention of conception." (It was not until 1971 that the statute was amended to delete the definition of contraception information as "filthy and vile." Even this amendment did not delete the inclusion of abortion devices, however.[54])

The torch of the family planning movement now passed to Emma Goldman. In 1910 her magazine *Mother Earth* was confiscated by Mr. Comstock (who was now acting as U.S. postal inspector). Comstock had by now become a self-proclaimed savior of public morals, and, according to one historian, had found sport baiting doctors who dared associate with family planners. (In one instance, "he had two women associates write to a Midwestern physician, claiming that their husbands were insane and that they feared that any children might inherit their insanity. When the doctor wrote them some simple advice, Comstock had him arrested and sent to seven years of hard labor."[55]) However, Comstock was forced to release the magazine after other inspectors found nothing obscene in it.[56] Although later tried for conspiracy in 1916, Goldman was acquitted. However, her ties to other radical causes, including anarchism and the antiwar movement, ultimately proved to be her downfall, and she was deported as an undesirable.[57]

The leadership vacuum was now filled by Margaret Sanger, who became known as the founder of the American birth control movement. Sanger first came to public notice in the aftermath of the affair of Sadie Sachs, who, having been advised that pregnancy would endanger her life, was rebuked by her doctor who told her "you want to have your cake and eat it too. Well, it can't be done," and coldly told her that her only recourse was to have her husband "sleep on the roof." Sanger later adopted the "sleep on the roof" phrase as the movement's slogan after Sadie later died an agonizing death in pregnancy, having apparently ignored the doctor's advice to give up intimacy with her husband as the only way to save her life.[58]

In her autobiography, Margaret Sanger described the deep effect that Sadie's death had on her: " 'Please tell me the secret' [Sadie had begged] . . . I really did not know what to say to her or how to convince her of my own ignorance; I was helpless to avert such monstrous atrocities . . . [After Sadie's death] I went to bed, knowing that no matter what it might cost, I was finished with palliatives and superficial cures; I was resolved to seek out the root of evil, to do something to change the destiny of [women] whose miseries were vast as the sky."[59]

Sanger's magazine, *The Woman Rebel,* coined the term family planning, although issues of the magazine were soon seized under the authority of the Comstock Act. Under the threat of a possible 45-year prison term, Sanger fled to England in 1914.[60] There she was introduced to Havelock Ellis, a contraception researcher, and Dr. Johanes Rutgers, who showed her a new kind of diaphragm he had developed.

Sanger returned to the United States in 1916 after old obscenity charges were dropped, but her husband was sent to jail for publishing *Family Limitation.*[61] After opening a birth control clinic in Brownsville, New York, Sanger was charged with the crime of selling contraceptive material. In her defense, she introduced for the first time the constitutional argument based on a right to privacy. However, the argument was rejected at that time.[62]

Sanger formed the New York Birth Control League in 1920, which published the *Birth Control Review.* She organized the First American Birth Control Conference, which was raided by the police, reportedly at the instigation of the Catholic archdiocese,[63] and Sanger was taken to jail. However, her work continued, organizing the World Population Conference in Geneva in 1927.[64] However, her star began to be partially eclipsed by the work of Mary Dennett, who founded the National Birth

Control League (later to become the Voluntary Parenthood League).[65] In England, Marie Stopes wrote the acclaimed *Married Love,* although publishers initially refused to publish it.[66]

One of Sanger's chief goals was to involve the medical profession in family planning. Although involving doctors in an activity considered as radical and dangerous as birth control was difficult, she succeeded in recruiting two doctors, Dorothy Bocker and later Hannah Stone, to launch a birth control research bureau.[67] Although legally restricted to giving contraceptive advice for medical purposes only, the clinic thrived until, in 1929, it was raided by the police. Sanger describes the raid: "Detectives were hurrying aimlessly here and there like chickens fluttering about a raided roost, calling to each other and, amid the confusion, demanding names, patients were sitting quietly, some of them weeping. Patrolmen were sweeping out the contents of medical cabinets seizing articles from the sterilizers and the case histories of women, some of whom had entrusted us with the knowledge that their husbands had venereal disease."[68] Sanger later tried to find out who instigated the raid and found that

Catholic patients, whose records had been purloined, received mysterious and anonymous telephone calls warning them if they continued to go to the clinic their private lives would be exposed . . . Catholic social workers, at a monthly meeting with officials of the Church had sought guidance in replying to parishioners, and the ecclesiastics had been shocked to find that a clinic existed. A Catholic policewoman had been summoned, Mary Sullivan, who had been chosen to wipe out the Clinical Research Bureau.[69]

The resulting trial (on the issue of whether the contraceptives served a medical purpose) became a circus, typified by the following dialogue between the prosecutor and the former Health Commissioner of New York. The exchange was initiated when the prosecutor asked the commissioner whether contraceptive information was given to persons regardless of their marriage status:

Dr. Harris: The Birth Control clinic is a public health work. Every woman desiring treatment is asked whether she is married.
Mr. Hogan: Don't they have to bring their marriage certificates with them?
Dr. Harris: No
Mr. Earnst: Did you ever know of a situation where a doctor dispatched a detective to find out whether his patient was married?

All the defendants were acquitted after the judge concluded that, "Good faith in these circumstances is the belief of the physician that the prevention of conception is necessary for the patient's health and physical welfare."[70]

Gradually, the practice of medicine became linked with family planning. Robert Dickenson succeeded in having obstetrics and gynecology recognized as a medical specialty, and formed the Committee for Maternal Health.[71] Major philanthropic organizations such as the Rockefeller Foundation were persuaded to fund such groups as the Bureau of Social Hygiene, which published a study of women,[72] and philanthropist Clarence Gamble also supported family planning causes.[73]

That family planning today is permitted at all is due in large measure to the dedicated efforts of these earliest pioneers in family planning who were willing to risk their own careers, reputations, liberty, and in some cases their own lives for the cause of family planning.

FAMILY PLANNING AND THE LAW

The Comstock Act prohibited the mailing or importation of contraceptive information and, until 1971, defined such material as "filthy and vile."[74] It was not, however, the only federal legislation relating to birth control. Section 305(a) of the Tariff Act of 1930 forbade the import of, among other articles, any writing urging treason, murder, obscene books, and "any article whatever for the prevention of conception or for causing unlawful abortion."[75] That the statute would lump contraception along with murder and treason as objectionable matters for import was indicative of the prevailing public mood toward family planning at that time. It was not until 1971, that Congress saw fit to delete the reference to contraception (although even then it left in the reference to abortion materials).[76] As recently as 1960, federal legislation was enacted forbidding the mailing of unsolicited matter "which is designed, adapted, or intended for preventing conception."[77]

Many state laws were even more stringent than the federal laws. In 1936, for example, a New York Statute made it a crime to "sell, give away, or advertise . . . any articles for the prevention of conception" except to physicians.[78] As recently as 1965, a draconian Connecticut statute forbade not just the mailing or sale of contraceptive devices, but their use as well, making it a crime to use "any medicinal article or instrument for the purpose of preventing conception."[79] In 1972, a Massachusetts law made it a felony for any one other than physicians or pharmacists to dispense birth control devices, and even then only to married persons.[80]

One of the first tests of these Acts came in the case of *U.S. v. One Package*.[81] In that case, Dr. Hanna Stone, the doctor associated with Margaret Sanger, ordered some pessaries from a doctor in Japan. She was charged with violation of the Tariff Act, which forbade the import of contraceptives and made no exception for imports of devices to be used by physicians in medical practice. The Court characterized the prosecutor's argument as a request that the statute be read literally on grounds that "in 1873, when the Comstock Act was passed, information now available as to the evils resulting in many cases from conception was most limited, and that . . . the language prohibiting the sale or mailing of contraceptives should be taken literally and that Congress intended to bar the use of such articles completely."[82] The Court, however, declined to so read the statute, finding that the Act's "design was not to prevent the import of . . . things which might intelligently be employed by conscientious and competent physicians for the purpose of saving life."[83]

The case of *One Package* is significant as one of a series of many decisions in which federal courts were confronted with clear language, but which if applied would lead to an absurd result. Torn between the jurisprudential values of strict construction and adherence to legislative guidance on the one hand, and their own common sense on the other, the Court's reasoning, though reaching a sensible result, did not appear sound. Justice Hand, in his concurring opinion, appeared even more nonplussed, conceding that "there seems to me substantial reason for saying that contraceptives were meant to be forbidden, whether or not prescribed by physicians, and that no lawful use of them was contemplated. Many people have changed their minds about such matters in the past sixty years, but the Act forbids the same conduct now as then; a statute stands until public feeling gets enough momentum to change it, which may be a long time after a majority would repeal it, if a poll were taken."[84] Nevertheless, Justice Hand declined to dissent, though he was obviously dissatisfied with the legal reasoning used to justify the result.

The jurisprudential dilemma that faced Judge Hand was to face the United States Supreme Court in the 1965 case of *Griswold v. Connecticut*.[85] It was not surprising, therefore, that the Justices split their votes in five separate opinions to resolve the case. Griswold, the Director of the Planned Parenthood League of Connecticut, and a Professor at Yale Medical School, challenged Connecticut's law forbidding all use of contraceptive devices. The plurality opinion of Justice Douglas adopted the argument, posed many years before by Margaret Sanger, that the U.S. Constitution created "penumbral rights of 'privacy and repose,' "[86] and concluded that

the present case concerns a relationship lying within the zone of privacy created by several fundamental constitutional guarantees. And it concerns a law which, in forbidding the use of contraceptives rather than regulating their manufacture or sale, seeks to achieve its goals by means of having a maximum destructive impact upon that relationship. Such a law cannot stand in light of the familiar principle, so often applied by this Court, that a 'governmental purpose to control or prevent activities constitutionally subject to state regulation may not be achieved by means which sweep unnecessarily broadly and thereby invade the area of protected freedoms'.[87]

The Chief Justice concurred that

the entire fabric of the Constitution and the purposes that clearly underlie its specific guarantees demonstrate that the right to marital privacy and to marry and to raise a family are of similar order and magnitude as the fundamental rights specifically protected . . . Although the Constitution does not speak in so many words of the right of privacy in marriage, I cannot believe that it offers these fundamental rights no protection.[88]

Justice White, on the other hand, was more concerned with the fact that the statute seemed to have no reasonable relationship to its professed goal, which the State claimed was to inhibit illicit sexual relationships. Since the statute forbade all couples, not just unmarried ones from using contraception, it did not appear to reinforce its own stated objectives. This fact, combined with the statute's effect of denying disadvantaged citizens access to medical assistance and information about proper methods of birth control, made the statute vulnerable to attack under the Fourteenth Amendment.[89]

But the reservations expressed by Judge Hand in *One Package* were also expressed by Justices Stewart and Black in dissent. While acknowledging that the Connecticut law is "every bit as offensive to me as it is to my brethren of the majority," the dissenters nevertheless voted to uphold the law. "Privacy," they said, is too "broad, abstract, and ambiguous [a] concept which can easily be interpreted as a constitutional ban against many things" deemed offensive, and thus purports to give federal judges the power to "invalidate any legislative act which [they] find irrational, unreasonable, or offensive."[90] This was indeed the same dilemma faced by Judge Hand, and one that was to face the Court again in the area of abortion rights (See chapter 6, infra).

In the 1972 Supreme Court case of *Eisenstadt v. Baird*,[91] William Baird gave a lecture on contraception to students at Boston University, and after the lecture gave a young woman a sample of Emko vaginal foam. He was convicted of the crime of exhibiting contraceptives and also of the crime of giving away the foam, both of which crimes carried 5-year prison terms. The Massachusetts Supreme Court reversed the conviction for lecturing on contraception and exhibiting contraceptive devices on grounds that the Massachusetts law violated the First Amendment. However, it upheld the conviction for giving away the foam.

Since the Massachusetts statute only made it a crime for lay persons to dispense contraceptive devices to unmarried persons, the Court first addressed the question of "whether there is some ground of difference that rationally explains the different treatment accorded married and unmarried persons."[92] To the argument of Massachusetts that the statute's purpose was to "preserve chastity . . . and engender in the State a virile and virtuous race of men and women," the Court responded that "it would be plainly unreasonable to assume that Massachusetts has prescribed pregnancy and the birth of an unwanted child as punishment for fornication," and thus "the effect of the ban on distribution of contraceptives to unmarried persons has at best a marginal relation to the preferred objective."[93] The Court concluded that "it is true that in *Griswold* the right of privacy in question inhered in the marital relationship . . . If the right to privacy means anything, it is the right of the individual, married or single, to be free from unwarranted government intrusions into matters so fundamentally affecting a person as the decision whether to bear or beget a child . . . On the other hand," the Court continued, "if *Griswold* is no bar to a prohibition on the distribution of contraceptives, the State could not, consistently with the Equal Protection Clause, outlaw distribution to unmarried but not to married persons."[94] The Chief Justice dissented on much the same grounds as the dissenters in *Griswold,* and expressed concern that the majority relied on "no particular provision of the Constitution."[95]

One of the most recent cases dealing with contraceptive rights was the 1981 case of *Youngs Drug Products v. Bolger.*[96] In that case, the plaintiff sold contraceptive products through wholesale distributors, and sought to supplement his product promotion by sending unsolicited informational pamphlets promoting the use of certain contraceptive products. This activity conflicted with the clear prohibitions of federal law forbidding the sending of any unsolicited matter designed "for preventing conception."[97] The U.S. District Court for the District of Columbia concluded that the statute could not forbid such mailings, but set forth a number of requirements that would have to be satisfied, such as the giving of notices and warnings on the envelopes mailing the material in order to protect people from unsolicited material they find offensive.[98]

If nothing else, the legal history of contraceptive rights in the United States reveals deep social, political, cultural, and religious resistance to the very concept of family planning. Overcoming this resistance obliged the Courts to extend the U.S. Constitution to its furthest limits, and according to many legal scholars, to compromise its jurisprudential principles of interpreting the law rather than usurping the legislative prerogatives of democratically elected representatives of the people.

Winning contraceptive rights in the United States has been, to use a vernacular, like "pulling teeth." The net result, however, is the right of every American to contraceptive information and methods. It remains to examine the degree to which the right has been translated into practical access. Education, parental guidance, religious dogma, and cultural values still play important roles. It further remains to survey and compare family planning programs in other countries, and to evaluate those findings and relate them to population policies and the environmental movement.

FAMILY PLANNING IN THE MODERN WORLD

Laws banning the use of contraception are no longer a major obstacle to the use of contraceptive devices in countries around the world. But religious, cultural, and political obstacles still remain. Although optimists point to falling fertility rates worldwide as an indication of the success of family planning programs,[99] the decreases in fertility reflect only declines in the *rate of growth*,[100] and not actual declines in population. Population in 1993 continued to grow at the rate of one human every one-third of a second.[101]

According to one recent report, even in China, which is often pointed to as the perpetrator of draconian family planning measures, "the effectiveness of family planning efforts has been routinely overstated. Most couples in China have two to three children, not the one child cited in official Chinese rhetoric . . . Tens of millions of rural couples are still without good access to family planning services."[102] Despite the improved availability of contraceptive methods in India, the average family still has four children.[103] As a result, one of the three additional human beings added to the planet each second is born in India or China.[104] Nevertheless, even rumors of family planning methods considered offensive by American lobbying groups has resulted in the cut-off of funds for family planning.

In 1986, for example, the U.S. Agency for International Development announced that it would withhold its modest $25 million contribution to the United Nations Fund for Population Activities because the fund allegedly supported a family planning program that "encourages abortion."[105] Despite protests that such cuts would deprive poor women of the right to plan their families, drastic cuts have been enthusiastically supported by such groups as the American Life Lobby, a spokesman for which claims that "birth control leads to abortion."[106] For similar reasons, President Bush sent a letter to Congressional leaders in 1989 threatening to veto a foreign aid bill that would have provided $15 million to the United Nations Population Fund.[107]

Tragically, however, studies reveal that it is the lack of access to birth control that results in abortion. In Mexico, for example, where one-third of all women are reported to have had abortions,[108] the Mexican Social Security Administration estimates that it has "prevented 360,000 abortions since family planning services began in 1972."[109] In Chile, a drastic decline in women seeking medical help in hospitals from complications resulting from illegal abortions was noted in 1965—the very year that family planning services began to be widely available.[110]

Education on contraception is just as important as the actual availability of contraceptive devices. Kasun may or may not be correct in characterizing sex education as "manipulating the hearts and minds and bodies of its people in a direction dictated by special interest groups"[111] and otherwise corrupting the young; but the fact remains that countries such as Sweden (where contraceptive devices are accessible to all and children at age 7 are introduced to such topics as menstruation, intercourse, masturbation, and contraception), has one of the lowest abortion rates in the world, a rate only one-third of that in the United States.[112] Another apparent by-product of sex education in Sweden is that the age at which Swedish girls have sex has risen by one year since 1980.[113] It thus appears to be no accident that the countries that provide their citizens with sex education and the broadest access to contraceptive devices are also the countries with the lowest abortion rates.[114]

In many cultural settings, the promotion of family planning can be most successful if taken out of the context of population control, and instead offered as a humanitarian option to women and their families. Indeed, family planning programs appear most effective where they are voluntary—but most important they must be truly accessible and not subject to political, cultural, or religious repression.

It is estimated that intercourse occurs 100 million times a day, resulting in over a million conceptions, of which half are unplanned.[115] A State Department survey of foreign populations has revealed that large percentages of the women worldwide would like to limit their family size, but are unable to do so because of the lack of access to contraceptive methods and devices.[116] "The presence of such women is highest where few services are available—it is 67% in Bangladesh where only 13% of couples use contraceptives; 22% in Costa Rica where 65% of couples are currently using contraceptives. A carefully monitored project in Matlab Thana in Bangladesh demonstrated that when high in quality family planning services were made available to poor villagers on a voluntary basis, contraceptive prevalence increased from 6.9% to 35.2%."[117]

Although socioeconomic factors have also been shown to be a significant effect on population growth rates,[118] the direct affect of contraception availability has been amply documented.[119] Nevertheless, studies also reveal that "only half of all women in the developing world have access to family planning. Worldwide . . . 100 million couples who want to delay or stop having children have no means of doing so."[120] With over 100 million births a year worldwide, it can readily be seen that voluntary family planning programs, if made widely available, could

achieve population stabilization. Unfortunately, however, even availability of contraceptive programs cannot prevent pregnancy if women
are subjected to cultural or religious pressure to have children they do
not want or cannot support. In many cases, husbands object to their
wives using contraception, either for reasons of "machismo" or because
they fear the sexual freedom it may give their wives. In such cases,
many women have had to opt for methods they would not otherwise
prefer (such as the IUD), in order not to alert the husband. And, as
noted, socioeconomic reasons and religious beliefs are also inhibiting
factors.

Tina Rosenberg has studied the availability and access to contraceptives in South America, and found that while wealthy and connected
women have no trouble obtaining contraceptives, poor women often find
their access restricted. She reports of the work of Dr. Fernando Tamayo
in Columbia who "routinely provided contraceptives to the wives and
daughters of presidents and cabinet ministers . . . Yet at the state-run
hospital for the poor where he also worked, the circumstances were
painfully different. 'I saw mothers curse their newborn children—they
couldn't afford to take care of them,' Tamayo said. 'But I wasn't allowed to prescribe contraception at the hospital; it was considered immoral.' "[121] Morality, it seems, was reserved for the poor and disadvantaged.

But Rosenberg also writes of the success of Profamilia, a family planing organization second only in size to Planned Parenthood Federation.
Profamilia has taken an active role in South America, distributing condoms and pills to thousands of small outlets and stores. But Profamilia
sometimes found local taboos hard to break. Rosenberg tells of Mer-
cedes Martinez, a family planning instructor working in a rural South
American province, who reported her experience with young rural
women. "They would say, 'My husband doesn't let me plan. He thinks
I'll prostitute myself.' I would explain that you can take pills or have an
IUD inserted without your husband finding out. And then there was religion. They'd say 'God sends children, and we shouldn't interfere,' Martinez said I'd say 'God also sends scientific methods so we can plan
families.' One by one, city by city, Profamilia began to convince."[122]

But for every success story, there are two disaster stories. The Department of International Economic and Social Affairs of the United Nations publishes an annual study on world population policies, and surveys the population policies of 170 member states. A review of the
policies of individual countries is not encouraging. The policies of Gabon
are not untypical. That country, in which life expectancy is 49, has an
official government policy to "increase the growth rate by raising fertility rates. The main goal of the population policy is to create an environment conducive to couples having larger families. In its effort to increase

population size, the government has set targets for the growth rate. It plans to achieve a 2.3 per cent growth rate by 1990, and a 3.0 per cent rate by 2000." [123]

A Family Planning Clinic in Kisii in Kenya reports little progress on the family planning front. In 1990 only two vasectomies were performed. The average woman of Kisii bears 8.5 children, compared to the Kenyan national average of 6.7 children per woman. As a result, according to the *Financial Times,*

As far as the eye can see, the District appears to be bursting under the sheer weight of rapid population growth. Almost all the arable land is being cultivated, including steep slopes. Plots are becoming smaller and are providing less income as holding are divided and bordered by hedges, making the fertile equatorial landscape resemble a cluttered chessboard. As farmers overwork the land, soil erosion and exhaustion of fertility are becoming more marked. The pressure on schools and health clinics is immense, and rural unemployment is growing, bringing increased social and domestic problems. The young are being forced off the land into migrating into urban centers . . . Kisii is Kenya's most populous district, but the population explosion is nationwide. [124]

In short, Kisii is a Malthusian village, a microcosm. One almost wishes one could send Simon, Kuznets, Godwin, and Kasun to Kisii to explain to the starving villagers that they should continue rejecting family planning because it represents unnecessary government intrusion in their lives and is evil, that as human beings they are the "ultimate resources," that technology and innovation will take care of them, that to plan their families is "immoral," and that in any case "God will provide." For good measure they might suggest that if they really want fewer children, they should let their husbands "sleep on the roof."

Although contraceptive use around the world has jumped from 8% in 1960 to almost 50% today, [125] the studies of Mauldin and Lapham (Studies in Family Planning) [126] have revealed that use is unevenly distributed. There are

a lot of family planning efforts . . . in a small number of countries; moderate efforts occur in a large number of countries; and weak or very little effort is found in an even greater number of countries. Strong programs were found in Asia; programs of moderate quality in some Latin countries—Cuba, Columbia, Chile, Costa Rica, and the Dominican Republic—and Asia. African family planning programs were uniformly weak; but weak programs were also found in Asia (Napal and Pakistan) and Latin America (Honduras, Guatemala, Brazil, and Mexico). [127]

Although there appears to be a strong statistical relationship between a country's per capita income and population growth, it appears that there are too many variables to make an absolute connection between the two. Nevertheless, it is not surprising to find that the countries with the highest population growth rates also have the lowest income per capita.

There are, of course, exceptions. Some industrialized countries have managed to make the lives of their citizens so intolerable that no one wants to have many children. In Rumania, for example, a low birth rate so alarmed the dictator Ceaucescu that he banned sex education, and censored all books on reproduction and sexuality.[128] All contraception was banned, leaving primitive and illegal abortions as the birth control measure of last resort (60 % of pregnancies ended in illegal abortion). A *Newsweek* investigative journalist reported that "women under the age of 45 were rounded up at their workplaces every one to three months and taken to clinics, where they were examined for signs of pregnancy, often in the presence of government agents—dubbed the 'menstrual police' by some Rumanians. A pregnant woman who failed to produce a baby at the proper time could expect to be summoned for questioning."[129] As a result of Romania's brutal policies, illegal abortions soared and infant mortality skyrocketed to 83 in every 1000 births (compared to 10 in Western European Countries).[130] If a woman did not produce a child, she was fined 10% of her salary, even if it was not possible for her to have a child.[131]

After the brutal dictator was finally overthrown, Breslau reported that "the rebels . . . quickly rescinded the policy. 'I could have killed Ceausescu for that law alone' said Maria Dulce from her bed at Bucharest's Municipal Hospital. The 29-year-old mother of two was recovering from a self-induced abortion. Her eyes were bruised with fatigue . . . 'Now that it is possible for a woman to be a woman again I'm mutilated' Dulce says through her tears. 'And now there is reason to have a child in this country.' "[132]

For those such as Kasun who are concerned about government intrusion in the area of family planning, Romania provides a instructive case history if not their idea of reproductive utopia. Unlike China, however, which endured international condemnation for its family planning policies, Romania's totalitarian experiment in repressing contraceptive rights received scant international attention.

BIRTH CONTROL METHODS

Only 10 years ago, the future looked bright for the development of new safe and reliable birth control methods. In 1980 a panel of experts compiled a list of 20 new birth control methods that they predicted would be available by 1990.[133] Although many of the methods and devices on the list were used and adopted in other countries, only a few actually reached the American market. (A low-dose oral contraceptive, the T380a IUD, a contraceptive sponge, and Norplant.) On October 29, 1992 the FDA finally approved Depo-Provera, but only after the Upjohn Company waited over 25 years for its approval.[134] Meanwhile 5 IUDs were pulled from the market, driven out by million dollar judgments and the threat of litigation. Carl Djerassi, one of the developers of the birth control pill, has observed that "The United States is the only country other than Iran in which the birth-control clock has been set back during the past 10 years."[135] Louise Tyrer, Vice-President for Medical Affairs of Planned Parenthood Federation, recently stated that "the outlook for contraception in the U.S. has become bleak."[136] Richard Lincoln of the Guttmacher Institute agrees: "If in the 1960's we saw the birth of a contraceptive revolution, then in the 1980's we are witnessing a failure of that revolution . . . In the U.S., where the pill and modern IUD were developed, contraceptive methods are disappearing faster than the new ones can be introduced."[137] By 1989, only one major drug company was even attempting to do research into birth control methods.[138] As a result, pregnancy rates for American teenagers are among the highest in the world.[139]

Meanwhile citizens in Sweden have access to a contraceptive implanted under the skin providing 5-year protection, Germany has an injectable contraceptive that gives 2-month protection, and China and Mexico have developed their own 1-month injectables.[140] A joint committee of the National Research Council and the Institute of Medicine has stated that "Without a drastic change in federal policy, the United States will continue to miss out on the plethora of new contraceptive technologies now being developed . . . These include contraceptive vaccines, a once-a-month pill to induce menstruation, reversible male and female sterilization, a hormone-releasing patch worn like a Band-Aid, and male contraceptives. The likelihood of any of these getting on the U.S. market before the year 2000 is negligible."[141] According to the Committee, the consequences of this failure will be "enormous" and will result in 2 million unwanted pregnancies and about 750,000 abortions.[142]

The dearth of devices available in the United States has resulted in resort to sterilization as the most prevalent method of birth control, as it has in other parts of the world where modern methods have not penetrated.[143] Unfortunately, however, sterilization is not always reversible, and is therefore an unsatisfactory method, especially for young couples who only want to defer childbirth. The Population Council reports that worldwide, the IUD is the second most prevalent method (20%), while the pill ranks third (with 45 million users).[144]

The Council has also reported the serious health consequences resulting from the lack of access to birth control devices. For example, mothers aged 17 or younger have a 46% higher relative risk of death than mothers aged 20–24.[145] Mothers at the other end of the age range carry increased medical risks for both themselves and their babies.[146] Neither rhythm nor "sleep on the roof" techniques appear to have substantially reduced the number of deaths from such medical risks.

PRIVATE POPULATION ORGANIZATIONS

There are a number of organizations with agenda related to population control. Many of them, such as the Center for Population Options, the Pathfinder Fund, Population Crisis Committee, the World Watch Institute, and Zero Population Growth have a more focused agenda, such as teenage pregnancy, sex education, or concerns about the relationship between population and economic welfare. Other major groups, such as Planned Parenthood Federation of America, have a broader program, and are dedicated to providing family planning options to as many people as possible, including the poor and underprivileged.

In many respects, however, these organizations suffer from some of the same disadvantages as the private environmental groups. Their efforts are dispersed, uncoordinated, compete for the same sources of funding, and sometimes work at cross-purposes (though less so than the environmental groups). Many of them are dedicated to women's rights and freedom of choice, while others stress the relationship between population growth, human well-being, and economic growth. While these may be admirable goals, few stress the role of population in the environment, or are willing to bridge the gap with environmentalists and unite in a common cause. Although the differences are often more political than philosophical in some instances, they often engage in the same kind of politics of neutralization in which environmental groups engage.

Only when these groups find common ground and common cause and recognize the relationship between population and environment will solutions be found that are compatible with both the environment and human dignity.

NOTES

1. Pranay Gupte, *The Crowded Earth: People and the Politics of Population* 48–49 (1984).

2. Stein, Policies, Not People, Cause Poverty, Some Argue, *Investor's Bus. Daily,* July 7, 1993, pp. A1, A2.

3. *Id.* citing statement of James Miller, Director of Research at the Population Research Institute in Gaithersburg, Md.

4. Croll, *China's One-Child Family Policy* (1985).

5. Cf. AAS22, pp. 559–560 (1930); cited in Cavanagh, *The Popes, The Pill and The People* (1964).

6. *Id.*, p. 14, citing de Conivg. Aduit ii: 12

7. *Id.*, p. 109.

8. *Id.* It should be noted that even Dr. Billings hedges his assertion with the word "immediate." It is just such hedges that justify the author in characterizing the Ehrlich/Simon debate only as one of timing, and not one of ultimate limits.

9. Gupte, *The Crowded Earth, supra,* note 1, p. 186.

10. *Id.*, p. 187.

11. *Id.*, p. 191.

12. *Id.*, p. 194.

13. Ehrlich, *The Population Bomb, supra,* Chapter 1, note 5.

14. Stein, Policies Not People Cause Poverty, *supra,* note 2.

15. *Id.*

16. *Id.*

17. *Id.*

18. Jacqueline Kasun, *The War Against Population: The Economics and Ideology of Population Control,* 159 (1988).

19. Citing Karl Pearson, *Life, Letters and Labors of Francis Galton* (4 vols., 1914–40), p. 159.

20. *Id.*, p. 160.

21. Kasun, *supra,* quoting Edward Pohlman, *How to Kill Population* 161 (1971).

22. *Id.*, pp. 206–207.

23. *Id.*, p. 43.

24. *Id.*, p. 43.

25. Albert Gore, *Earth in the Balance, supra.*

26. *Id.*, p. 83.

27. *Id.*, p. 82, citing James E. Carter, Farewell Address: Major Issues Facing the Nation, in *Vital Speeches of the Day,* vol. XLVIII, no. 8, February 1, 1981, p. 22.

28. *Id.*, p. 83, citing Statement of Honorable M. Peter McPherson, Administrator, Agency for International Development Before the Senate Foreign Relations Committee (April 1, 1981).

29. Kasun, *supra,* p. 209.

30. *Id.*, p. 209.

31. *Id.*, p. 207.

32. *Id.*, p. 38, citing Sassone, *Handbook on Population* 99 (1978). For a response to the suggestion that such concentrations of Population are viable, see discussion of "Netherlands Fallacy," *supra,* Chapter 2.

33. *Id.*, p. 13 (The Foreword)

34. *Id.*

35. *Id.*, on back cover.

36. *Id.*

37. *Id.*

38. *Id.*

39. See, e.g., Simon, Miller, and Billings as quoted in Gupte, *supra.*

40. See Chapters 1 and 2.

41. *Supra,* Chapter 2.

42. On Population [1926 (1820)], cited in Kurt Back, *Family Planning and*

Population Control 31 (1989). This book presents the most concise and up-to-date history of the family planning movement yet found by the author.

43. *Illustrations and Proofs of the Principle of Population* (1822), cited in Margaret Sanger, *Margaret Sanger: An Autobiography* 126 (1971).

44. Back, *supra,* p. 32.

45. Douglas, *Pioneer of the Future: Margaret Sanger* 66 (1970).

46. *Id.,* p. 67.

47. Cited *id.,* p. 33.

48. Cited *id.*

49. *Id.,* p. 34.

50. *Margaret Sanger: An Autobiography, supra,* p. 127. The sentence was later suspended.

51. *Id.,* p. 127.

52. *Id.*

53. Ch. 258 §2, 17 Stat. 598 (Mar. 3, 1873) codified as amended at 18 U.S.C. §1461.

54. Pub. Law No. 91–662 §3(2)(3) (1971). Also deleted were references to contraception in Paragraphs 2 and 3.

55. Lader & Meltzer, *Margaret Sanger: Pioneer of Birth Control* 44 (1969).

56. Back, *supra,* p. 42.

57. *Autobiography, supra,* p. 89.

58. *Id.*

59. *Id.,* p. 92.

60. *Autobiography, supra,* pp. 109–120.

61. Back, *supra,* p. 51.

62. *Id.,* p. 52.

63. *Id.,* p. 52.

64. *Id.,* p. 56.

65. *Id.,* p. 53.

66. *Id.*

67. *Autobiography, supra,* pp. 358–368.

68. *Id.,* p. 404.

69. *Id.,* pp. 407–408.

70. *Id.,* p. 409.

71. Back, *supra,* p. 71.

72. *Id.*

73. *Id.,* p. 72.

74. 18 U.S.C. §1461; 19 U.S.C. §1462.

75. Ch. 497, Title 3 §305, 46 Stat. 688 (June 17, 1930).

76. Pub. Law No. 91–662 (1971).

77. 39 U.S.C.A. §3001 (derived from Pub. Law No. 86–682) (Sept. 2, 1960).

78. N.Y. Penal Laws.

79. Conn. Gen. Stat. §§53–32, 54–196 (1958 rev.)

80. Mass. Ann. Laws, Ch. 272 §21.

81. 86 F.2d 737; Consol. Laws Ch. 40 §1145.

82. 86 F.2d 737 at 739.

83. *Id.*

84. Hand, J. concurring; 86 F.2d 727 at 740.

85. *Griswold v. Connecticut*, 381 U.S. 479, 85 S.Ct. 1678, 14 L.Ed.2d 510 (1965).

86. 381 U.S. 479 (1965).

87. *Id.*, p. 485.

88. *Id.*, p. 495.

89. *Id.*, p. 503.

90. *Id.*, p. 509.

91. *Eisenstadt v. Baird*, 405 U.S. 438, 92 S.Ct. 1029, 31 L.Ed.2d 349 (1972).

92. *Id.*, p. 448.

93. *Id.*, p. 454.

94. *Id.*

95. *Id.*, p. 471.

96. *Youngs Drug Products v. Bolger*, 526 F. Supp. 823 (1981).

97. 39 U.S.C. §3001(e).

98. *Id.*

99. Moffett, Fertility Rates Decline in Third-World Nations, *Christ. Sci. Mon.*, July 8, 1992, p. B16.

100. *Id.*

101. See Chapter 2, note 1.

102. New Reports Critique Family Planning Programs in World's Two Most Populous Nations, *Population Crisis Committee Press Release*, Sept. 14, 1992; Mixed Results Mark Asian Family Planning, Sept. 15, 1992, p. B2.

103. *Id.*

104. *Id.*

105. Schmid, U.S. To Withhold Funds for U.N. Family Plan, *Philadelphia Inquirer*, Aug. 28, 1986, p. D8.

106. Mower, U.S. Rule on Birth Control Is Criticized, *Philadelphia Inquirer*, Aug. 27, 1985, p. A6.

107. Devroy, Bush Hints at Veto of Foreign Aid Bill; President Denounces Provision to Fund Population-Control Agency, *N.Y. Times*, Oct. 10, 1989, p. A28.

108. M. Peter McPherson, Address on International Family Planning, *Dept. St. Bull.*, March, 1986, p. 43.

109. *Id.*

110. *Id.*

111. Kasun, *supra*, p. 155.

112. Elsner, *AIDS Tempers Sweden's Liberal Attitudes on Sex*, Sec. 1, p. 2, pt. 1, col. 1 (Monograph; April 23, 1989).

113. *Id.*

114. See UN Survey on Global Sex and Fertility Trends, *Boston Globe*, June 25, 1992, p. B6.

115. *Id.*

116. McPherson, *supra*.

117. *Id.*

118. See, e.g., Donaldson, Modernizing Family Planning, *Society*, July/Aug. 1988, p. 11.

119. McPherson, *supra*.

120. Statement issued by the Population Council, and cited in Moffett, *supra*.

121. Rosenberg, Winning the Trojan War, *Washington Monthly,* July/Aug. 1991, p. 18.

122. *Id.,* p. 20.

123. *World Population Policies,* United Nations (1989).

124. Ozanne, Kenya Fights Its Baby Boom, *Financial Times,* reprinted in *World Press,* July, 1990, p. 67.

125. Moffett, *supra.*

126. Mauldin and Lapitam, *Studies in Family Planning* (1972), cited and discussed in Donaldson, *supra,* p. 14.

127. *Id.,* p. 14.

128. Breslau, Ceausescu's Cruel Law, *Newsweek,* Jan. 22, 1990, p. 35.

129. *Id.*

130. *Id.*

131. *Id.*

132. *Id.*

133. Podolsky, Sorry, Not Sold in the U.S., *U.S. News & World Report,* Dec. 24, 1990, p. 65.

134. Leary, U.S. Approves Injectable Drug as Birth Control, *N.Y. Times,* Oct. 30, 1992, p. A1. Cited in Update, *International Family Planning Perspectives,* Mar. 1993.

135. Podolsky, *supra.*

136. Zinman, An Era of Promise Unfulfilled: We Have Many Methods of Contraception, But Our Unintended Pregnancy and Abortion Rate Are Among the Highest in the World, *Newsday,* Feb. 28, 1989, p. 7.

137. *Id.*

138. *Id.*

139. Podolsky, *supra.*

140. Roberts, U.S. Lags on Birth Control Development, *Science,* Feb. 23, 1990, p. 901.

141. *Id.* (as summarized by L. Roberts).

142. *Id.*

143. Dourlen-Rollier, Family Planning and the Law, *World Health,* April, 1989, p. 7.

144. Ross, Mauldin, Green, and Cooke, *Family Planning and Child Survival Programs,* Population Council, 1992, p. 1.

145. *Id.,* p. 6.

146. *Id.*

6   Abortion

[P]opulation growth, [and] pollution . . . tend to complicate the [abortion] problem.

Roe V. Wade (1973)[1]

That abortion practices might have an effect on the environment was first recognized by Plato and Aristotle, who thought of abortion as a means of preventing overpopulation.[2] (It will be recalled that Plato first observed the effects of overpopulation on the erosion of soils in Attica.[3])

Certainly in modern times, however, abortion has never been a preferred method of birth control or preventing overpopulation. Abortion has become the means, however—often a last desperate resort—for women deprived of access to safe and effective contraceptive methods and devices. (Indeed the relationship between contraceptive availability and abortion is so strong that when England experienced a brief "pill scare," the abortion rate jumped almost overnight.[4])

Not surprisingly, the countries that provide the broadest access to contraception enjoy the world's lowest abortion rates. In the Netherlands, for example, where contraceptives are widely available and the people are educated as to their use, the abortion rate of .018 is one of the lowest in the world—despite the fact that abortion is legal.[5] In Romania under Ceaucescu, by contrast, which banned all contraception, 60% of all pregnancies were aborted, despite a draconian ban on all abortions and enforcement by secret police.[6]

In between these two extremes falls Italy and the United States. The withdrawal of contraceptives in the U.S. market has already been discussed, and explains its higher abortion rate.[7] In Italy, the explanation for a higher rate was provided by the Health Ministry, which blamed its high numbers on "ignorance about contraception."[8] In 1983 the Ministry "launched a $3 million campaign to encourage birth control to avoid abortion," declaring that the purpose of the campaign [was] to fight the ignorance and the cultural backwardness which still condition and inhibit women in Italy, by giving them [contraceptive] instruments . . . By informing women about adequate specific use of birth control, we can avoid a great number of abortions due to use of contraceptives.''[9]

Given such compelling data, one might assume that those opposing abortion would be the most enthusiastic advocates of contraception. Unfortunately, as Chapter 5 documented, this is not the case. The Reagan and Bush administrations, which opposed abortion, engineered a reduction of AID's family planning budget from $300 million in 1985 to $270 million in 1990.[10] In June of 1991, the Supreme Court upheld an administration policy of denying funds to any family planning organization dispensing contraceptives if the organization advised patients of abortion options.[11] U.S. agencies have forbidden the import of contraceptives proved safe and effective in other countries.[12]

The result of such policies has been the tragic death of 200,000 women a year from illegal abortions worldwide.[13] Studies showing that contraceptives "improve the health of women most effectively by preventing the most dangerous pregnancies"[14] have not moderated the stance against contraceptives by antiabortion groups. The Pope's *Humanae Vitae* continues to condemn both abortion and contraception.[15] Some antiabortion groups oppose contraception because they consider many contraceptives (such as the IUD) to be abortificants; others who oppose contraceptives appear to be latter-day followers of Comstock (who considered contraceptives to be obscene, "vile, and filthy").[16] One of the few consolations is that not all of the rank and file pay attention to their leaders. A 1988 survey revealed that "the abortion rate among Catholic women is 30% higher than among Protestant women.''[17]

Although the figure of 200,000 women who die annually from illegal abortions has been documented by the World Health Organization,[18] antiabortion activists have professed skepticism of these figures.[19] Perhaps more revealing than such global estimates is the report of a single hospital in overpopulated Kenya (which outlaws abortion) that it admits between 40 and 60 women *every day* suffering from the effects of illegal abortions.[20] Even in countries where abortion is legal (such as Bangladesh), the closing of a U.S. funded clinic drove desperate women back to dangerous abortions performed by untrained personnel using primitive methods.[21]

A 1992 survey of 132 countries with populations of 1 million or more revealed that only 25 countries permit abortion on demand up to a certain point of gestation, 55 require specific medical or social reasons (such as rape or incest), and 52 permit abortion only when the life of the mother is endangered.[22] According to a recent study, of the 40–60 million abortions performed every year around the world, "10–25 million are illegal."[23] The toll in human suffering represented by the illegal abortions has been described by an abortion law scholar: "The tale of death that illegal abortions caused is well known; the personal tragedies that tale recounts [are] widespread, and evident in every social stratum. Paradoxically the tale has been so often told that many listeners have become anesthetized to the human pain it reflects."[24]

HISTORY OF ABORTION

Both the philosophical question of when life begins and the religious question of when a fetus is "ensouled" have been debated for thousands of years. The ancient Greeks and Romans had something to say about it, and virtually no era of human history has escaped the moral dilemma these questions have posed. That no consensus has ever been reached—even within religious denominations and among those with moral conviction—might alone be testament to the futility of any one segment of society attempting to impose its moral view by force of law or dogma. But even when—for brief periods in history—a moral view has been imposed, hypocrisy and cynicism have undermined the foundations of the authority asserted.

Aristotle proposed that a mother have an abortion if the state was unable to accommodate the child.[25] However, he was one of the first philosophers to make the distinction based on fetal movement (later known as "quickening"), insisting that any abortion be conducted before there is "sensation and life."[26] Plato also saw abortion as a means of attaining an optimum population.[27]

Historians differ, however, on the import of Hippocrates' Oath "not to give a deadly drug, [and] not to give a woman an abortifacient pessary."[28] Some have suggested that "the 'deadly drug' is one type of abortifacient which is rejected along with the pessary"[29]—in other words, neither pessaries nor other deadly drugs should be given to a mother since they might endanger her. (In this context it should be recalled that one dubious method of abortion is to give the mother a poison sufficient to kill the fetus without killing the mother.) Others have read into the oath a prohibition against doctors performing abortions. In any case, Soranos of Ephesus (A.D. 98–138), "the most learned of Greco-Roman gynecologists," attributes to Hippocrates a writing in which Hippocrates himself "told a girl how to accomplish an abortion by jumping."[30]

Noonan, a noted abortion historian, has noted that "in the Mediterranean world in which Christianity appeared, abortion was a familiar art."[31] Soranos set forth in a treatise of the day the most common and familiar methods of abortion: "purging the abdomen with clysters; walking about vigorously; carrying things beyond one's strength; bathing in sweet water which is not too hot; bathing in decoctions of linseed, mallow, and wormwood; applying poultices of the same decoctions; injecting warm and sweet olive oil; being bled and then shaken after softening by suppositories."[32] Given these other less dangerous methods of abortion it is not surprising that Hippocrates would forbid the use of "deadly drugs" or "pessaries" as a means of inducing abortion.

By Medieval times, St. Thomas Aquinas had adopted the Aristotelian notion of quickening. Aquinas "was clear that there was actual homicide when an ensouled embryo was killed. He was equally clear that ensoulment did not take place at conception,"[33] and stated in *Politicorum* that "seed and what is not seed is determined by sensation and movement."[34]

Martin Azplicueta, "the guide in moral questions of three Popes, and the leading canonist of the 16th century,"[35] was a consultant to the Sacred Penitentiary, "the Roman Tribunal for deciding cases of conscience submitted to confessors."[36] Historian Noonan has noted that Azplicueta stated in *Consilia* that "the rule of the Penitentiary was to treat a fetus over forty days as ensouled. Hence therapeutic abortion was accepted in the case of a fetus under this age."[37]

On October 29, 1588, however, Pope Sixtus V launched a campaign against the prostitutes of Rome by issuing the bull *Effraenatam* that declared abortion to be homicide regardless of the age of the fetus. Punishment was to be excommunication, and only the Holy See could grant absolution from the excommunication.[38] Though this appeared to be plainly inconsistent with existing dogma, Sixtus, in a fit of pique and in apparent exasperation with the Roman prostitutes, nevertheless justified his precedent-breaking bull by rhetorically asking, "Who would not punish such cruel lust with the most severe punishments?"[39] (Implied in the answer was that a prostitute, when faced with the severe punishment of excommunication, would choose to carry an unwanted child as a lesser form of punishment.)

Sixtus V's bull, issued in the heat of a campaign against Roman prostitutes, and apparently based on the dubious assumption that an unwanted child was God's retribution for lust, mercifully did not stay in effect long. Only 2 years later, after Sixtus died, the new Pope Gregory XIV, noting that "the hoped for fruit had not resulted," issued restrictions in 1591 on *Effraenatum*, "repeal [ing] all its penalties except those applying to a fetus which had been ensouled."[40] Thus the dogma of Aquinas and Azplicueta was restored.[41]

It was not until almost 300 years later, in 1869, that God revealed to Pope Pius IX that St. Thomas Aquinas, Azplicueta, and Gregory XIV had all been wrong, and that the abortion of any fetus, *regardless of quickening,* was grounds for excommunication.[42] Thus the bull issued by

Sixtus V in his campaign against the prostitutes over 300 years before was restored.

There followed a series of even more extreme declarations, including one issued by the Pope in 1889, that "it was not 'safe' to teach in the Catholic schools that a craniotomy necessary to save the mother's life was lawful, although without it both mother and child would die."[43] The culmination of such proclamations was the *Humanae Vitae* of 1968, which condemned not only abortion, but all forms of artificial birth control.[44]

The Catholic Church is not alone in its condemnation of abortion, however, and is joined by a number of protestant groups and other religions. The Southern Baptist Convention, the Mormons, Jehovah's Witnesses, and the Eastern and Russian Orthodox Church all oppose abortion, although some, like the Mormons, do not advocate specific legislative proposals.[45] Orthodox Judaism also opposes abortion but regards it as a religious question and is therefore against any government interference in the matter.[46] The Union of American Hebrew Congregations, however, supports the right to abortion, as does the Moslem religion for any reason in the first 40 days of pregnancy.[47] The Moslems base the right to abortion not on the Koran, but on the Hadith (the sayings of Muhammad as collected by the ninth century scholar Al-Bukhari), which states the fetus is "40 days in the form of seed, then he is a clot of blood for a like period, then a morsel of flesh for a like period, then (at 120 days) there is sent to him the angel who blows the breath of life into him."[48]

In the case of Christians, reference to abortion has been found in the Bible Chapter of *Jeremiah* 1:15 ("Before I formed you in the womb I knew you, and before you were born I consecrated you"), and *Exodus* 21:22 ("When men strive together, and hurt a woman with child, so that there is a miscarriage, and yet no harm follows, the one who hurt her shall be fined . . . and he shall pay as the judges determine. If any harm follows, then you shall give life for life, eye for eye, tooth for tooth"). Predictably, the ambiguity of such passages has resulted in widely varying interpretations by the Christian denominations. Some, such as the Lutherans, avoid a confrontation within their ranks by simply agreeing to call on "couples and individuals [to] explore all issues."[49]

Other major world religions, such as Hinduism, Buddhism, and Shintoism, are ambivalent on the issue or take no firm position.[50] Of course, most religions (other than the Catholic Church) are far less strict on the question of birth control than abortion. Unfortunately, however, the distinction between birth control and abortion has become blurred by findings or opinions that some methods thought to be purely methods of birth control (such as the intrauterine device) are in fact abortificants.[51]

ABORTION LAWS

Given the theological notions of ensoulment and quickening, it is perhaps not surprising that in 1800 abortion before quickening was legal in every jurisdiction in the United States.[52] This state of the law reflected the common law of England, which could be traced back to the thirteenth century when Henry de Bracton's law treatise provided that "if anyone . . . causes an abortion, if the foetus be . . . animated, he commits homicide."[53] When Coke wrote his legal commentaries in the first part of the seventeenth century, the doctrine of quickening was well established.[54] Cyril Means' study of the common law of abortion concludes that, "As Coke's language indicates, and as decisions afterwards made clear, an abortion before quickening, with the woman's consent, whether killing the foetus while still in the womb, or causing its death after birth alive was not, at common law, an indictable offense, either in her or in her abortionist. It was not a crime at all."[55]

The Roman Civil Law fixed the time of ensoulment as 40 days after conception,[56] while the common law fixed the time at "quickening," which varied among women, "but ordinarily takes place between the sixteenth and eighteenth week."[57]

Early precedent in American Courts was set by the 1812 case of *Commonwealth of Massachusetts v. Bangs,* which declared that "if an abortion [is] alleged and proved to have ensued, the averment that the woman was quick with child at the time is a necessary part of the indictment."[58] Thereafter, abortions flourished, and techniques were widely published in manuals such as William Buchan's *Domestic Medicine* (1816), Samuel Jenning's *The Married Lady's Companion* (1808), John Burns' *Observations on Abortion* (1808), Joseph Brevitt's *The Female Medical Repository* (1810), and Richard Reece's *Lady's Medical Guide* (1833).[59] Although perceived earlier as a practice resorted to mostly by poorer women who had gotten into trouble and wished to preserve their reputations, the "dramatic surge of abortion in the U.S. after 1840 was attributed to . . . the increasing use of abortion by white, married, Protestant, native-born women of the middle and upper classes who either wished to delay their childbearing or already had all the children they wanted."[60] Mohr has observed that "the enduring resiliency of the quickening doctrine throughout the period from 1840 through the 1870's indirectly substantiates the likelihood of high abortion rates during that period."[61]

Beginning around 1860, resistance to abortion began to surface—not surprisingly from religious groups—but from the medical profession. Its prestige enhanced by such medical advances as Lister's work on sepsis in 1865, the medical profession began a campaign to "protect their turf," lobbying for licensing laws and other legislation to protect the public from quacks and incompetents. "Doctors found a receptive audience among legislators, who tended to be both atavistic and protective of their women's medical safety. [Thus] physicians were able to bring about a major revision of official American policy toward abortion, a practice which had been viewed in the United States with considerable tolerance in the early decades of the 19th century."[62]

Inasmuch as the medical professions' campaign against abortion began before the Pope's surprising 1869 reversal of abortion dogma, it was perhaps not surprising that religious groups played little or no role in the doctors' campaign. In 1884, Dr. J. Miller evaluated the role of religious groups in the antiabortion campaign, remarking with some exasperation that "There are some divines who do take the bold stand, but they are unpopular, and their work bears little fruit, and that of poor quality."[63] Mohr has noted that "the anti-abortion crusade won limited support during the 1860's from a few denominations that appeared to be more worried about falling birthrates among their adherents than about the morality of abortion itself."[64]

Some doctors, however, did profess a broader concern than their own professional well-being. In 1868 the *New York Tribune* quoted doctors who "have declared that were it not for immigration, the white population of the United States would actually fall off,"[65] thus joining others who were concerned that free abortion might adversely affect racial balance against the white population.

The final blow to abortion rights came when the antiobscenity crusaders joined the campaign. Acting under the authority of his 1873 Act for the "Suppression of . . . Obscene Literature and Articles for Immoral Use," Comstock "became the country's best known pursuer of abortionists for the remainder of the 1870s. In each of the years from 1873 through 1877 he probably prosecuted more abortionists, usually through their advertisements, than any other person in the United States."[66]

The coalition of doctors and antiobscenity crusaders was effective in turning public opinion. Between 1840 and 1880 over 40 states passed antiabortion laws, and by 1900 the war against abortion rights was virtually complete: abortion, without regard to quickening, was forbidden throughout the United States.[67]

The increasingly draconian laws appeared to have little affect on actual abortion rates, however. Tribe has observed that "the early twentieth century was remarkably free from debate about abortion, remarkably so because it appears that women continued to have abortions in roughly the same proportions as before criminalization . . . it seems that as many as one in three pregnancies was terminated by induced abortion during this era."[68]

Tribe cites two episodes that helped to turn the tide back toward abortion rights for women. In 1962, Sherri Finkbine, who had ingested thalidomide, which causes hideous birth defects in children (such as no arms, and flippers for legs), was denied the right to an abortion in the United States and had to flee to Sweden to get an abortion. She found out later that her embryo had been horribly deformed.[69] During the 1962–1965 outbreak of rubella, which causes birth defects, some doctors conducted abortions that violated abortion laws, leading to the indictment of nine doctors in California (the San Francisco nine).[70] Shortly after Finkbine's abortion, a Gallup poll revealed that 52% of Americans supported her right to the abortion; 32% opposed it.[71] The stage was set for a return to abortion rights.

Hawaii repealed its abortion law in 1970, as did New York by one vote in the New York Legislature. A dramatic last minute change of one vote by a Catholic legislator carried the day. Martin Ginsberg had originally planned to vote for keeping the law, believing that it would pass in later years anyway. However, his wife told him: "In the meantime thousands of women will be butchered in underground abortion."[72] At the last moment, Ginsberg rose, in the State Assembly, stating, "I am terminating my political career, but I can not in good conscience sit here and allow my vote to be the one that defeats this bill—I ask that my vote be changed from 'no' to 'yes.' "[73] Ginsberg's vote did indeed ruin his political career.[74] But after Alaska and Washington joined the ranks of states giving freedom of choice to women, the stage was set for *Roe. v. Wade*.

ROE V. WADE

Although *Roe v. Wade* has become the legal focal point of the abortion debate in the United States, that decision was a logical extension of the 1965 case of *Griswold v. Connecticut* (discussed in Chapter 5), a case less known by activists in the abortion debate. It will be recalled that *Griswold* held that the right to use contraceptives "concerns a relationship lying within the zone of privacy created by several fundamental constitutional guarantees."[75] Although the Supreme Court did not at that time make a distinction between types of contraceptive devices, the decision clearly pertained to the typical contraceptives in use, such as the IUD and the pill. Since the IUD (and sometimes the pill) acts by preventing the implantation of a fertilized egg into the uterus, thus causing the fertilized egg's destruction, *Griswold,* as a practical matter, legalized the act of destroying a fertilized egg. *Roe* simply extended that decision to include the right to destroy a fertilized egg after implantation. Since the appellees in *Roe* argued that life began at "conception" (i.e., at the time the egg is fertilized), their argument was one that might better have been made in *Griswold* than *Roe*. Indeed, most of the other legal arguments against the decision in *Roe* were in fact resolved in Griswold.

One of the strongest arguments by the dissent in *Griswold* began by observing that the "right of privacy" was "a broad, abstract, and ambiguous concept . . . which can be interpreted as a constitutional ban against many things."[76] This statement in itself did not accuse the majority of violating an important jurisprudential principle—that is, the principle of seeking guidance from authority rather than usurping prerogatives reserved to the legislative branch, or to the states, by the Constitution. If the majority in *Roe*—after honestly seeking the guidance of legislative, constitutional, and judicial precedent—concluded that the right of privacy encompassed the right of a woman to control her own body by using contraceptive abortifacients, the decision would not be in violation of that jurisprudential value. If, on the other hand, the majority preconceived a desired result, and then used a legal doctrine that was conveniently "amorphous" to justify that result, then they would be acting as superlegislators rather than judges, and violating the jurisprudential responsibilities assigned them under the separation of powers provisions of the Constitution. The result would be not a rule of law, but the rule of man.

In fact, Justice Black came very close to making just such an assertion when he stated that the majority's decision was based on its feeling that the "evil qualities they see in the law make it unconstitutional."[77] After confiding that the Connecticut law was "every bit as offensive to me as it is to my brethren in the majority,"[78] he proceeded to lecture the majority on the jurisprudential dangers of allowing personal beliefs of good and bad to cloud constitutional conclusions:

If these formulas based on "natural justice," or others which mean the same thing, are to prevail, they require judges to determine what is or is not constitutional on the basis of their own appraisal of what laws are unwise or unnecessary. The power to make such decisions is of course that of a legislative body . . . No provision of the Constitution specifically gives such blanket authority to Courts to exercise such a supervisory veto over the wisdom and value of legislative policies and to hold unconstitutional those laws which they believe unwise or dangerous.[79]

Justice Stewart joined in the dissent, stating that "I think this is an uncommonly silly law . . . But we are not asked in this case to say whether we think this law is unwise, or even asinine. We are asked to hold that it violates the United States Constitution. And that I cannot do."[80]

The legitimacy of any judicial decision must ultimately depend upon the jurisprudential integrity of the judges who render it. In the strict sense, therefore, the key to the validity of the most common criticism of *Griswold* and *Roe* lies buried in the minds of the judges who wrote the opinions. Nevertheless, a more objective measure of validity can be sought in the judicial precedent upon which the Court relied.

One of several cases upon which the majority relied in *Griswold* (and *Roe*) was *Pierce v. Society of Sisters,* decided in 1925.[81] In that case, the State of Oregon passed a law requiring that every child attend public school, thereby depriving children and their parents of the right to send their children to private or religious schools. The Court relied upon the "fundamental theory of liberty upon which all governments in this Union repose," and found that the law violated the Fourteenth Amendment by depriving children and their parents of "liberty" and undermining the relationship between parent and child. The same arguments made against the decisions in *Griswold* and *Roe* could certainly have been made in *Pierce*. First, the drafters of the Fourteenth Amendment probably did not have parent–child relationships specifically in mind when they wrote the Amendment (the "original intent" argument). Second, the Court used the "amorphous" concept of liberty and applied it to a particular state law.

Likewise, in *Eisenstadt v. Baird,* decided prior to *Roe,* the Court held that "if the right to privacy means anything, it is the right of the individual . . . to be free from unwarranted intrusions into matters so fundamentally affecting a person as the decision whether to bear or . . . a child."[82]

Thus the majority in *Roe* had substantial precedent upon which to base their decision that the right of privacy is founded on the "Fourteenth Amendment's concept of personal liberty and restriction upon state action," and is "broad enough to encompass a woman's decision whether or not to terminate her pregnancy."[83]

The Court in *Roe* was less persuasive, however, when it attempted to justify its determination that the right of a woman to have an abortion is a "fundamental right" by referring to lower court decisions holding that the right of privacy covers the right to an abortion. In fact, lower Court decisions were sharply divided,[84] and the argument was vulnerable to Justice Rhenquist's retort that the right could hardly be "so rooted in the traditions and conscience of our people as to be ranked as fundamental"[85] when a majority of states had outlawed abortion. (Of course, if state legislatures never passed laws that violated the Fourteenth Amendment, there would, by definition, never be occasion for its application.)

The Court in part explained away the existence of state laws prohibiting abortion by considering arguments that their original purpose had been the one advocated by the medical profession, namely the health and safety of the women. That purpose was not served where medical advances in abortion techniques had advanced to the point where early abortions were safer than childbirth.[86] Such a purpose did serve a legitimate state interest in the later stages of pregnancy, however.[87]

The Court did not consider the argument that the state had a legitimate interest in discouraging "illicit sexual conduct," because even the appellants conceded that the abortion statute did not further such an interest since it made no distinction between unwed and married mothers.[88]

The Court took more seriously, however, the contention that the state had an interest in protecting prenatal life, that the unborn child was a "person" entitled to protection under the Fourteenth Amendment, and that the rights of the unborn child must be weighed against any other rights of the mother. Such a contention would have to rest upon a finding that a fetus is a person.

The Court could find nothing closer to a definition of person than that provided by the Fourteenth Amendment itself, which refers to "persons born or naturalized in the United States." The Court therefore concluded that the word "person" as used in the Fourteenth Amendment did not include a fetus,[89] and declined to address the question of "when life begins" on grounds that if theologians, philosophers, and doctors could not agree, the judiciary should not presume to find the answer.

Although the Court reviewed the long history of theological and philosophical debate on the question, it did not review the medical debate. Had it done so, it would have found a debate as sharp as that engaged in by the theologians and philosophers. Dr. John Wilke of the National Right to Life Committee, for example, maintains that "Contained within the single cell who I once was, was the totality of everything I am today."[90] Dr. Charles Gardner, on the other hand, explains that "there is no program to specify the fate of each cell. Rather a cell's behavior is influenced at each stage by its location within the developing body pattern of the embryo. Each new stage brings new information, information that changes as the body pattern changes. And each cell will respond to this new information in a somewhat random way."[91] Dr. Gardner points out that even identical twins from the same egg with the same DNA have different fingerprints, thus proving that "the fertilized egg is clearly not a prepackaged human being. There is no body plan, no blueprint, no tiny being preformed and waiting to unfold . . . [T]he particular person that it might become is not yet there."[92]

There is even debate on when "conception" occurs. The American Medical Association defines it as occurring at the time the fertilized egg is actually implanted in the uterus.[93] Some prolifers, however, contend that conception takes place before implantation at the time the egg is fertilized by the sperm. In light of the fact that doctors estimate that "two thirds of all fertilized ova fail naturally to implant in the uterus," Tribe has asked rhetorically, "who among us really believes that we are now faced with a tragedy in which two-thirds of the people who have come into existence" have been killed in such a way.[94] Obviously, the further one goes back in the reproductive process, the more ridiculous the argument becomes, as in the bumper sticker that reads "sperms are people too."

In any case, the Court in *Roe* may have had difficulty in believing that even the appellants truly believed that a fetus was a human being, since most state abortion laws were totally inconsistent with that belief. For example, most of the state laws provided for exceptions in such cases as rape, incest, or at least where the life of the mother was in danger. If a fetus is a person, it is presumably no less a person by virtue of having been conceived by an act of rape or incest; and there are no provisions in the murder laws of any state that permit the killing of one innocent person in order to save the life of another. If prolifers truly believed that a fetus was a person, consistency would require that the State's most severe penalty (death, in many states) be imposed for abortion. In light of the thousands of abortions that occurred when abortion was illegal, women who had abortions or took an abortion pill would have to be rounded up and killed *en masse*—a prospect from which even "prolifers" would probably shrink.

However, none of the state laws banning abortion provided penalties equal to those for killing a child or adult. (Indeed, only Nazi Germany is known to have prescribed the death penalty for abortion.) In addition, many state laws purported to punish only the abortionist, and not the mother who requested the abortion. This too is inconsistent with the contention that a fetus is a human being, since murder statutes hold that one who hires a person to kill another person is equally responsible for the death.

The Court in *Roe* did concede, however, that the state has two legitimate interests in regulating abortion. First, there is an interest in the health and safety of the mother, which is served by regulating abortion during the later stages of pregnancy when abortion might be unsafe. Second, the state does have "a legitimate interest in protecting the potentiality of human life;" however, that interest becomes "compelling" only in the later stage of pregnancy.

With regard to the first interest, the Court noted that after the first trimester of pregnancy, the health risk to the woman exceeded that of childbirth. Therefore, the first trimester of pregnancy was a reasonable cut-off point for determining when the state's regulation of abortion reasonably related to a legitimate and compelling state interest in the health and safety of the mother. After the first trimester, therefore, the state may regulate abortion to the extent that its regulation reasonably relates to the protection of maternal health.

With regard to the state's legitimate interest in protecting potential human life, the "compelling point is at viability. This is so because the fetus then presumably has the capability of meaningful life outside the woman's womb. State regulation protective of fetal life after viability thus has both logical and biological justification. After viability, the state may ban abortion entirely, except where necessary to preserve the life of the mother.''

Since the decision in *Roe,* prolife legislators in some states have attempted to take maximum advantage of *Roe's* recognition of a state interest in the potential of human life. Again and again, the Supreme Court has been asked to pass on a wide variety of state-imposed restrictions on abortion, ranging from a requirement that abortion be approved by an "abortion hospital committee"[95] to a requirement that a minor's parents be notified before an abortion is performed.[96]

The Supreme Court has approved regulations requiring the mother to sign an informed consent to the abortion,[97] the submission of a postabortion pathology report,[98] and that second-trimester abortions be performed in a licensed clinic.[99] In *Webster v. Reproductive Health Services,* the Supreme Court upheld the power of the states to forbid public employees from performing abortions.[100]

The Court has disapproved regulations requiring that written consent be obtained from the parent of an unmarried woman under the age of 18,[101] that all abortions be performed in a hospital,[102] that an attending physician be required to inform the patient of the emotional complications of abortion,[103] that second-trimester abortions be performed in acute-care facilities,[104] that parental or spousal consent to abortion be obtained,[105] that a woman wait 48 hours after advisement before obtaining an abortion,[106] that the patient be given advisement designed to affect her choice of abortion,[107] and that certain abortion records be made public.[108]

Since 1973, all of the Supreme Court decisions on abortion have been based on the underlying principles set forth in *Roe v. Wade.* In 1992, however, the strongest legal assault since 1973 was launched against *Roe* in the case of *Planned Parenthood v. Casey.*[109] Although the specific state regulations at issue involved the requirement of spousal consent and a 24-hour waiting period, the State of Pennsylvania asked the Supreme Court to reverse outright *Roe v. Wade's* basic guarantee under the Fourteenth Amendment of the right of a woman to obtain an abortion. The Court came within a whisker of doing just that.

In an epic opinion of unusual length and detail, the plurality opinion acknowledged the long, bitter, but continuing debate surrounding abortion. But the tone of the opinion clearly reveals the hope that it would finally put to rest the fundamental question of the basic right of a woman to obtain an abortion. "Liberty finds no refuge in a jurisprudence of doubt,"[110] Justice O'Connor intoned for the plurality. But despite pleas to reverse years of precedent, as the Court had done at least twice before in its history (in *West Coast Hotel v. Parrish*[111] and *Brown v. Board of Education*),[112] the Court recognized that "the immediate question is not the soundness of *Roe*'s resolution of the issue, but the precedential force that must be accorded to its holding."[113] The Court concluded, after exhaustive analysis, that "the basic decision in *Roe* was based on a constitutional analysis that we can not now repudiate."[114]

Justice Blackmun, while dissenting on the plurality's view of one of the Pennsylvania regulations, nevertheless reasserted the principles of *Roe v. Wade*. But he was not optimistic that this case would be the last world. "Three years ago" he recalled, "four members of this Court appeared to 'cast into darkness the hopes and visions of every woman in this country' who had come to believe that the Constitution guaranteed her the right of reproductive choice . . . I do not underestimate the significance of today's joint opinion. Yet I fear for the darkness as four justices anxiously await the single vote necessary to extinguish the light."[115]

Justice Blackmun's fear was not understated. The four dissenting Justices in *Casey* were direct: "We believe *Roe* was wrongly decided, and that it can and should be overruled."[116] In response to the plurality's hope that this case would finally resolve the abortion issue, the four dissenting Justices closed their opinion on a distinctly ominous note.

"It is no more realistic for us in this case" said the dissenters, "than in the Dred Scott case involving slavery, to believe that this issue can be 'speedily and finally' settled . . . Quite to the contrary, by foreclosing all democratic outlet for the deep passions this issue arouses, by banishing the issue from the political forum that gives all participants, even the loser, the satisfaction of a fair hearing and an honest fight, by continuing the imposition of a rigid national rule instead of allowing for regional differences, the Court merely prolongs and intensifies the anguish. We should get out of this area we have no right to be, and where we do neither ourselves nor the country any good by remaining."[117]

The Presidential election of 1992 may prove to have been pivotal in the legal battle over abortion. With four of nine justices committed to overruling *Roe,* President Clinton's choice of a new Justice in 1993 has provided a cushion of one extra justice on the prochoice side of the Court.

ABORTION POSTSCRIPT

There may be some merit in the argument of the dissenting Justices in *Casey* that democratic debate rather than judicial fiat might produce a more lasting compromise and acceptance of an abortion decision by the citizenry of the United States.[118] But such considerations, as well as ones of a purely legal character, were considered by the majority in *Roe,*

and the issue was decided. Certainly the Court's reversal of precedent
on substantive due process (under pressure exerted by President Roosevelt when he threatened to pack the Court the "switch in time that saved
nine") does not provide a good example for reversing *Roe,* a decision
upon which millions of women have relied over a period of 20 years.
Nor would a reversal of *Roe,* given the honest moral and philosophical
debate over abortion over thousands of years, have the same force of
moral conviction that *Brown v. Board of Education* had in reversing an
American policy of apartheid condemned by all civilized nations.

A reversal of *Roe* now, after so many years, would undoubtedly damage the moral authority of the Court far more than continued reliance on
established precedent, whatever analytical weaknesses there may have
been in the original *Roe* decision. An equally forceful argument can be
made that *Roe* helped to defuse a volatile issue by deciding it on a purely
intellectual and Constitutional plain. Although the image of bitter confrontations taking place today between prochoice and prolife groups
might not appear to support this view, one wonders if 50 different legislative battles, with abortion rights at stake in each, would not provoke
even more bitter confrontations, drawing even more funds and resources
for bitter battles than are now consumed by opposing groups. Given the
hardened views and extreme tactics now employed by abortion groups,
it may be unduly optimistic to suggest that legislative defeats would be
accepted any more gracefully than judicial ones by the losing side.

Although 50 different legislative battles might indeed take into account
"regional differences," the result would very likely be close decisions
in many states; the United States itself would be "balkanized" on the
issue. No doubt a vast underground railroad would arise as people trav-
eled from states where abortion was legal to those where it was not.
And for those who could not afford such travel, the tools of the back-
alley and illegal abortionist would no doubt take the same deadly toll as
they always have.

RELATIONSHIP OF ABORTION TO FAMILY PLANNING
AND POPULATION

Few women would ever choose abortion as a family planning alternative to safe, reliable, and convenient contraceptive methods. But many
who oppose abortion, also oppose contraception. Where contraceptives
are unavailable or impractical, abortion becomes the birth control
method of last resort. A deadly cycle begins when the young and uneducated are denied sex education and information on contraception. After
pregnancies occur, many of the same people who prevented the dissemination of birth control devices now also oppose abortion. Finally, if they
are successful in forcing a woman to have an unwanted child, they now

resist being taxed the necessary millions to provide welfare benefits for the unwanted children, millions of whom are then doomed to lead lives of desperate poverty and misery.

Sixtus V's notion that bringing an unwanted child into the world is God's just retribution and punishment for irresponsible sexual behavior has no place in a world where 45,000 children die each day from neglect and starvation. Although the Court in *Roe* made one brief reference to population and the environment in their opinion, they discussed it no further. But abortion must be addressed not only by those concerned about human dignity, but also by those concerned about the environment.

The link between abortion and the environment may not be immediately apparent; but abortion, until a better world is achieved and contraceptives are more widely available, will remain an important means not only of exercising a woman's constitutional right to reproductive freedom, but of ensuring that the Malthusian consequences of starvation and misery do not serve as substitutes for controlling population by the most humane and voluntary methods mankind can devise.

NOTES

1. 410 U.S. at 116 (1973).

2. John T. Noonan *et al.*, *Morality of Abortion* 23 (1970).

3. Plato, *supra* Chapter 4, note 2.

4. 40–60 Million Abortions Performed Each Year in World, *Boston Globe,* Oct. 9, 1986, pp. 3–12.

5. Abortion Rate in U.S. High, *Miami Herald,* June 3, 1988, p. 14A.

6. Breslau, Ceausescu's Cruel Law, *Newsweek,* Jan. 22, 1990, p. 35.

7. See Chapter 5, *supra.*

8. *Id.*

9. *Id.*

10. Horgan, Exporting Misery: A U.S. Abortion Ruling Affects Women's Health Worldwide, *Scientific American,* Aug., 1991, p. 16.

11. Hogan, *supra.*

12. *Id.* See Chapter 5, *supra.*

13. Source: World Health Organization (WHO) in Jacobson, Abortion in a New Light, *World-Watch Reader,* p. 287.

14. *Id.,* p. 288.

15. *Humanae Vitae, Acta Apostolica Sedes,* 60 (1968).

16. See Chapter 5, *supra,* note 53.

17. *From Abortion to Reproductive Freedom: Transforming a Movement* (M. Gerber Fried, ed.) (1990).

18. Jacobson, *supra,* p. 287.

19. *Id.*

20. Barth, U.S. Abortion Policy Abroad Is Disastrous, *Newsday,* June 7, 1989, p. 15A.

21. *Id.*

22. Where Other Nations Stand, *Star Tribune,* June 30, 1992, p. 8A.

23. 40–60 Million Abortions Performed Each Year in World, *Boston Globe,* National/Foreign Section, Oct. 9, 1986, p. 12.

24. Laurence H. Tribe, *Abortion: The Clash of Absolutes* 35 (1990).

25. *Politics* 7.16, 1335, cited in Noonan et al., *The Morality of Abortion: Legal and Historical Perspectives* 5 (1970).

26. *Id.*

27. *The Republic* 5.461, cited in Noonan, p. 5.

28. Edelstein, *The Hippocratic Oath: Text, Translation, and Interpretation* 3 (1943), cited in Noonan, *supra,* p. 5.

29. Edelstein, cited in Noonan, *supra,* p. 5, note 4.

30. Hippocrates, The Nature of the Child, in *Oeuvres* (E. LIttre, ed.) 7:409 (1834–1861), cited in Noonan, p. 5, note 6.

31. Noonan, *supra,* p. 4.

32. *Id.*

33. *Id.,* p. 23.

34. *Id.,* p. 23, note 79.

35. *Id.,* p. 27.

36. *Id.*

37. Navarrus, Consilia, 5.22, in 4 *Opera* (1951), cited in Noonan, p. 27, note 95.

38. *Effraenatam, I Codicis Juris Foutes* (P. Gasparri, ed.) (1927), cited in Noonan, p. 33, note 11.

39. Noonan, p. 33.

40. *Sedes Apostolica, I Codicis Juris Foutes* 330–331, cited in Noonan, p. 33, note 112.

41. Abortion before the fetus was ensouled was not considered homicide. According to Tribe, however, it was still condemned in the same manner as masturbation and contraception. Tribe, *supra,* p. 31.

42. *Id.*

43. To the Archbishop of Lyons (May 31, 1889), Denzinger, n. 1889; cited in Noonan, p. 41, note 142.

44. *Humanae Vitae, Acta Apostolica Sedes,* 60; 481–503 (1968), cited in Noonan, p. 45.

45. Faith and Abortion: Where the World's Major Religions Disagree, *Washington Post,* Jan. 23, 1990, p. 212.

46. *Id.*

47. *Id.*

48. *Id.*

49. *Id.*

50. *Id.*

51. Ancient practice, *supra,* note 32, pp. 55–56.

52. Mohr, *Abortion in America* 3 (1978).

53. 3 De Bracton, *The Laws and Treaties of England,* ii 4, quoted in Davis, The Law of Abortion and Necessity, 2 *Mod. L. Rev.,* 126, 133 (1938) and cited in Means, The Law of New York Concerning Abortion and the State of the

Foetus 1964–1968: A Care of Cessation of Constitutionality, 14 *N.Y. Law Forum,* 409, 419 (Fall 1968).

54. Means, p. 420.

55. In 1803, however, Parliament passed for the first time a law making abortion before quickening a crime. Mohr, p. 5.

56. Means, p. 412.

57. *Id.*

58. *Commonwealth of Massachusetts v. Bangs,* 9 Mass. 386, 387 (1812).

59. Mohr, pp. 6–9, 61.

60. *Id.,* pp. 46–47.

61. *Id.,* p. 73.

62. *Id.*

63. *Id.,* p. 195.

64. *Id.*

65. *Id.,* p. 180.

66. Source: "Reports of Persons Arrested . . . Committee for the Suppression of Vice (1873–1882), cited *Id.,* p. 197.

67. *Id.,* p. 226.

68. Tribe, *supra,* citing Luker, *Abortion and the Politics of Motherhood* 32 (1984).

69. Tribe, p. 37.

70. *Id.,* p. 38.

71. *Id.*

72. *Id.,* p. 48.

73. *Id.* citing Kovach, Abortion Reform Is Voted by the Assembly, *N.Y. Times,* April 10, 1970, p. 1.

74. *Id.,* p. 49.

75. 381 U.S. 479, 485 (1965).

76. 381 U.S., p. 509 (Black dissenting).

77. 381 U.S., p. 507.

78. 381 U.S., p. 507.

79. 381 U.S., p. 512.

80. 381 U.S., p. 527 (Stewart dissenting).

81. *Pierce v. Society of Sisters,* 268 U.S. 510, 45 S.Ct. 571, 69 L.Ed. 1070 (1925).

82. 405 U.S., p. 454 (1972).

83. 410 U.S., p. 153.

84. See cases cited in 410 U.S., pp. 154–155.

85. *Snyder v. Mass.,* 291 U.S. 97, 105 (1934), cited by Rhenquist in 410 U.S., p. 174.

86. Tietze, Morality with Contraception and Induced Abortions 45 *Studies in Family Planning* 6 (1969); Abortion Morality, 20 *Morbidity and Mortality* 208, 209 (June 21, 1971) (HEW, Public Health Service); cited in 410 U.S., p. 149, note 44.

87. 410 U.S., p. 150.

88. 410 U.S., p. 148.

89. 410 U.S., p. 158.

90. Quoted in Tribe, p. 117.

91. *Id.*

92. *Id.*

93. *Id.*

94. Gardner, Is An Embryo a Person, *Nation,* Nov. 13, 1989, p. 57; cited and discussed in Tribe, p. 118.

95. *Doe v. Bolton,* 410 U.S. 179, 93 S.Ct. 739, 35 L.Ed.2d 201 (decided immediately after *Roe*).

96. *Indiana Planned Parenthood v. Pearson,* 716 F.2d 1127 (1983).

97. *Planned Parenthood Assoc. v. Danforth,* 428 U.S. 52, 96 S.Ct. 2831, 49 L.Ed.2d 788 (1976).

98. *Planned Parenthood Assoc. v. Ashcroft,* 462 U.S. 476, 103 S.Ct. 2517, 76 L.Ed.2d 733 (1983).

99. *Simopoulos v. Virginia,* 462 U.S. 506, 103 S.Ct. 2532, 76 L.Ed.2d 755 (1983).

100. *Webster v. Reproductive Health Services,* 492 U.S. 490, 109 S.Ct. 3040, 106 L.Ed.2d 410 (1989).

101. 428 U.S. 52 (1976).

102. *Akron v. Akron Center for Reproductive Health,* 462 U.S 416, 103 S.Ct. 2481, 76 L.Ed.2d 687 (1983).

103. *Id.*

104. *Planned Parenthood Assoc. v. Ashcroft,* 103 S.Ct. 2517 (1983).

105. *Roe v. Gerstein,* 428 U.S. 901 (1975).

106. *Womens Services v. Thorne,* 103 S.Ct. 3102.

107. *Thornburgh v. American College of Obstetricians and Gynecologists,* 476 U.S. 747, 106 S.Ct. 2169, 90 L.Ed.2d 779 (1986).

108. *Id.*

109. *Planned Parenthood of Southeastern Pennsylvania v. Casey,* 112 S.Ct. 2791, 120 L.Ed.2d 674 (1992).

110. *Id.*

111. *West Coast Hotel Co. v. Parrish,* 300 U.S. 379, 57 S.Ct. 578, 81 L.Ed. 937 (1937), overruling the "substantive due process" cases that had blocked much of President Roosevelt's New Deal Legislation [see, e.g., *Lochner v. New York,* 198 U.S. 45, 25 S.Ct. 539, 49 L.Ed. 937 (1905)].

112. *Brown v. Board of Education,* 347 U.S. 483, 74 S.Ct. 686, 98 L.Ed. 873 (1954), striking down school segregation and overruling *Plessy v. Ferguson,* 163 U.S. 537, 16 S.Ct. 1138, 41 L.Ed. 256 (1896).

113. 112 S.Ct. 2791.

114. *Id.*

115. *Id.*

116. *Id.*

117. *Id.*

118. Indeed, there is some scholarly support for this position.

7   Immigration

To those who would look to the incoming of those of foreign birth, I would say "cast down your bucket where you are." Cast it among those who have tilled your fields, cleared your forests, builded your railroads and cities, and brought forth the treasures from the bowels of the earth. We shall stand by you with a devotion that no foreigner can approach, ready to interlac[e]) our industrial, commercial, civil and religious life with yours.

Booker T. Washington, from his "most famous address" (at the 1895 Atlanta Exposition to an audience of powerful white employers and businessmen)[1]

The history of human immigration is as old as the history of the human race. The earliest humans were nomads, leaving one region in search of virgin lands that offered new opportunities. The migration of the earliest humans from Africa was but the first of many in the history of mankind.

A discussion of the effect of immigration on population and the environment might begin by revisiting the Kenyan district of Kisii, which was discussed in Chapter 5 as a microcosm of the world environment. It should be recalled that Ozanne, a journalist traveling in that district, observed that

as far as the eye can see, the District is bursting under the sheer weight of rapid population growth. Almost all the arable land is being cultivated, including steep slopes. Plots are becoming smaller and are providing less income as holdings are divided and bordered by hedges, making the fertile equatorial landscape resemble a cluttered chessboard. As farmers overwork the land, soil erosion and exhaustion of fertility are becoming more marked. The pressure on schools and health clinics is immense, and rural employment is growing, bringing increased social and domestic problems. The young are being forced off the land into migrating [elsewhere].[2]

I saved discussion of the last sentence of Ozanne's observation for this chapter, because it reveals that immigration has historically been a significant method of deferring Malthusian consequences. It has been noted that such consequences do not occur uniformly and simultaneously around the world. Even when its consequences occur locally, however (as when throngs of Irish, long teetering on the brink of starvation, confronted agricultural disaster in the form of "potato rot"), the quest for the means of deferring Malthusian consequences can cause dramatic social upheaval. The Irish achieved deferral by immigrating to America by the millions (3.5 million alone between 1830 and 1860).[3] (The other means, industrial and agricultural technology and innovation have been discussed in previous chapters.[4])

In 1993, 45,000 children died every day from starvation and neglect. While this is greater in absolute terms than at any time in human history, anti-Malthusians point out that in terms of percentage of the world's population this number is smaller than at the time of Malthus. Starvation is not uniformly occurring around the world, and there are still plenty of places where humans have enough to eat—thus proving to the anti-Malthusians that there is no reason to control population.

Anti-Malthusians concede that in some countries, technological and agricultural innovation and economic growth have failed to take root. Those countries have been unable to provide sufficient food and decent living standards for their teeming and growing populations. For such countries, immigration is a means of deferring Malthusian consequences.

Anti-Malthusians have a number of historical cases in point to vindicate their premise. For millions of the Irish living in the 1840s, the harsh Malthusian overpopulation remedy of starvation was avoided by immigrating to America. For millions of others in Europe, where forests were being depleted, arable soils were being eroded, and social and economic conditions were becoming intolerable, immigration also became the preferred method of deferral. Virgin lands, uncut forests, clean rivers, clean air, and fertile untilled soil all awaited the earliest arrivals. Immigration enabled the anti-Malthusians to point to the European migrations as proof that Malthus' predictions did not have to come true.

The migration of the poor and underprivileged also solved a number of problems for their parent countries. By the early 1800s, many European countries, such as Ireland, were beginning to be confronted with some very awkward choices. Government policies encouraging birth control were not only out of the question, but were virtually unmentionable (see Chapter 5). But the very existence of large numbers of destitute and desperate people was a threat to the established order. (The French Revolution provided example enough of what could happen to those in power when too many of their subjects suffered from the Malthusian disease of hunger.)

The European migrations proved to be a Godsend to all parties concerned. America, of course, benefitted from the labor provided by the immigrants in developing vast new areas of virgin territory. The immigrants found new land and resources that provided new opportunities for the creation of wealth, and the freedom that enabled them both to achieve and enjoy that wealth. And the European countries were only too glad to relieve Malthusian pressures by sending off their wretched, tired, "huddled masses" to lands thousands of miles away.

The population of Europe increased by 100 million people in the 40 years from 1807 to 1847, putting enormous strains on both the economies and environment of Europe.[5] Garrett Davis, writing in 1849, saw a direct relationship between the expansion of the European population and emigration policies: "The area of Europe is but little more than that of the United States, and from its higher northern positions and greater population of sterile lands, has a less natural capability of sustaining population. All her western, southern, and middle states labor under one of the heaviest afflictions of nations—they have a redundant population."[6]

By 1843 the aggregate population of Germany and Ireland alone was rising by 2 million people per year.[7] The effects of this population growth were observed by Davis: "2.3 million of the Irish people [are] in a state of destitution. Large masses of people, in many countries, not only want the comforts of life, but its subsistence, its necessaries, and are literally starving." Davis noted that "England, many of the German powers, Switzerland, and other governments, have put into operation extensive and well-arranged systems of emigrating and transporting to America their excess of population, and particularly the refuse, the pauper, and demoralized, and the criminal."[8]

The link between the Malthusian pressures of population and government emigration policy was clear to an observer of the time: "The governments know that they have an excess of population. They feel more intensely its great and manifold evils, and for years they have been devising and applying correctives, which have all been mainly resolved into one—to drain off into America their surplus, and especially their destitute, and vicious population. By doing so, they not only make more room and comfort for the residue, but they think—and with some truth—that they provide for their own security, and do something to avert explosions which might hurl kings from their thrones."[9]

England, for example, found emigration to be an excellent way of getting rid of undesirables, particularly criminals. When it was pointed out to British authorities that an expanding population might have the Malthusian result of land needed for food production being divided up into ever smaller and inefficient parcels, Parliament responded by enacting the primogeniture laws, which permitted only the eldest son to inherit estates of land. Second and third sons were often the first on the ships headed for America.

During the 1840s over 4 million Germans emigrated to America.[10] A shortage of farmland in Scandinavia triggered the departure of 1.5 million Scandinavians during the period 1870–1900. Between 1880 and 1920, overpopulation in Austria, Czechoslovakia, Italy, and Austria was relieved by the emigration of over 8 million people to the United States. Over 2.5 million Jews from Eastern Europe fled religious prosecution, while a million Poles escaped grinding poverty and political repression.[11] In the aftermath of revolution in Mexico, grinding poverty provided the impetus for the first wave of Mexican immigration; over 700,000 emigrated from Mexico alone during the period 1910–1920.[12]

During the 1930s U.S. immigration policies were finally tightened, and, more important, enforced. Less than 500,000 immigrants were admitted to the United States during that entire decade.[13] By the 1940s, however, immigration had begun to rise again as a result of more liberal laws. In 1942, the "Brocero" program was initiated, which allowed American farm growers to take advantage of cheap, temporary Mexican labor.[14] In the 1950s, immigration laws were substantially relaxed, making it far easier for relatives of Americans to immigrate.[15] In 1965 the system of determining eligibility by national origin was repealed, but 20,000 were allowed in annually from any one country.[16]

The 1980 Refugee Act allowed the immigration of anyone with a "well-founded fear of prosecution on account of race, nationality, membership in a particular social group or political opinion."[17] The 1986 Amnesty law provided that anyone who had deliberately violated U.S. immigration laws, and had managed to continue to violate the laws since 1982 without getting caught, would be given the right to seek permanent residency.[18] No such dispensation was given to those who had unsuccessfully sought legal entry during this period. Sanctions against employers of illegal aliens were imposed, however.[19] In 1992, immigration limits were raised for certain favored countries with population problems (such as Ireland, which still forbade abortion).[20]

As a result of these changes in the laws, immigration soon skyrocketed, exceeding 7 million people during the 1980s.[21] In 1992 alone over a million people immigrated to the United States. Of these, 227,000 were legally admitted based on claims of "asylum." Not surprisingly, in light of such U.S. laws as the Amnesty Program, which made many legal applicants for immigration feel like "suckers," over 200,000 people entered illegally.[22]

The impact of these numbers on the growth of the U.S. population is significant. Although the population impacts vary from region to region, the example of California is indicative of a trend. A recent study reveals that the population of that state is now growing at a rate faster than "India, Indonesia . . . and Bangladesh."[23] The report states that immigration "account[s] for about half of the state's growth and contribute[s] to the other half with high birth rates." [24]

It is interesting to speculate as to what policies the countries exporting undesirables might have adopted had the Malthusian escape valve of emigration not been available. Would authoritarian and corrupt regimes have had to adapt their laws and social policies to accommodate their starving millions? Would countries like Ireland have had to consider family planning programs, or even abortion? In any case, it is difficult to imagine that these governments would not, had they had no choice, have found more humane alternatives for their people than mass starvation. Despite the claims of Simon and others, "technological innovation" and "better farming methods" could not save the teeming millions of Irish who in the 1840s were faced with potato rot. Without emigration, millions of Irish and other Europeans would have starved, in a process of population "self-correction" by the cruel means that Malthus had predicted. (One wonders how Malthus' writings would have been viewed at that time had there been such a catastrophe.) Very simply emigration saved European governments from having to adopt policies of reform that a starving population would have demanded. It also bought time until other means could be found to defer the spectre of Malthusian consequences.

CURRENT POLICIES

The policies of emigration and immigration are much the same today as they were 100 years ago. "Exporting" governments still rely on emigration as a means of ridding themselves of undesirables; and some governments still seek to get rid of those whom they fear might destabalize the existing power structure, or exert pressure for reforms. "Importing" governments rely on immigration as a means of reaping economic benefits and profits by taking advantage of the poverty and desperation of many of the immigrants.

Perhaps the most dramatic example in recent years of a country using emigration as a means of getting rid of undesirables was that of Cuba, which in 1980 decided to put American immigration laws to the test by emptying prisons and mental hospitals and allowing the inmates to sail directly to America. Within 5 months, over 125,000 "Mariels" had entered the United States. The Mariel Entrant Tracking System later estimated that at least 40,000–80,000 of the immigrants were convicted criminals. [25] A report issued by the head of the System recounted interviews with four Mariel criminals who were asked "how many of these characters who came with you were out of Cuban prisons" responded that everybody was. [26] Although an embarrassed U.S. government later claimed that the number of criminals among the Mariels was not that high,[27] psychological profiles of the first two thousand Mariels (who ended up in an Atlanta penitentiary) revealed that "only 50 were considered normal, were sane."[28] In any case, shortly after the boatlift, arrests of Cubans in New York City jumped to between 2000 and 3000 a year, compared to 214 the year before the boatlift.[29] Twelve percent of the homicides in Las Vegas were attributed to Mariels.[30]

More common is the practice of a human-exporting country to rely on emigration as a means of relieving itself of an excess population for whom it cannot provide opportunities for earning a decent standard of living. Already noted in Chapter 5 has been the failure of many third world and developing countries to provide women with adequate access to family planning methods and contraceptive devices. In many countries women are denied the legal right to an abortion. This failure is sometimes explained by cultural traditions or religious teachings. Reforming these laws and policies might have some unpleasant and awkward political ramifications. It is not surprising that most leaders of such countries would prefer not to deal with issues, or even to bring them into the open for purposes of discussion. The bitter experience and example of the United States in dealing with these issues (see Chapters 5 and 6) would itself give pause to third world leaders contemplating reforms in the area of family planning and abortion.

It is not surprising, therefore, that human-exporting countries have preferred to rely on emigration to solve their population problems, and to take advantage of the developed nations' indulgent immigration policies, rather than tackle the politically daunting task of internal reform. Certainly it is more politically popular and rewarding for third world leaders to express "outrage" at any efforts by importing countries to enact more restrictive immigration policies, or worse yet, actually enforce existing ones. But reliance on emigration as an escape valve for Malthusian population pressures in human-exporting countries would not be possible were it not for the silent but effective connivance of special economic interests in the human-importing countries.

Immigration policies in the United States are often criticized because of the social and economic impact that such policies have. While there is currently fierce debate over the extent of these alleged impacts, the debate itself is fundamentally misdirected when viewed in the context of evaluating the effects of population on the environment.

Resolution of the debate between Ehrlich and Simon over when the limits of population growth will be reached has thus far been avoided by concluding that limits to growth, whenever reached, cannot ultimately be avoided. It has further been concluded that the risks of slowing population growth too soon are outweighed by slowing the growth too late. Moreover, the effects of an expanding population on the environment have been noted, not the least being the elimination of one living species per day to make room for more humans. Slowing that rate of growth in the most humane ways possible is essential to the goal of avoiding Malthusian consequences. It was seen in Chapter 5 that population could be stabilized today through purely voluntary means if family planning methods were available to all who desired to use them.

The tragedy of present immigration policies is not so much the relatively short-term economic and social consequences of those policies. Of greater concern is that emigration, encouraged by the lax immigration policies of the human-importing countries, has come to be relied on as the alternative to the more difficult process of internal reform of family planning policies. As long as this situation persists, there will be little incentive for human-exporting countries to deal with their population problems. If immigration laws were tightened, however, population issues would have to be dealt with directly. Family planning policies, if reformed, would stabilize population, and eliminate the need to export humans in the first place. This in turn would lay the foundations for the improvement of living conditions, as well as relieve the environment from the pressures of population growth.

Unfortunately, however, environmental factors are rarely considered in immigration policy. However, the motivations behind immigration policy, as well as the factors considered in formulating policy, including the social and economic effects of immigration, must be understood in order to pursue immigration reforms that would serve the cause of environmental preservation.

THE EFFECTS OF IMMIGRATION POLICY

The effects of American immigration policy are currently the subject of fierce debate.[31] Effects are best understood, however, in the context of the goals and objectives of those who enact the immigration laws. The effects of immigration on labor are a case in point.

After the American Civil War, the abolition of slavery released a vast pool of unskilled workers into the labor market. Propitiously, however, the industrial revolution then taking place required millions of unskilled laborers to man the factories and assembly lines. There loomed the prospect of a labor shortage. The opportunities for the unskilled appeared to bode well for the economic prospects of America's African-Americans. Release from bondage, by itself, would be insufficient to enable African-Americans to assimilate into American society and reap the benefits of economic prosperity. Without economic opportunity, the advantages of education and training would also be denied. It was essential that African-Americans be permitted to take advantage of the opportunities provided by America's industrial revolution.

But it was not to happen. The prospect of a labor shortage was viewed with alarm by the privileged classes, and particularly by America's robber barons and titans of industry. A labor shortage meant that the working class would have increased bargaining power—the power to demand higher wages and humane working conditions. It meant also that corporations and employers, when faced with worker resistance to low wages and abysmal working conditions, would not have the luxury of firing workers or hiring strike-breakers. Moreover, racial prejudice inhibited the hiring of African-Americans.

There was, of course, a way to avoid both the labor shortage and the necessity of hiring African-Americans. That way, of course, was to import teeming throngs of impoverished workers from overpopulated Europe. That such a policy could be implemented under the guise of promoting the "American dream" as set forth on the Statue of Liberty made it all the more attractive as a policy; but, more important, it made it possible to persuade the policymakers in Congress to pass the legislation that made it possible.

Not everyone in America failed to see what was happening, however. Booker T. Washington, the great African-American educator, tried valiantly to alter the course of this policy, which he knew was so disastrous to the aspirations of millions of African-Americans. He was invited to speak at the Atlanta International Exposition on September 18, 1895, and the President of the United States was scheduled to appear. Washington was determined to set forth his views on immigration policy.

That he was invited to speak was considered remarkable at the time. In his autobiography, Washington explained how the invitation came about:

As the day for the opening of the exposition drew near, the board of directors began preparing the program for the opening exercises. In the discussion from day to day of the various features of this program, the question came up as to the advisability of putting a member of the Negro race on for one of the opening addresses. It was argued that such recognition would mark the good feeling prevailing between the two races. Of course there were those who were opposed to any such recognition of the rights of the Negro, but the board of directors had their way, and voted to invite a black man to speak on opening day.[32]

Washington was apprehensive about giving the address. "I knew," he later recalled, "that this was the first time in the entire history of the Negro that a member of my race had been asked to speak on the same platform with white southern men and women on any important national occasion. I was asked now to speak to an audience composed of the wealth and culture of the white south, yet there would be present a large number of northern whites."[33]

That he was not asked to speak on any particular topic only increased his apprehension. "I was determined" he later said,

to say nothing that I did not feel from the bottom of my heart to be true and right. I felt that the board of directors had paid a tribute to me. They knew that by one sentence I could have blasted, in a large degree the success of the exposition. The papers, North and South, had taken up the discussion of my coming speech, and as the time for it drew near this discussion became more and more widespread. Not a few of the Southern white papers were unfriendly to the idea of my speaking. From my own race, I received many suggestions as to what I ought to say. I prepared myself as best as I could for the address, but as the 18th of September drew nearer, the heavier my heart became, and the more I feared that my effort would prove a failure and a disappointment.[34]

His apprehensions were increased by predictions that his speech would be a failure.

I had been told that while many white people were going to be present to hear me speak, simply out of curiosity, and that others who would be present would be in full sympathy with me, there was a still larger element of the audience which would consist of those who were going to be present for the purpose of hearing me make a fool of myself, or, at least, of hearing me say some foolish thing, so that they could say to the officials who had invited me to speak, "I told you so."[35]

"As I remember it now," says Washington in his autobiography, "the thing that was uppermost in my mind was the desire to say something that would cement the friendship of the races and bring about hearty cooperation between them. So far as any outward surroundings were concerned, the only thing that I recall distinctly now is that when I got up, I saw thousands of eyes looking intently into my face."[36]

To those black members of the audience who had been contemplating emigration as a way of improving their lives, Washington told the story of a ship lost at sea. Suddenly, the ship

sighted a friendly vessel. From the mast of the unfortunate vessel was seen a signal, "water, water; we die of thirst!" The answer from the friendly vessel at once came back, "cast down your bucket where you are." A second time the "water, water; send us water" ran up from the distressed vessel, and was answered "cast down your bucket where you are." The captain of the distressed vessel, at last heeding the injunction, cast down his bucket, and it came up full of fresh sparkling water from the mouth of the Amazon river. To those of my race who depend on bettering their condition in a foreign land, I would say "cast down your bucket where you are." Cast it down in agriculture, mechanics, in commerce.[37]

Then Washington looked to the white members of his audience, those powerful titans of industry, employers who needed labor to keep their factories running and producing goods. "To those [of you]," he said, "who look to the incoming of those of foreign birth, 'cast down your bucket where you are.' " If they but did so, Washington eloquently promised that "we shall stand by you with a devotion that no foreigner can approach, ready to interlac[e] our industrial, commercial, civil and religious life with yours."[38]

The speech was well received. The editor of the *Atlanta Constitution* wrote "I do not exaggerate when I say that Professor Booker T. Washington's address yesterday was one of the most notable speeches. The whole speech is a platform upon which blacks and whites can stand with full justice to each other."[39] The *Boston Transcript* said "The speech dwarfed all the other proceedings and the Exposition itself. The sensation that it has caused in the press has never been equalled."[40] Washington met the President, and was later offered $50,000 from a lecture bureau, which he politely refused on grounds that he could not enter into "arrangements that seemed to place a mere commercial value upon my services."[41]

Despite the acclaim over Washington's performance, however, his words were not heeded. The profit motive for the industrialists was too great, as was the danger of a labor shortage altering the balance of economic power between the privileged and working classes. Racial prejudice continued to be a major factor in the denial of economic opportunity to African-Americans. Immigrants continued to pour into America, eliminating almost entirely the labor shortage that had so alarmed the robber barons.

But were the fears of Washington justified? One recent study has tracked the average American unemployment rate against levels of immigration for the period 1946–1989. Immigration for the period 1941–1951 was scarcely one million. As immigration levels increased to 2.5 million in the 1960s, 4.5 million in the 1970s, and 7.3 million in the 1980s, unemployment levels rose commensurately. Under Truman the average unemployment rate was 4.6%, under Eisenhower and Kennedy the rate was 4.9%, under Nixon 5.8%, Carter 6.5%, and under Reagan 8.9%.[42] Unemployment rates more recently may understate the extent of unemployment as large segments of the population of unskilled workers have given up attempting to enter the labor market.

Such aggregate figures do not, in themselves, prove cause and effect. Yet many statistics and events appear incongruous. In 1987, at a time when the unemployment rate of African-American teenagers approached 80%, "the garment makers in Los Angeles were pleading with the Immigration and Naturalization Service to allow them to import workers,"[43] on grounds that there was a "labor shortage" of unskilled workers.

During the 1970s, most large office buildings in Los Angeles hired union workers as janitors, paying $9 an hour plus benefits. Almost all the employees were African-American. Then the building managers learned that they could do exactly what the robber barons did during the industrial revolution. They hired independent contractors, who in turn hired immigrants willing to work for the minimum wage with no benefits. Thousands of African-Americans lost their jobs, and wages remained depressed.[44]

The taking of American jobs by illegal immigrants is sometimes justified on grounds that they are taking jobs no American will take. In fact, it is not the dirty nature of the work that keeps Americans from taking such jobs, but the depressed wages. For example, unionized jobs in garbage disposal are sought after by Americans if the wages and benefits are sufficient to feed a family, despite the dirty nature of the work.

The tide of immigrants permits racial discrimination to flourish. A *Chicago Tribune* survey of employers who hired illegal immigrants revealed the following reasons for not hiring Americans: "I don't think black people want to work in Chicago"; "The blacks are the most unreliable help you can get, whereas the illegal immigrants are reliable"; "the black people we've got here are uneducated and unskilled"; "black workers have high absenteeism and poor work habits."[45] In light of such expressions of blatant racial prejudice, the question must be asked as to what these employers would do if the illegal immigrants were not available to perform jobs at low wages. Would they just go out of business, or would they turn to African-Americans, offering work-training programs and other opportunities?

The American Congress can pass civil rights laws. But no law can prevent employers from paying minimum wages that only desperate immigrants can afford to take. Had Washington's plea in 1895 been heeded, African-Americans today would be the beneficiaries of their fair share of economic prosperity. But similar pleas today still go unheeded.

In 1965, just when the hopes of African-Americans were being raised by the Civil Rights Act, Congress acted to nullify the economic hopes of millions of African-Americans by allowing in additional millions of immigrants.[46] Over 25 million immigrants were added to the U.S. population between 1970 and 1990, dashing the hopes of millions of African-Americans.[47]

A 1992 Study for Immigration Studies has concluded:

When blacks ask why their economic plight has not improved since the Civil Rights Act took effect in 1965, one answer is that the Immigration Act passed the same year. Since then, the importation of millions of foreign workers into U.S. inner cities has done two things: It has provided an alternative supply of labor so that urban employers have not had to hire available black jobseekers, and the foreign workers have oversupplied labor to low-skill markets. That has kept the jobs in a seemingly perpetual state of declining real wages which are incapable of lifting unskilled black workers out of poverty . . . Whether intended or not, the present immigration policy is a revived instrument of institutional racism.[48]

Despite a 1992 Harris Poll that revealed that 63% of African-Americans feel that immigrants were taking jobs from them,[49] their pleas have not been acknowledged any more than those of Booker T. Washington were in 1895.

Aside from the effects of immigration on wage levels and the direct economic impact on American minorities, what are the net benefits and burdens of immigration on the American economy? Although this is currently the subject of fierce debate, no one denies that immigrants make a contribution. Corporations benefit immensely from low wages, as they have ever since the Civil War.

A study by Gary Imhoff has concluded that benefits of immigration are reaped primarily by the rich. He notes that "if an influx of illegal professionals could lower the wages of the overpaid, of doctors and lawyers, rather than the wages of the poor, then there might be some economic benefit to their coming to this country. But doctors and lawyers would not allow that to happen. Instead, it is low-wage labor markets, the wages at the bottom that are being depressed."[50] The Study concludes that immigration "widens the differences between classes in the United States; it keeps down the price of hiring a maid or a gardener for the rich while it makes things worse for the poor."[51]

Supporters of increased immigration argue that the United States does benefit from the influx of some highly educated immigrants in high-tech industries. They point to the "brain-drain" as an example of how the United States benefits by luring such people away from their impoverished native lands. *Business Week* recently gloated that "the U.S. is reaping a bonanza of highly educated foreigners."[52] Although the percentage of highly skilled immigrants is small compared to unskilled immigrants, the fact that other countries, many of them poor, have spent scarce funds educating the privileged few who then immigrate to the United States taking their skills with them, hardly seems an admirable justification for America's lax immigration laws.

Other arguments in favor of immigration hardly merit discussion. Social historian Thomas Nichols, for example, has argued in his essay "America Should Welcome Immigration," that "vast sums have fallen to immigrants and their descendants by inheritance, for every few days we read in the papers of some poor foreigner becoming the heir of a princely fortune, which in most cases, is added to the wealth of his adopted country."[53]

It has more reasonably been suggested that even though immigration benefits the rich, some of the benefits may trickle down to the middle class. For example, not all of the cost savings of low wages are retained by the wealthy; a portion of the cost savings may be passed on in the form of lower prices for some products. While many Americans might indeed benefit from lower prices of some goods the same might be said of prices of goods produced by the slave labor of political prisoners in China. Many, if not most Americans, however, would be willing to pay a little higher price for goods not made by exploiting the poor and wretched. They might also be willing to pay slightly higher prices if it meant new job opportunities for unemployed African-Americans—opportunities that all the Civil Rights laws have failed to provide. In New York City, a torrent of hundreds of thousands of illegal Chinese immigrants has caused fancy restaurant prices to fall. However, the influx of illegals has caused the dish-washing wages of all illegals to fall to $700/month from $1200/month just 4 years ago.

In any case, however, any benefits must be weighed against the costs. In California, Los Angeles County estimates that 23% of its school budget goes to educate recent immigrants.[54] Over 12,500 illegal immigrants are in California state prisons alone, at a cost of $20,000 each—or a total that approaches half a billion dollars.[55] Santa Clara County estimates that 40% of its welfare recipients are recent immigrants.[56] The *San Diego Union-Tribune* cited the case of the daughter of a Mexican millionaire who obtained $130,000 in Medi-Cal payments after crossing the border to obtain care at the San Diego Medical Center.[57]

It has been argued that, at the federal level, immigrants may now be contributing more in social security premiums than they now receive in benefits. Even if this is true, however, "federal costs for the citizen children of ineligible children of alien parents, including Medicaid and Aid to Families With Dependent Children, ha[s] risen from approximately $57.7 million in 1988–89 to $140.5 million in 1990–91, and could reach $533 million by the year 2000."[58] Public assistance and education costs of immigrants cost $2.2. billion in 1990.[59] At the state and local level costs are also spiraling. Governor Wilson of California recently demanded $1.5 billion from the federal government to help defer the costs of state and local services to immigrants.[60]

A COALITION OF INTERESTS

A 1992 Roper Poll revealed that the vast majority of Americans, including African-Americans and Hispanics, want stricter immigration laws and enforcement.[61] Of those polled in California 63% believed that there were too many immigrants in the state.[62] A 1992 Louis and Harris Poll revealed that a majority of African-Americans believe immigration is bad for the country.[63] Other polls, including one conducted by Hispanic Opinion and Preference Research Inc., revealed that "70% of Hispanics did not want Latin Americans to be given preferential treatment in immigration."[64] An Immigration and Naturalization poll revealed that only 11% of Hispanics would like to see more visas granted for people from Mexico.[65]

Why then, in a democratic society, are present immigration policies continued? The answer lies in a coalition of interests. The Mexican government, under pressure to provide for an exploding population, sees emigration as a politically more popular policy than confronting the population problem directly by advocating family planning programs, dealing with the issue of abortion, or taking on the Catholic Church. Wealthy American industrialists and employers do not wish to lose access to an easily exploitable pool of cheap labor, or be forced to turn to the large pool of currently unemployed African-Americans. The result is the passage of immigration laws that reflect both greed and hypocrisy. Caught in the middle is the hapless immigrant whom the American Border Patrol cannot even protect from robberies and beatings along the border.[66]

Perhaps the most cynical aspect of American immigration laws is that there is only the barest pretense of enforcing them. In the 1980s the number of border patrol agents patrolling both the Mexican and Canadian borders was "smaller than the number of transit police of New York City's buses and subways."[67] The assignment of only a few hundred agents to enforce employer sanctions across the entire United States has made a mockery of the employer sanctions bill. Needless to say, a powerful business community has not pushed for more resources to be allocated for such enforcement. Thus, the 1986 Amnesty program, billed as a "compromise" by rewarding long-term violators of immigration laws with residency in exchange for prosecuting employers who hire illegal aliens, has turned out not to have been a compromise at all, but rather a cynical ploy to avoid the inconvenience of having to enforce the immigration laws against the most blatant violators of U.S. laws.

Thus, despite the rising tide of public opinion in favor of reform, there is unlikely to be meaningful reform as long as powerful business interests can continue to exploit the misfortunes of the Third World's underclass, and as long as countries such as Mexico can relieve their population pressures by condoning and even encouraging the exploitation of their citizens by American business interests

Even the legal entry of 800,000 people in 1992 was not enough to satisfy those who seek to exploit immigrants; they also wanted to make sure that the annual flow of 200,000 illegal immigrants was not disrupted. A proposal to impose a one dollar tax on immigrants to fund a modest increase in the number of border patrol agents was met with cries of outrage. Proposals to build a high-tech laser fence across the border to

enable agents to efficiently intercept smugglers have also met with outrage. The arguments against such a fence are twofold: the first is that it
would not work, and would therefore be a waste of money; the second
is that it would work, in which case it is compared to the "Berlin Wall"
(as if a wall built to keep people in can be compared to a wall to keep
illegals out). The Mexican government has also let it be known that they
would consider any such effective methods of controlling immigration to
be an "affront"—although the Mexican government's strict enforcement
of its own immigration laws on its southern border with central America
apparently does not qualify as an affront.

Similar proposals to issue tamperproof I.D. cards, or to install a computerized network that could instantaneously verify electronically the
social security numbers of job applicants, have been met with protests
as well, despite the fact that such a system would be no more burden-
some than existing credit-card verification systems. Most exploiters of
immigrants are perfectly happy with a system that allows an illegal immigrant's use of cheap counterfeit documents to insulate the employer
from meaningful sanctions.

Some who have resisted meaningful reform have suggested that the
immigration problem (if there even is one) could be solved simply by
"enforcing the labor laws." While all laws should certainly be enforced,
the notion that a government unable to muster enough border patrol
agents to intercept even a small percentage of illegal border crossings
could somehow patrol the thousands of back-alley sweatshops around
the nation and monitor their employment practices is not easily compre-
hended. Even if a small handful of such enterprises could be shut down
through extended legal action, they would doubtless reappear in a matter
of hours or days in some other nameless alley. In any case, the dismal
record of enforcing employer sanctions provides little grounds to believe
that "enforcing the labor laws" would be any more successful in preventing the exploitation of illegal immigrants.

There is hope, however, that if Americans begin to see that such reform might lead to the kind of social and economic justice so long denied
to its most deprived citizens, and for which Booker T. Washington was
such an eloquent advocate, the interests of all citizens may ultimately
be served. True immigration reform would also lead to third world countries facing their own population problems and finding solutions that
would serve the interests of all their citizens.

IMMIGRATION AND THE ENVIRONMENT

The economic and social problems associated with immigration have
thus far dominated the current debate over policy. But it is now clear
that global population problems around the world will never be solved if

countries are permitted to use emigration as a means of deferring Malthusian consequences. For one thing, a day of reckoning must come. At some point the receiving country too will be filled to capacity.

Only recently have environmental groups come to recognize the relationship of immigration policies to the environment. Nevertheless, groups such as the Sierra Club and the Audubon Society, while considering the issue, have thus far hesitated to take an active role. The Federation for American Immigration Reform, which was formed by board members of population-control groups, has expressed its view that groups such as the Sierra Club are "avoiding immigration out of fear of being labeled racist or xenophobes."[68]

In California, a group calling itself Californians for Population Stabilization, noting that "all ethnic groups—blacks, whites, Latinos—favor lower levels of immigration," claims that "environmental arguments are crucial to the political debate over immigration because they are persuading more and more liberals to join the anti-immigrant base."[69]

Meanwhile, in 1993, the Sierra Club was only conducting "internal discussions," but the head of the Club's population committee has acknowledged that "there are already too many of us. Short of wars or plagues, reducing immigration and fertility levels are the only ways of meeting the goal of 'stabilizing or reducing population.' "[70]

While acknowledging an environmental component to the immigration issue, however, no major environmental group has made any major policy statements in this area. Nor have any major family planning or population control groups taken a clear stand on immigration issues. Even the limited discussions taking place have acknowledged only the Nimbyism aspect of immigration, the notion that immigration harms a nearby environment because additional people make demands on resources.[71] Thus, the Californians for Population Stabilization emphasize that "urban areas compete with farms and wildlife for water. New subdivisions put pressure on fragile ecosystems such as the Sierra and raise the demand for timber. Already overcrowded Yosemite becomes even more so."[72]

In fact, the major threat to the environment comes not from the fact that humans already living move from point A to point B. The true threat comes from the failure to initiate family planning programs—a failure made possible and convenient by the lax immigration policies of human-importing nations. As an expanding human population expands its habitat and demand for resources, there is less room, and fewer resources left for the rest of the world's creatures. The current immigration policies of the human-importing countries accelerate this process.

The citizens of Kisii must be reminded. There will not always be someplace else to move to.

NOTES

1. Hawkins, *Booker T. Washington and His Critics* 24–27 (1974). Ellipses indicating deletions have been omitted.

2. Ozanne, Kenya Fights Its Baby Boom, *Financial Times,* reprinted in *World Press,* July 1990, p. 67.

3. *Immigration: An American Dilemma* 3 (B. Ziegler, ed., 1953).

4. *See* Chapters 1 and 2.

5. *Immigration: Opposing Viewpoints* 27 (W. Dudley, ed., 1990), Garrett Davis, *America Should Discourage Immigration.*

6. *Id.*

7. *Id.*

8. *Id.*

9. *Id.,* p. 28.

10. In charts accompanying Moss, American Dream Conquers Troubles For the Newcomers, *USA Today* and Usdansky, Price of Immigration Alienate Taxpayers, July 14, 1993, p. A6.

11. *Id.*

12. *Id.*

13. Kershner, Why Immigration Laws Are So Hard to Change, *San Francisco Chronicle,* June 21, 1993, p. A7.

14. *Id.*

15. *Id.*

16. *Id.*

17. *Id.*

18. *Id.*

19. *Id.*; see also Richard Boswell, *Immigration and Nationality Law* (1992).

20. *Id.*

21. *Id.*

22. *Id.*

23. Kershner, California Leads in Immigration—and Backlash, *San Francisco Chronicle,* June 21, 1993, p. A1.

24. Lamm and Imhoff, *The Immigration Time Bomb* 62–63 (1985).

25. *Id.*

26. *Id.*

27. *Id.*

28. *Id.*

29. *Id.*

30. *Id.*

31. See, e.g., Kershner, *supra,* notes 13 and 23.

32. Booker T. Washington, The Atlanta Exposition Address, in *Booker T. Washington and His Critics* 21 (1962, 1974), p. 21.

33. *Id.*

34. *Id.,* p. 22.

35. *Id.,* p. 24.

36. *Id.*

37. *Id.,* p. 25. Ellipses indicating deletions are omitted.

38. *Id.*
39. *Id.*
40. *Id.*, p. 28.
41. *Id.*
42. Lamm, *supra.*
43. Kershner, supra, p. A6.
44. *Id.*
45. Lamm, *supra,* p. 154.
46. Kershner, supra, p. A7.
47. Center for Immigration Studies, Despair Behind the Riots: The Impediment of Mass Immigration to Los Angeles Blacks, *Scope,* Summer 1992, pp. 1–3.
48. *Id.*
49. The Immigrants, *Business Week,* July 13, 1992, p. 119.
50. Lamm, *supra,* p. 156.
51. *Id.*
52. The Immigrants, *supra,* p. 118.
53. Nichols, America Should Welcome Immigration, in *Opposing Viewpoints, supra,* p. 20.
54. Kershner, *supra,* p. A6.
55. *Id.*
56. *Id.*
57. *Id.*
58. Miles, Blacks v. Browns, *The Atlantic Monthly,* Oct. 1992, p. 60.
59. *Id.*
60. *Id.*
61. Kershner, supra, p. A7.
62. *Id.*
63. The Immigrants, *supra,* p. 119.
64. Lamm, *supra,* p. 204.
65. *Id.*
66. Lamm, *supra,* pp. 30–33.
67. Lamm, *supra,* p. 206.
68. Kershner, p. A6.
69. *Id.*
70. *Id.*
71. *Id.*
72. *Id.*

8 · Economic Growth

It is scarcely necessary to remark that a stationary condition of capital and population implies no stationary state of human improvement. There would be as much scope as ever for all kinds of mental culture and more and social progress; as much room for improving the Art of Living and much more likelihood of its being improved.

John Stuart Mill (1857)[1]

There is conceptual as well as linguistic significance to the fact that the words "economy" and "ecology" are both derived from the same Greek root oikos, meaning home.[2] Although the former modern derivation describes the home's wealth and prosperity, the latter relates to its livability.

The debate over the effects of population on economic growth is no less contested than the debate over the effects of population on the environment. Nevertheless, a resolution of the first debate may have serious practical consequences in terms of environmental policy. If, for example, it is determined or believed that population growth is necessary for economic growth, advocates of population control face an uphill battle in convincing policymakers to adopt policies that will harm the economic interests of their constituents. If population growth is not a precondition to economic growth, or even a drag, then those who favor economic growth may have common ground with those who favor policies that would control population growth. But would those two groups then have common ground with environmentalists? These are the questions that are explored in this chapter.

It should first be recognized that the question of the relationship between population and economic growth is more narrow than the question already considered, namely how many people the earth can support. This is because implicit in the term "economic growth" is the notion that such growth will bring a rise in per capita income, and not just a rise in gross product. Nevertheless, this more narrow question must be considered because of the implications the answer has in affecting state policy.

It will be recalled that the traditional view of population was that large populations were a primary indicator of a nation's wealth. Modern adherents of this view include P. Bauer, who has concluded that "rapid population growth has not been an obstacle to sustained economic growth either in the Third World or the West;"[3] Kuznets, who argues that "large numbers of people mean larger numbers of able and talented people who, by interacting with each other, discover and disseminate improvements in technology;"[4] F. Glahe, who claims to have discerned that "Developing nations with the highest population growth rates have achieved the highest economic growth,"[5] and observed that "there is no law of diminishing returns with respect to technology;"[6] Colin Clarke, who has noted that "the costs per head to society for a modern infrastructure of transportation and other facilities declines as population grows, thus facilitating an increase in net income per person;"[7] Julian Simon, who argues that a greater population allows greater use of methods of mass production;[8] and J. Kasun, who concludes that "while resources are always scarce relative to the demands that human beings place on them, there is no indication of imminent, absolute limits."[9]

Such views are certainly comforting, since they suggest that mankind faces no hard choices, and need not be concerned about an exponentially rising population. Women can have as many children as they want, since this will only add to their community's wealth, guardians of morality are free to take an absolutist moral view about the effects of contraceptive use on sexual promiscuity, and "prolifers" can maintain a purely moral position against abortion without concern about the effects of their position on the human condition.

There is validity to some aspects of the arguments advanced. From a microeconomic standpoint it is true that a particular firm can continue to grow at a high rate only if the market for its product expands. An expanding population will increase aggregate demand. Whether this will result in an increase in per capita consumption is another matter. Per capita income can increase only to the extent that economic growth exceeds the growth in population. (In the United States between 1950 and 1970, for example, population grew by 35% while per capita income increased by 51%.[10]) It is certainly true, as Simon suggests, that a population can be so small that there is no opportunity to take advantage of economies of scale or to use efficient methods of mass production. But it is also known that there are optimum sizes of productive enterprises, above which diseconomies of scale occur.

Likewise, there is some validity to Colin Clarke's point about spreading the cost of infrastructure overhead. But once all highways and bridges are jammed to capacity, the overhead is already spread to its maximum and additional population growth will not spread the cost further or more efficiently. Ehrlich has pointed out that the results predicted by Clark have not occurred, as in his "announcement in 1969 that India would within a decade be the most powerful country in the world because of its growing population." [11]

Kasun, besides citing the findings of Clark, Simon, Kuznets, and Glahe (among others), relies on data purporting to show that there is no statistical relationship between rates of population growth and rates of economic growth. In her book *The War on Population,* Kasun presents a diagram purporting to show the lack of any such relationship. [12] On the vertical axis of the diagram is the average annual rate of growth. On the horizontal axis is the average annual rate of population growth. On the plane of the two axes are 106 unidentified dots, apparently spread out randomly. The conclusion she draws from this chart is that "there is hardly any relationship at all . . . Many countries with high rates of population growth have high rates of per capita output growth, while the converse is also true." [13]

The problem with Kasun's chart (and thus her conclusion) is that it makes no distinction between countries that have a large preexisting economic base and those that do not. Thus, a desperately poor third world country with a high rate of population growth but that raised its annual per capita income from $100 to $110 would appear on the chart as a country with an exceedingly high 10% growth rate—indeed twice or three times as high as Japan or the United States. (Of course the cause of the $10 increase in per capita income might reflect nothing more exciting than a rise in the price of cocoa that year.) Although this country's unidentified dot might appear to be randomly mixed in with the United States or Japan (which have lower rates of population growth), such data are hardly convincing evidence of Kasun's conclusions that there is no relationship between population growth and economic growth.

Kasun also relies on another chart. This one contains a selected list of named countries in Asia. [14] It shows, for example, that two of the countries with the highest population densities (Hong Kong and Singapore) have among the highest per capita incomes, while a country such as Burma, with one of the lowest population densities, also has among the lowest per capita incomes. Kasun also points to the Netherlands and Japan as examples of countries with high population densities and high per capita incomes, concluding from these data that "there is no evidence that more densely settled countries tend to have lower levels of per capita income and output." [15]

Such analyses are vulnerable to Ehrlich's counter of the "Netherlands Fallacy." It will be recalled that Ehrlich, in response to the example of the Netherlands as a country with high population density and high income, pointed out that "the Netherlands can support 1,031 people per square mile only because the rest of the world does not. In 1984–86 the Netherlands imported 4 million tons of cereals, 130,000 tons of oils, and 480,000 tons of pules. It took some of these relatively inexpensive imports and used them to boost their production of expensive exports"[16]— thus their high GNP. The same sort of response can be made about Japan, which is almost entirely dependent on the rest of the world for a variety of resources such as oil and timber.

Several additional points may also be made about using GNP as a measure of economic growth when comparing rates of population growth. In 1972, Nordhaus and Tobin, in their essay "Is Growth Obsolete?,"[17] developed a measure of economic welfare (MEW) as an alternative to the measure of gross national product (GNP). This measure included factors not considered by GNP, such as the value of leisure. Tobin and Nordhaus concluded that MEW in the United States grew at only one-sixth the rate of GNP over the period 1947–1965.[18]

In the 1992 article "Growth Without Progress,"[19] John Cobb set forth an index of sustainable economic welfare (ISEW) that included a number of economic factors not listed in either MEW or GNP. It assumes, for example, that economic well-being is best indicated by measuring one's relative, rather than absolute, economic status. (People in the wealthiest societies are not necessarily the happiest, as indicated by national suicide rates.) In addition, ISEW considers the distribution of existing income. Thus, it judges that "an increase of average income in the poorest 20% of the population adds more to overall economic well-being than an increase on the part of the richest 20%."[20]

Cobb's index also takes into account the use of nonrenewable natural capital that is consumed, such as nonrenewable natural resources. Al Gore has pursued a similar theme in his book *Earth in the Balance,* noting that when a country cuts down trees, "the money received from the sale of logs is counted as part of that country's income. The wear and tear on the chain saws and logging trucks will be entered on the expense side of the ledger, but the wear and tear on the forest itself will not."[21] Cobb goes further, and introduces the element of "net international position," which assumes that "financing the purchase of goods for immediate consumption whether by borrowing money or by selling capital assets is not a sustainable practice."[22] Thus, both make the point that the consumption or sale of a nonrenewable resource should not be considered as part of national product.

An analogy might be made to the case of an individual who inherits a house and a million dollars, which he puts in the bank. If he withdraws the money, and spends it in order to consume, he will eventually run out of money. Just as the "nonrenewable" money he spends on consumption should not be considered as "product," so the production of oil and gas (less the labor needed to extract it) should not be considered as part of the GNP.[23]

All of these proposed measures attempt to consider factors that cannot be precisely quantified, but that ultimately relate to the quality of life. As John Kenneth Galbraith has observed, "the penultimate western man, stalled in the ultimate traffic jam and slowly succumbing to carbon monoxide, will not be cheered to hear from the last survivor that the Gross National Product went up by a record amount."[24]

In any case, it does not appear that the question of whether population growth is related to economic growth will be resolved by reference to statistics. In fact, there appear to be too many factors involved in economic growth for the answer to be found in statistical relationships alone. For example, political systems can also have an effect, as in the case of the brutally repressive regimes of Burma or Rumania that simply made the lives of everyone so miserable that no one wanted to have children. Low population growth may be an effect as well as a cause of economic growth. In many poor countries, a child is considered a financial asset, someone who, along with many brothers and sisters, can help in the fields or provide for their parents in old age. Likewise, in wealthy countries, children are a financial liability. One recent study of the cost of raising children in industrialized nations has revealed that the average cost of raising a child exceeds twice the annual income of the parents.[25] Certainly a country with few people can be poor (such as Burma) while a country can be rich in spite of, rather than because of a high population (the Netherlands). But certain economic laws, such as the law of diminishing returns, cannot be avoided by simply denying that they exist. One would be better off denying the laws of supply and demand, or the law of gravity.

Thus when Nancy Birdsall writes that the idea that population growth slows per capita income rests on the assumption that "with rapid increases in the number of workers, each worker produces less in relation to the land and capital each has to work with,"[26] it is not an adequate response to say, as Kasun does, that this assumption has "been neither verified nor questioned by official policy-makers; they have simply been taken on faith."[27] One can certainly argue, as Simon does, that the law of diminishing returns can be deferred by technological innovation, but this is far different than claiming the law is not valid.

It will be recalled that no attempt was made to resolve the question of how many humans the earth can support; it was simply concluded that the risks of slowing growth too soon were outweighed by the risks of slowing growth too late. It is suggested that the more narrow question of the relationship between population growth and economic growth requires no answer, because any answer would not affect the fundamental question of policy. Population growth should be retarded because the

risks (including environmental ones) outweigh the minimal risks of slowing growth too soon. It was acknowledged that one of the risks of slowing population too soon was that there might be a risk of slightly slower
economic growth. One reason that this relatively minimal risk was as-
sumed was that the environmental effects of population growth may be
even worse if it is true, as Kasun and Simon maintain, that population
growth spurs economic growth.

It will be recalled that a wealthy consumer in one of the industrialized
nations emits 10 tons of carbon into the atmosphere, compared to one-
tenth of a ton by a poor person in a Third World country. It has been
estimated that on average, an American baby born in 1973 will consume
50 tons of food, 10,000 pounds of fertilizer, 21,000 gallons of gasoline,
13,000 pounds of paper (forest), and 52 tons of iron and steel.[28] The
American baby will consume 50 times as much steel, 250 times as much
gasoline, and 300 times as much plastic as his counterpart in an undevel-
oped nation.[29] Thus, the industrialized nations, which account for one-
fourth of the population, consume almost 90% of the world's natural resources.[30]

While such disparities in income and consumption may be questioned
as a matter of social justice, the difference in impact on the earth's life-
support system is of more concern to the environmentalist. Holdren has
created a model that measures total environmental impact by multiplying
population size by per capita consumption by environmental impact per
unit of consumption $(I = PCU)$.[31] Using this model, it has been determined that the American baby's impact on the environment approaches
50 times that of the peasant baby born in an underdeveloped country.[32]
On the basis of such calculations, Miller has concluded that "based on
environmental impact, the United States is the most overpopulated
country in the world."[33] Of particular concern are statistics showing that
the rate of impact on the environment may even exceed the rate of economic growth. During the period 1950–1970, for example, per capita income in the United States increased by 51%, amounts of environmentally harmful emissions increased by up to 1900%.[34]

If the statistics reveal one indisputable fact, however, it is that population growth is not a precondition to economic growth. Countries, such
as those in Western Europe, that have slowed or stabilized their populations are enjoying economic growth. Thus policies should be instituted
that first, promote population stabilization, and second, promote economic growth in a stabilized population. There are a number of economic policies that can be pursued to achieve economic growth at the
same time that population is stabilized. An example of one such policy
is free trade, the current debate over which raises issues about how such
policies might be promoted.

FREE TRADE

The North American Free Trade Agreement provides a current case study for analysis of many of the issues already discussed, including immigration, the effects of population growth on economic growth and the environment, and the role of government and private environmental organizations.

Until relatively recently, trade between nations was considered a means of exerting national power and obtaining economic advantage over other nations. The export monopolism and mercantilist policies that dominated most of the eighteenth century,[35] and the imperialism of many Western nations during both the eighteenth and nineteenth centuries, reflect this view of international trade. Nations erected trade barriers to protect domestic industries from competition, on the short-sighted theory that such barriers would maintain domestic industries and employment ("Protectionism"). Before the widespread adoption of the income tax in the twentieth century, trade-inhibiting tariffs were an important source of government revenues.

It was not until 1701 that the economic wisdom of such policies was challenged, in a tract entitled *Considerations of the East-India Trade* by an anonymous author.[36] Schumpeter has identified this tract as one of the first to recognize the underlying principle of comparative advantage.[37] Although this principle can be explained by a complicated set of equations, a simple hypothetical illustrates the principle.

For the sake of simplicity, assume that there are only two countries (Arctic and Tropical), and that the citizens of each consume only two products, ice-cubes and oranges. (Assume further, for the sake of simplicity, that the costs of transportation are negligible in relation to the value of each product.) However, both countries have set up trade barriers—Arctic to protect its local orange industry, and Tropical to protect its local ice-cube industry. With its available resources, Arctic is able to produce 8 units of ice-cubes, but only 2 units of oranges (for a total GNP of 10 units). This is because in order to grow oranges in the cold Arctic, special heated greenhouses must be built. Tropical is able to grow 8 units of oranges, but only 2 units of ice-cubes (also for a total GNP of 10 units). This is because it must build expensive, capital-intensive factories to produce the ice-cubes. Thus the total GNP of the two countries combined is 20 units, which must be divided among the entire populations of each.

Then the leaders of both countries read about the law of comparative advantage. They overcome the determined political opposition of their local industries, and lower trade barriers between the two countries. Arctic now "specializes" in producing ice-cubes, at which it is very efficient. By diverting resources formerly used for producing oranges (at which it was very inefficient), it can now produce 100 units of ice-cubes (although no oranges). Tropical stops trying to produce ice-cubes, and instead produces 100 units of oranges, for which it has the perfect climate. Each country then trades its product for that of the other country, so that there is now a total GNP of 200 to share among the citizens of both countries. Per capita consumption in each country rises by a factor of 10.

However, it should be noted that the transition from a state of high tariff barriers to one of free trade involves temporary dislocations. Orange workers in Arctic and ice-cube makers in Tropical will temporarily be put out of work. It is the responsibility of each country to provide for these workers during the transition period. A variety of methods are available to soften the impact of transition. For example, the transition may be phased in over a period of time to give local industries time to adjust. Workers can be given job training, or temporary assistance. Despite the temporary economic dislocations, however, in the long-term, everyone will be better off if free trade is permitted.

Although this hypothetical is oversimplified, it illustrates the basic law of comparative advantage. It further illustrates how government policy can directly affect economic growth without relying on an increase in population to increase aggregate demand.

The effect of free-trade barriers on economic growth was revealed most dramatically in 1929, after the Republicans passed the Smoot-Hawley Tariff Act. This bill had been promised in an election campaign to "protect American jobs." Of course, it did nothing of the sort. Tariffs cut imports by 77%, other countries retaliated, and world trade declined by 50%, ushering in the Great Depression in which almost a third of all Americans lost their jobs.[38]

Despite such economic tragedies brought on by protectionism, however, political demagogues and special interest groups continue to advoate such policies as a way of winning votes. In 1933, for example, the North American Free Trade Agreement was the subject of fierce debate.[39] Special interests representing those industries that would be affected during a transition period argued against the treaty.[40] Such opposition was clearly understandable given the disruptions, albeit temporary, that free trade might cause to noncompetitive industries. It was clear, however, that free trade between the United States and Mexico would increase productivity on both sides of the border, raise living standards, and raise the wages of Mexican workers. The rise of Mexican wage levels would reduce the incentives for the immigration of Mexican labor to the United States. Senator Bill Bradley of the U.S. Senate said he feared that if the treaty were rejected, the "Mexican economy would falter dramatically, creating a return to the old politics where demagogues fight bitterly for power while democracy is shunted aside. With half the population of Mexico under the age of 19, a terrible Mexican economy will produce millions of illegal immigrants flooding into America''[41] (see Chapter 7). Since rises in per capita income have historically resulted in lower birth rates, the effect on population pressures in Mexico, and thus on the environment, would therefore be beneficial.

Surprisingly, environmental groups joined labor in opposing the treaty, creating an odd coalition. The argument of the environmental groups was that the treaty would force American firms to compete with Mexican firms, which not only enjoy lower labor costs, but also have lower costs because they are not required to comply with strict environmental laws. Close examination of laws and economic circumstances reveals how the environmental groups, by failing to recognize population issues, have devoted their time and resources to the wrong side of an issue.

With regard to jobs, it should be noted that beginning in 1986, when tariff barriers between Mexico and the United States first began to be lowered, U.S. exports to Mexico increased by 230%.[42] More important to American workers was the fact that American jobs related to exports paid an average of ''$3500 more per year than those unrelated to international trade.''[43] The Secretary of the U.S. treasury has reported that the United States, which had a trade deficit with Mexico before tariffs were lowered, enjoyed a $5 billion surplus in 1992. In 1992, he reported that ''we sold $40 billion worth of goods. That is up $25 billion in just five years. Some 600,000 Americans now work at jobs directly linked with exports to Mexico. With [the North American Free Trade Agreement], we expect them to rise to 900,000.''[44] The Secretary stated that he feared if the treaty were rejected as a result of special interest groups, including environmental groups, Mexico could ''reverse itself and many U.S. jobs could disappear.''[45]

Although some critics claimed that the treaty would result in American firms going to Mexico to take advantage of low wages,[46] the fact was that prior to the relaxation of tariffs in 1986, many American firms did move to Mexico in order to sell there without paying the high tariffs.[47] Free trade reduced the incentive for American firms to move to Mexico, since they were able to sell in Mexico without paying tariffs.

Nevertheless, some labor groups continued to maintain that lower wages would lure American firms to Mexico. However, it has been pointed out that labor costs are only one factor a firm considers in deciding whether to relocate. ''Companies also consider productivity, transportation, and technology.''[48] The adequacy of infrastructure is also critical. As the former U.S. Ambassador has pointed out, ''if low wages were all that mattered, Haiti and Bangladesh would be industrial giants.''[49]

In any case, the wages of Mexico in 1993 were far above the $.60 an hour claimed by treaty critics. Adolpe has noted that fringe benefits account for 25–35% of wages. Many foreign companies have tried to pay even higher wages, but were prevented by Mexico's own policies of restraining inflation (the Pact for Stability and Growth).[50] Moreover, Mexico's labor laws have been described as "some of the toughest labor laws in the world . . . Mexico's laws have been the model for the labor laws of other countries."[51] Mexican labor laws require the training of employees on company time, the sharing of 10% of profits with workers, employer contributions for pensions and housing funds, Christmas bonuses, and a prohibition against firing at will.[52] Indeed, it has been noted that "so strict are the Mexican labor laws, that attorneys caution their clients that they had better be very sure they want to start a permanent establishment in Mexico."[53]

Despite the claims of American environmental groups, Mexico has spent billions on environmental programs. An EPA official stationed at the Mexican embassy has written that the Mexican government has spent $3.5 billion for an "Integrated Air Pollution Program" initiated in 1990.[54] An "Integrated Environmental Plan for the United States/Mexico" was developed by the Mexican Environmental Agency[55] in concert with the EPA, and released to the public on August 1, 1881.[56] The Plan "focuses on the environmental concerns of the border area, including water quality, hazardous wastes, air quality, and chemical emergencies."[57] Mexico was the first country in the world to sign the Montreal Protocol, which limits the emissions of substances depleting the ozone, signed the Convention for the International Trade in Endangered Species, and is active in the research on Global Climate Change.[58]

In response to such initiatives, and the prospect of an improvement in Mexican living standards that would help to stem the flow of illegal immigrants to the United States, a coalition of American environmental organizations filed a federal law suit to block the treaty by alleging that the treaty required the filing of an Environmental Impact Statement. Although the lawsuit was summarily dismissed by a federal judge, the environmental groups persisted until, in July 1993, they found a sympathetic judge willing to hold up the treaty on grounds that no Environmental Impact Statement was filed. The Clinton Administration, which had been working hard to negotiate side agreements addressing all environmental issues, appealed the decision.

Once again, the efforts of environmental groups were misdirected, in this case by distorting provisions of an environmental act. Such misdirection can be explained by noting the failure of such environmental groups to recognize that the fundamental cause of environmental damage is not economic growth, but an exponentially rising population.

BALANCING THE EQUATION

It will be recalled that Holdren's simple formula for determining aggregate environmental impact $(I = PCU)$ incorporated three elements: population, consumption (per capita), and the environmental impact of each unit of consumption. Thus, aggregate environmental impact can be reduced by reducing any one of the three components of the equation. Government has focused on the third component, unit impact. Thus, for example, cars are required to have catalytic converters, thereby reducing the amount of emissions per automobile. As already noted, however, most environmental regulations have accomplished little more than what a former EPA Administrator described as the "circle game"[59]—transferring pollution from one medium to another, or simply transferring pollution from rich areas to poor ones (Nimbyism). (Although the EPA administrator condemned such programs as worse than no program at all, his words do not appear to have been heeded by government policymakers.) Most environmental groups have supported this approach, as have many high-profile environmentalists such as Vice-President Al Gore. Although billions have been spent on such programs, the net effect on unit impact has been relatively small (see Chapter 3).

A second environmental approach has been taken by some scholars, and more cautiously by some policymakers. This approach focuses on the second component of the Holdren equation, per capita consumption. Professor Benson, at a 1992 Free Trade Symposium, stated this approach boldly: "Lesson Number One: The costs of traditional economic growth exceed the benefits and will lead to environmental collapse. Therefore, free trade, which promotes that growth, is a fundamentally misguided public policy."[60] Though this "lesson" is boldly stated in a law review article, it encompasses the hidden agenda of the environmental groups opposing the North American Free Trade Treaty. (The more visible agenda is the purported concern for environmental laws relating to unit impact.) The argument appears to be as follows: if free trade is permitted, countries that participate will experience an increase in wealth and per capita consumption. Thus, aggregate environmental impact will be affected. In other words, it is better if countries such as Mexico remain in poverty, because, as a poverty-stricken nation, its impact on the environment will be less; or as Professor Daly has put it, "for all 5.4 billion people presently alive to consume resources and absorptive capacities at the same per capita rate as Americans or Europeans is ecologically impossible."[61]

The "lesson" of course is absolutely true—true in the sense that a reduction in any of the three Holdren components will reduce total environmental impact. Bold as this lesson is, however, it is easy to see why policymakers must use caution in adopting it. It is, after all, a call for reducing living standards, or more bluntly a plea for poverty. It is difficult to imagine a politician running on a platform of "elect me, and I promise to make you less well off—all in the interest of protecting the environment." (It is probably just as difficult for environmental groups to concede that their real concern about the free trade treaty is not the loss of American jobs, but their fear that Mexico might prosper economically, and thus increase the impact on the environment.)

How then can policymakers, who cannot afford to be as forthright as the scholars in proposing poverty as a remedy for pollution, make such an approach palatable? Vice-President Al Gore appears to have accomplished just that in his book *Earth in the Balance*. His proposal is couched deep in his book in Chapter 13, titled "Environmentalism of the Spirit." After taking to task those who "complain bitterly about the (Catholic Church's) opposition to birth control," Mr. Gore proceeds to indorse the "Pope's powerful and penetrating analysis of the ecological crisis," and suggests that the Pope should be "recognize[d] as an ally" in the environmental cause. What is this penetrating analysis? It is that, "Faced with the widespread destruction of the environment . . . we cannot continue to use the good of the earth as we have in the past . . . society is given to . . . consumerism while remaining indifferent to the damage which [it] cause[s]."[62]

Although few may doubt the Pope's penetrating analysis, or that of Al Gore, there are a few questions left unanswered in their suggested approach. Would people in industrialized nations be "grandfathered" as part of any policy toward poverty? That is, would they be permitted to continue their high levels of consumption, even as countries such as Mexico are deprived of the opportunity for economic growth? Or must people in industrialized society agree to reduce their consumption levels to those of people in Third World nations? If the answer to the last question is no, we may expect to encounter some resistance to the Pope's and Gore's policy by people now living in desperate poverty. Nevertheless, "environmentalism of the spirit" still has a nice (politically acceptable) ring to it, and sounds much more palatable than Professor Benson's more scholarly version that states that "the costs of traditional economic growth exceed the benefits and will lead to environmental collapse."

There is, however, a third approach, a description of which is reserved for the next and final chapter.

NOTES

1. Cited in G. Tyler Miller, *Living in the Environment: Concepts, Problems, and Alternatives* 328 (1975).

2. *Id.*, p. 325.

3. Bauer, *Equality, The Third World, and Economic Delusion* (1981); cited in Jacqueline Kasun, *The War Against Population* (1988).

4. Paraphrased by Kasun, *supra,* p. 55, citing S. Kuznets, Population Change and Aggregate Output, in *Demographic and Economic Change in Developing Countries, a Conference of the Universities* 324–340 (1960).

5. Paraphrased by Kasun, *supra,* p. 56, citing F. Glahe and Dwight Lee, *Macro Economics: Theory and Applications* 189 (1981).

6. *Id.*

7. Paraphrased by Kasun, *supra,* p. 50, citing Clarke, *Conditions of Economic Progress* (1957).

8. Simon, *supra,* Chapter 2.

9. Kasun, *supra,* p. 57.

10. See Barry Commoner, The Environmental Cost of Economic Growth, in Ridker, *Population, Resources and the Environment: The Commission on Population Growth and the American Future Research Reports,* Vol. 111, Washington D.C., U.S. Government Printing Office (1972), cited in Miller, p. 16.

11. Ehrlich, *The Population Explosion* (1990).

12. Kasun, *supra,* p. 49, Chart 2-1.

13. *Id.*, p. 48.

14. *Id.*, p. 52, Chart 2-2.

15. *Id.*, p. 52.

16. Ehrlich, p. 39.

17. William Nordhaus and James Tobin, Is Growth Obsolete, in *Economic Growth* (1972), cited in Cobb, Growth without Progress, 15 *Loy. L.A. Int. Comp. L. J.* 45, 51–55 (1992).

18. *Id.*

19. *Id.*

20. *Id.*

21. Albert Gore, *Earth in the Balance* 184 (1993).

22. Cobb, *supra,* p. 55.

23. Cobb's calculations are actually more sophisticated, taking into account the estimated cost of producing gas from renewable corn sources. However, the loss of certain types of forests is considered nonsustainable.

24. Cited in Miller, *supra,* p. 331.

25. Miller, *supra,* p. 110, Chart 8-3.

26. Birdsall, Population Growth and Poverty in the Developing World, 5 *Population Bulletin* 14 (Dec. 1980), cited in Kasun *supra,* p. 47.

27. Kasun, *supra,* p. 47.

28. Miller, p. 15.

29. *Id.*

30. *Id.*

31. Holdren, Ehrlich v. Commoner: An Environmental Fallout, *Science,* 177, 242–247, cited by Miller, *supra;* see also Ehrlich, *supra.*

32. Miller, p. 13.

33. Miller, p. 15.

34. Commoner, *supra,* cited in Miller, p. 16.

35. See Hecksher, *Mercantilism* (1931).

36. Schumpeter, *History of Economic Analysis* 373–374 (1954, 1963).

37. *Id.*

38. See, e.g., Bonker, *America's Trade Crisis,* 58–60, 81–83 (1988).

39. In fact, the treaty represented a consolidation of previous policies of tariff reduction.

40. State Support of NAFTA Overshadowed by Special Interest Efforts, *N.Y. Times,* July 21, 1993, p. C16.

41. Senator Bill Bradley, The Longer View of NAFTA, *N.Y. Times,* July 21, 1993, p. C12.

42. Lucey, The Lies of Nafta's Critics, *N.Y. Times,* July 13, 1993, p. A15.

43. See Cobb, *supra.*

44. Lloyd Bentsen, The Post-Protectionist Era? *N.Y. Times,* July, 21, 1993, p. C11.

45. *Id.*

46. Lucey, *supra.*

47. *Id.*

48. *Id.*

49. *Id.*

50. Adolpe, The Marketing of an Agreement: Misinformation and Misunderstanding Plague the Harmonious Implementation of NAFTA, *The Recorder,* July 21, 1993, p. 8.

51. *Id.*

52. *Id.*

53. *Id.*

54. Alonzo, Mexico, in Symposium: Free Trade & The Environment in Latin America, 15 *Loy. L.A. Int. Comp. L. J.* 87, 92 (Dec. 1992).

55. Known as SEDUE; *Id.,* p. 93.

56. *Id.*

57. *Id.*

58. *Id.,* pp. 95–96.

59. See note 1, Chapter 3.

60. Benson, The Threat of Trade, the Failure of Policies and Law, and the Need for Direct Citizen Action in the Global Environmental Crisis, 15 *Loy. L.A. Int. Comp. L.J.* 1, 7 (Dec. 1992).

61. Daly, From Adjustment to Sustainable Development: The Obstacle of Free Trade 15 *Loy. L.A. Int. Comp. L. J.* 33, 38 (Dec. 1992).

62. Gore, *supra,* pp. 262–263.

9   Putting It All Together—The Theory of Environmental Malthusianism

Environmental policy today is directed primarily toward controlling the unit impact component of Holdren's equation, $I = PCU$. Virtually all of the 2% of GNP that the United States allocates to protecting the environment is dedicated to the cause of reducing the effect on the environment of mankind's tools of living. It has been such a fruitless and counterproductive effort that ecology now threatens to replace economics as the "dismal science."

Billions of the dollars spent on the "environment" actually are spent on financing the confrontations between special interest groups in society, on litigation, propaganda, and bureaucracy. Private groups pursuing narrow interests siphon off billions of tax-deductible dollars. What money is left is spent primarily on funding what former EPA Director Thomas called the "circle" game—taking pollution from one medium and dumping it in another. Even he had to concede that such policies were worse than no environmental policy at all. Billions more of taxpayer's dollars are spent on Nimbyism—taking pollution from point A, and dumping it at point B, where the surrounding community is politically or economically impotent. At their worst, such policies take the form of the politics of exclusion—simply keeping the tide of polluting humanity away from the environs of the politically powerful.

It is not surprising that the results of such policies have been catastrophic to the environment. As we have seen, the debate over *when* limits are reached need not be resolved. The fact is that the limits will be reached, and the risks of waiting to take action exceed the risks of acting too soon.

One species of life continues to be exterminated every day to make room for humans expanding at the rate of one every third of a second. The burning of fossil fuels and forests continues to contribute to global warming,[1] plastics production and use of fluorocarbons continue to degrade the protective ozone layer,[2] water tables are dropping around the

world,[3] and waste continues to accumulate in piles as big as the Great
Pyramid of Giza.[4] Radioactive wastes with half-lives of thousands of
years sit in storage containers; landfills are leaking their poisons; 2.7
billion pounds of atmospheric contaminants are released into the air;
soot particulates alone kill 60,000–80,000 people annually.

Defenders of traditional environmental policy point to isolated environmental improvements as examples of progress. In the United States
the Clean Air Act and the mandating of pollution control devices in automobiles have been cited for their modest contributions to improving the
quality of air. In fact, the attempt to control emissions from automobiles
provides a classic example of the "circle game." In the mid-1960s California enacted some of the toughest laws regulating pollution from automobiles, requiring the installation of exhaust control devices in cars.
While these tough new controls did indeed result in a modest 12% reduction in hydrocarbon levels, they also *increased* noxious nitrogen oxide
emissions by 28%. One study of the auto emissions laws has concluded
that as a result of such laws, "one pollution problem has been traded
for another."[5]

In any case, the modest decreases in hydrocarbon emissions per automobile were more than offset by increases in the number of automobiles.
Each year, more than 4 million automobiles are added to the American
supply of motor vehicles.[6] For every one additional American added to
the population, almost two motor vehicles are added.[7] Worldwide the
problem is even more severe, as developing countries try to realize the
American dream of two cars in every garage. In South Korea alone, for
example, the number of cars increased from a little over 100,000 in 1970
to over 2 million in 1988.[8] Almost half a million cars were added in 1988.
India recently doubled its car fleet to over 3 million, and China is adding
over half a million per year.[9] If the poorest countries of the world ever
realize the American dream, the number of cars will increase by eight
times—but that is only if the population does not grow, which of course
it will.

The developed countries can afford the expensive technology necessary to make modest reductions in the emission of certain pollutants
from such sources as automobiles (albeit at the expense of increases in
other types of pollutants). Most countries, however, are too poor to afford such expensive technology. Even in developed countries that can
afford the technology, however, any modest reductions are completely
neutralized as population rises, and the number of units emitting pollution increases.

It was noted in Chapter 1 that isolated areas of the developed countries have enjoyed reductions in pollution over the past 20 years. It is
true, for example, that England managed to clean up much of the
Thames River by building expensive water purification plants. In 1858,

the Thames was so polluted that people near the river had to use rags soaked with chloride to be able to breath.[10] By 1979 the Thames was producing salmon for the first time in centuries.[11]

But for every celebrated example of the modest contributions of environmental technology in the richest countries, there are untold disaster stories elsewhere. In India, for example, the Benares River is a cesspool of typhoid and cholera caused not just by all the typical industrial wastes, but by such other causes as raw sewage and the dumping of 10,000 dead humans and 60,000 dead animals.[12] One study has revealed that 98% of the teeming millions living near the river suffer from stomach ailments.[13]

Recognizing the hopelessness of relying on technology to cure the environmental ills caused by a rising population around the world, some have found solace in the fact that poor countries may never grow economically, and thus may not raise their levels of consumption of pollution up to those of the industrialized world. Professor Benson's "lesson" that "economic growth . . . will lead to environmental collapse" may be recalled, as well as Professor Daly's view that for all the world's population to "consume resources at the same per capita rate as Americans is ecologically impossible" (see Chapter 8).

Harrison has studied the question of what a "reduction in consumption solution to the environmental problem would require. He assumes a model in which by the year 2100, the population of the world is consuming and producing waste at the present rates of the United States and Europe. He notes that the environment's ability to absorb the pollutant's of such a consuming population is limited, since the waste-carrying capacity of such mediums as water is "fixed and absolute. And it is these ceilings, rather than absolute shortages of resources, that will impose ever tighter limits" on economic activities. The more people there are, the lower our pollution 'rations' will be. For example, the International Panel on Climate Change has set a ceiling of 2.8 billion tons of carbon in the atmosphere. Beyond this limit the atmosphere will not remain stabilized. At such ceiling levels, each human would be allotted 0.53 tons of carbon per year, or about the same level as "Burkina Faso, the 13th poorest country in the world."[14]

It thus appears that mankind has some hard choices. It can proceed as it has, ignoring the environment and watching as the ceilings for pollutant levels for human support are exceeded. This is already occurring in places such as Benares; *or,* the industrialized world can agree to reduce its consumption levels to Burkino Faso; *or,* those living in poor countries can be denied the opportunity to experience economic growth, thus preventing ecological disaster.

Another proposed alternative, that of reducing unit impacts, cannot achieve success if population increases at the present rate. First, the technology required to make even modest reductions in industrial pollution is very expensive and beyond the affordability of poor countries.

Second, most of this technology, even when applied, proves a basic ecological law: "everything is connected to everything." The environment is like a three-legged table; adjustments made at one point have an effect elsewhere: reduce hydrocarbons, increase nitrous oxides; reduce reliance on burning coal that emits particulates into the air and causes acid rain, increase nuclear waste. Neither such utopian energy sources as windpower (against which environmentalists are already crusading) nor solar power (with panels covering 90% of the globe) are viable ways of producing mankind's energy needs in the foreseeable future.

Third, attempts to reduce unit impact have historically degenerated into the "circle game" of transferring pollution from medium A to medium B, or Nimbyism. In many cases, even the most sophisticated technology is unable to do much more.

There is another reason why the "reduction in consumption" is neither practical nor realistic. The technology on which many rely as a means of postponing indefinitely the day of Malthusian reckoning is a vital component of economic growth. People did not invent the great machines of industrial society as an academic exercise. They did it to get rich, so that they could improve their condition in life. One need only compare the number of technological innovations produced by a capitalist society, in which wealth is the reward for technological innovation, with communist societies, where such rewards are not given.

It does not appear realistic to suggest that consumers in industrialized nations would be willing to reduce consumption to the levels that this solution would require. True, it may be possible to prevent the poorest nations from increasing their standard of living. Some critics of the North American Free Trade Agreement have freely conceded that they believe economic growth and prosperity would hurt the environment. But such a solution does not seem fair to those who are now so economically deprived. As a matter of social justice, a policy of deliberately avoiding economic growth cannot be justified. Nor does it appear seemly for those in the richest nations enjoying high rates of consumption to tell the poor in Third World nations that it is up to them to help the environment by giving up their aspirations to consume at the level of Americans or Europeans.

ENVIRONMENTAL MALTHUSIANISM

It is the first component of the Holdren equation that should be the focus of policy: population. If population is stabilized, policies directed toward unit impact can slowly and modestly improve environmental conditions without the threat of neutralization by a rising tide of units.

Economic growth in impoverished nations can be promoted without fear of harming the environment. Indeed, as conditions improve in these countries, experience shows that fertility rates decline. Nor will it be necessary to ask American and Europeans to reduce their standard of living; to reduce the economic incentives for technological innovation would greatly inhibit the technological progress necessary to buy time in order to avoid Malthusian consequences while population is being stabilized.

What is suggested is a fundamental reordering of priorities. Existing policy in the United States directs 2% of the GNP toward essentially vain efforts to reduce unit impact. The bulk of those resources must be shifted toward stabilizing population. As stabilization or reduction in population is achieved, proportionate increases in consumption per capita can rise without creating additional harm to the environment.

A policy of population stabilization will require a great deal more than handing out condoms. It will require a fundamental change in the way policy is formulated and directed.

First, although contraceptive rights have come a long way since 1965 (when not all American states even permitted the use of contraceptives), over half the women in the world are today denied access to contraceptives. Many more are denied essential information and counselling with regard to the use of contraceptives. It has already been noted that simply making contraceptive devices and information available to every woman who wanted them could achieve population stabilization.

Sex education and information on reproduction must be made available to all. Government should look at the education programs in Sweden, where declines in teenage pregnancy and abortion were directly attributed to such programs.

Coercive programs must be avoided. Family planning programs cannot be made to work in the long-term if coercion is used. When liberalization comes to China, there is likely going to be a severe backlash against the coercive measures of the government. In fact, such a backlash has already occurred in India, when coercive programs of sterilization brought down the government and put back the cause of family planning at least 20 years.

Governments must not only permit or condone family planning, they must actively promote it. Money spent on family planing is far more cost-effective in reducing environmental impact than the current ineffective, but expensive environmental policy of attempting to control impact by playing the circle game or engaging in Nimbyism.

Abortion must be recognized as a fundamental right of a woman. As such, it must be afforded to all women, not just those who have the means to pay for it. With 45,000 innocent children now starving to death every day, governments can no longer emulate Sixtus V's campaign against the prostitutes by insisting that poor women bear unwanted children as punishment for their sexual activities.

Religious leaders must reexamine their own history, and return to the sound principles of their greatest theologians, such as Thomas Aquinas and Pope Gregory XIV, whose doctrine of quickening withstood the test of hundreds of years of religious thinking. It should be recalled that prior to 1869, no moral Christian would ever have entertained the view that the interests of a barely fertilized egg were superior to the life of the mother.

Private environmental groups must recognize their common cause with population groups, and unite to forge policies that recognize the critical link between population and the environment. Their task, even when they are united, will be daunting. There is resistance worldwide to family planning. Never again can there be a world "environmental" conference that declines to even invite those concerned about world population. Environmental groups in particular must recognize the futility of promoting Nimbyism or circle-game policies, and direct their resources and energies to stabilizing population as the most effective long-term environmental policy.

Immigration policy must be linked directly to environmental policy. It is not in the interests of either the human-importing or the human-exporting countries to allow policies of emigration to provide a politically expedient means of relieving an internal population explosion. A population explosion must be dealt with directly by facing whatever political and cultural obstacles a humane policy of family planning requires.

Economic growth must be encouraged. But population growth can no longer be relied on to provide an unending increase in demand for products. It is the interest of living humans, not potential humans not yet conceived or born, that must command society's attention. Recognition of this simple principle would go far in ensuring decent living standards of human dignity and social justice for all of mankind. Economic growth will continue to spur the technological progress necessary to raise living standards. It will also provide the technology for finding cleaner, more sustainable kinds of energy. Technology can also be used in ways to limit the effects of human consumption on the environment.

There is nothing wrong with specific policies directed toward unit impact. Such legislation as the Clean Air Act has provided some environmental relief, and should be continued. But such types of legislation should not be relied on as providing long-term solutions to the problem of environmental deterioration. At most, they should be looked at as buying time while population is stabilized. Thereafter, such policies can make a more permanent contribution to improving the environment.

There is also nothing wrong with promoting pet environmental causes, such as recycling, using biodegradable products, turning off the lights, bathing in cold water, walking to work, eating organic foods, and the like. Such habits may (or may not) have a marginal beneficial effect; the danger, however, is that we will do these things, and then pat ourselves on the back and think that we have done our part for the environmental cause. The fact is that we have not done our part unless we, along with all mankind, become part of the long-term solution—helping to stabilize population by actively supporting programs designed to achieve it. The greater the success of voluntary family planning programs, the greater the per capita consumption that will be possible without reaching the environmental ceilings or capacities of the air, water, and soil to sustain us.

During the 1992 Presidential campaign, a sign posted prominently in the Democratic headquarters reminded all the campaign workers of what the election was all about: "It's the Economy, Stupid." Today, a similar sign should be posted in the headquarters of environmental groups, and directed toward all those concerned about long-term solutions: "It's the Population, Stupid."

NOTES

1. Ehrlich, *The Population Explosion*, p. 112.
2. *Id.*, p. 124.
3. *Id.*, p. 129.
4. *Id.*
5. G. Miller, *Living in the Environment: Concepts, Problems, and Alternatives*, p. 318.
6. Miller, p. E-133.
7. *Id.*
8. P. Harrison, *The Third Revolution* (1992), p. 273.
9. *Id.*
10. Harrison, p. 202.
11. *Id.*
12. *Id.*, p. 303.
13. *Id.*, p. 283.
14. Miller, p. 318.

Selected Bibliography

Back, K. *Family Planning and Population Control*. Boston: Twaynne Pub., 1989

Bauer, P. B. *Equality, the Third World and Economic Delusion*. Cambridge: Harvard University Press, 1981.

Bonker, D. *America's Trade Crisis*. Boston: Houghton Mifflin, 1988.

Boserup, Ester. *Population and Technological Change: A Study of Long Term Trends*. Chicago: University of Chicago Press, 1981.

Boswell, Richard. *Immigration and Nationality Law*. Durham: Carolina Academic Press, 1992.

Bureau of the Census. U.S. Department of Commerce, Economics and Statistics Administration, 1991.

Cavanaugh, R. *The Popes, the Pill and the People*. Bruce, 1964.

Childe, V. G. *Man Makes Himself*. New York: Mentor, 1951

Chiras, D. *Environmental Science: Action for a Sustainable Future*. Menlo Park, CA: Benjamin/Cummings, 1991.

Clarke, C. *Conditions of Economic Progress*. New York: Macmillan, 1957.

Cohen, M. N. *The Food Crisis in Prehistory, Overpopulation and the Origin of Agriculture*. New Haven: Yale University Press, 1977.

Croll, E. *China's One-Child Family Policy*. New York: St. Martin's Press, 1985.

Demographic and Economic Change in Developing Countries, a Conference of the Universities. Princeton: Princeton University Press, 1960.

Douglas, E. T. *Pioneer of the Future: Margaret Sanger*. New York: Holt, Rhinehart & Winston, 1970.

Ehrlich, Paul. *The Population Bomb*. New York: Ballantine, 1968.

Ehrlich, Paul. *The Population Explosion*. New York: Simon & Schuster, 1990.

From Abortion to Reproductive Freedom: Transforming a Movement. M. Gerber Fried, ed. Boston: South End Press, 1990.

Glahe, F., and Lee, Dwight. *Macro Economics: Theory and Applications*. New York: Harcourt Brace, 1981.

Glendon, Mary. *Abortion and Divorce in Western Law*. Cambridge: Harvard University Press, 1987.

Gore, Albert. *Earth in the Balance*. New York: Phime, 1993.

Gupte, P. *The Crowded Earth: People and the Politics of Population*. New York: W. W. Norton, 1984.

Harrison, P. *The Third Revolution*. I.B. Taurus, 1992.

Hawkins, H. *Booker T. Washington and His Critics*. Lexington: D. C. Heath, 1974.

Immigration: An American Dilemma. B. Ziegler, ed. Boston: D. C. Heath, 1953.

Immigration: Opposing Viewpoints. W. Dudley, ed. San Diego: Greenhaven Press, 1990.

Kasun, J. *The War against Population: The Economics and Ideology of Population Control*. Ignatius Press, 1988.

Kuznets, S. *Population, Capital and Growth*. New York: Norton, 1973.

Lader, L., and Meltzer, M. *Margaret Sanger: Pioneer of Birth Control*. New York: T. Croswell, 1969.

Lamm, D., and Imholf, G. *The Immigration Time Bomb*. New York: E. P. Dutton, 1985.

Livi-Bacci, Massimo. *A Concise History of World Population*. Oxford: Blackwell Pub., 1989.

Malthus, Thomas. *Essay on Population*. 1798.

Malthus, Thomas. *Essay on the Principle of Population*, 7th ed. London: Dent, 1967.

Meadows, Donella, et al. *The Limits to Growth*. New York: Universe Books, 1972.

Meadows, Dennis L., et al. *The Dynamics of Growth in a Finite World*. Cambridge: Wright-Allen Press, 1974.

Meadows, Dennis L., and Meadows, Donella. *Towards Global Equilibrium*. Cambridge: Wright-Allen Press, 1973.

Meadows, Donella, and Meadows, Dennis L. *Beyond the Limits*. Chelsea Green Publishing Company, 1992.

Miller, G. *Living in the Environment: Concepts, Problems, and Alternatives*. Belmont: Wadsworth Publishing Company.

Mohr, J. *Abortion in America*. Oxford: Oxford University Press, 1978.

Noonan, John T., et al. *Morality of Abortion: Legal and Historical Perspectives*. Cambridge: Harvard University Press, 1970.

Pearson, K. *Life, Letters, and Labors of Francis Galton*, 4 Vols. Cambridge: Cambridge University Press, 1914–40.

Plato. *Critias*. A. E. Taylor, trans. In *Plato, Collected Dialogues*. Princeton: Princeton University Press, 1963.

Pohlman, Edward. *How to Kill Population*. Philadelphia: Westminster Press, 1971.

Ricardo, P. *The Principles of Political Economy and Taxation*. London: Dent, 1964.

Ridker, R. *Population, Resources and the Environment: The Commission on Population Growth and the American Future*. Research Reports Vol. III. Washington D.C.: U.S. Government Printing Office, 1972.

Sanger, Margaret. *Margaret Sanger: An Autobiography*. New York: Dover, 1971.

Sassone, P. *Handbook on Population*. Santa Ana, 1978.

Schumpeter, J. A. *Capitalism, Socialism and Democracy*, 2nd ed. New York: Harper & Sons, 1947.

Schumpeter, J. A. *History of Economic Analysis*. Oxford: Oxford University Press, 1954.

Schumpeter, J. A. *History of Economic Analysis*. New York: Oxford University Press, 1954, 1963.

Seredich, J. *Your Resource Guide to Environmental Organizations*. Irvine: Smiling Dolphins Press, 1991

Simon, J. C. *Theory of Population and Economic Growth*. London: Blackwell, 1986.

Smith, Adam. *The Wealth of Nations,* Vol. 1 London: J.M. Dent, 1964.

Tribe, L. *Abortion: The Clash of Absolutes*. New York: W.W. Norton, 1990.

U.S. Government Publication. *Environmental Protection Agency Manual*.

World Resources Institute. *World Resources*. New York: Oxford University Press, 1992.

Index